KU-437-175

Scotland and the Union
1707–2007

For
Margaret Begbie

Scotland and the Union
1707–2007

Edited by
T. M. Devine

Edinburgh University Press

© editorial matter and organisation T. M. Devine, 2008
© the chapters their several authors, 2008

Edinburgh University Press Ltd
22 George Square, Edinburgh

Typeset in Adobe Sabon
by Servis Filmsetting Ltd, Manchester, and
printed and bound in Great Britain by
Antony Rowe Ltd, Chippenham, Wilts

A CIP record for this book is available from the British Library

ISBN 978 0 7486 3541 2 (hardback)
ISBN 978 0 7486 3542 9 (paperback)

The right of the contributors to be identified as authors of this work
has been asserted in accordance with the Copyright, Designs and
Patents Act 1988.

CONTENTS

FIGURES AND TABLES

CONTRIBUTORS

Neal Ascherson   Writer and journalist; honorary lecturer in the Institute of Archaeology, University College London.

Karin Bowie   Lecturer in History, University of Glasgow.

Ewen A. Cameron   Reader in Scottish History, University of Edinburgh.

John Curtice   Professor of Politics, University of Strathclyde.

T. M. Devine   Sir William Fraser Professor of Scottish History and Palaeography, University of Edinburgh.

Richard J. Finlay   Professor of Scottish History, University of Strathclyde.

Charlie Jeffery   Professor of Politics, University of Edinburgh.

Allan I. Macinnes   Professor of Early Modern History, University of Strathclyde.

W. L. Miller   Edward Caird Professor of Politics, University of Glasgow.

Alexander Murdoch   Senior Lecturer in Scottish History, University of Edinburgh.

Christopher A. Whatley   Professor of Scottish History and Vice-Principal and Head of the College of Arts and Social Sciences, University of Dundee.

PREFACE

On 1 May 2007 the parliamentary Union between England and Scotland achieved its 300th anniversary and to mark the occasion a series of lectures and debates were held in the University of Edinburgh. The public response was remarkable. Venues such as the McEwan Hall and the Assembly Hall were filled to capacity with well over 4,000 people attending the four events which took place between January and April 2007. The series also attracted great interest from the national and international media. The fact that the future of the Union was itself a central element in the May 2007 elections to the Scottish Parliament added huge contemporary relevance to the discussions.

This book has been published as a direct result of the 'Scotland and the Union' series. Most of the chapters which follow are versions of the presentations which were given during the course of the programme, while others have been specially commissioned to ensure coherence and fuller coverage of key aspects of the long relationship between the two ancient nations of England and Scotland since 1707. The debate format which was an important part of some of the original events has been retained. For instance, the origins of the Union remain an issue of considerable dispute among scholars as is evident from the differing perspectives offered by Allan Macinnes and Christopher Whatley in Chapters 4 and 2, respectively. Throughout, the focus of the book is on the experience of the Union from the perspective of Scotland, although it is hoped that English readers will also find its contents of interest. There is surely no more vital issue in Scottish politics today than the future of the Union but that question must also be a matter of considerable significance for all citizens of the United Kingdom. The tercentenary of 1707 has predictably produced a number of studies on the origins of 1707. However, this book is the first to attempt an examination of the entire three hundred years of this historic association, while the topic is brought fully up to date by including chapters on the post-devolution era. The subject is approached from different disciplinary perspectives with historians and political scientists all contributing to the overall analysis.

It is a special pleasure to thank all those whose support and help has brought this project to a conclusion. In no small measure the success of the original public events was due to the professionalism and enthusiasm of the administrative staff of the School of History, Classics and Archaeology together with Communications and Marketing and Development and Alumni Services in the University of Edinburgh. Without the essential contributions of Jane Denholm, Kristin Flood, Jo Morrison, Ailsa Vamplew and Deephi De-Silva Williams the project would not have been possible. I called them the 'A Team'; they richly deserved the title.

The Principal and Vice-Chancellor of the University, Professor Sir Tim O'Shea, the Head of the College of Humanities and Social Science, Professor Vicki Bruce and Head of the School, Professor Douglas Cairns, could not have been more supportive of the endeavour. Mr Simon Fennell, a distinguished graduate of the School and currently a member of staff of Goldman Sachs, was our chief benefactor and so enabled the series to be carried through successfully without any financial concerns.

The staff of Edinburgh University Press were most helpful and I am particularly grateful for the professional advice and guidance of Esmé Watson who saw the project through from first commission to final publication.

My thanks also go to my academic colleagues in this venture, not only for their contributions but also for their patience and fortitude when confronted with some tight deadlines and editorial interventions.

Finally, and not for the first (or last) time, I am most grateful to Margaret Begbie who held the whole publication together and kept the editor and contributors firmly on the right track. To her, this book is very warmly dedicated.

Tom Devine
University of Edinburgh
November 2007

1

THREE HUNDRED YEARS OF THE ANGLO-SCOTTISH UNION

T. M. Devine

I

In an oft-quoted remark, the former Canadian Prime Minister, Pierre Trudeau, during a speech in Washington, DC in 1969, observed to his American audience that 'living next to you is in some ways like sleeping with an elephant: no matter how friendly and even-tempered the beast, one is affected by every twitch and grunt'.[1] Trudeau's memorable simile could, of course, be applied to any relationship between a large, powerful country and a close neighbour, much weaker in political, economic and demographic terms. It certainly might refer to the Anglo-Scottish connection. In 1707 the English outnumbered the Scots by over five to one. By 1901 that disparity had widened further to ten to one. England has always been the senior partner in the relationship with the sovereign Parliament meeting in London as the seat of government and the political, social and cultural establishment of the United Kingdom also heavily concentrated in the south. Yet, despite the obvious possibilities for domination, assimilation or even exclusion by the senior partner, the Union of the two countries has survived for three hundred years. May Day 2007 marked the tercentenary of the Treaty of 1707 being enacted in law. For the first half of the eighteenth century, the new connection was fragile and could easily have fractured. Also, since the 1960s, the option of withdrawal from the Union has appealed to a substantial minority of Scots though, thus far, not to a majority. However, since the later eighteenth century, until very recent times, the Anglo-Scottish connection has been remarkably stable and indeed rarely questioned, far less opposed, by political interests north of the Border.

In the 1840s, when nationalist insurrection rocked the capitals of Europe, Scotland was undisturbed. Between then and the First World War, any articulated concerns about the Union were concerned with refinement and improvement not repeal. The National Association

for the Vindication of Scottish Rights, formed in 1853, voiced a
number of grievances, which included the plea that Ireland received
more generous treatment than Scotland, that the United Kingdom
should always be designated 'Great Britain' and that the Scots merited
an increase in the number of MPs at Westminster. These, however,
were essentially cosmetic adjustments and none of them were of
serious consequence. The Association itself did not last long (it was
wound up in 1856) and attracted few figures of significant influence.
It was resentment that the Irish were receiving a better deal than the
Scots during the debates over Irish Home Rule that once more triggered interest in Scottish constitutional reform. In 1881, for example,
the earl of Rosebery memorably remarked that Scotland was 'mum-
bling the dry bones of political neglect and munching the remainder
biscuit of Irish legislation'.[2] Soon a fully-fledged and politically significant Scottish Home Rule movement was under way. This was not,
however, a radical attempt at separation or even federalism. The aims
of the Home Rulers were essentially both modest and moderate. They
sought to devolve Scottish business to Edinburgh in order to make the
sovereign Parliament in London more efficient. After all, at this time,
most Scottish commentators believed that the Union was vital to
the nation's progress, an enlightened act which had liberated the
country from the anarchy, poverty and fanaticism which to them had
scarred its pre-1707 past. To endanger such an invaluable relationship was simply unthinkable. The Union was an accepted and immov-
able part of life which now required no defence. It was a telling fact
that when the Scottish Unionist Association emerged in 1912 out of
a merger between the Scottish Conservatives and Liberal Unionists,
the Union referred to in its title was not that of 1707 but the Irish
Union of 1801. The Anglo-Scottish Union required no such vindication or protection.

Yet to earlier generations of Scots and to later historians there
was nothing inevitable about the survival of the Union. Mere geographical proximity between two different states does not, of course,
guarantee the durability of any political association. Indeed, far
from being typical, it may well be that the Anglo-Scottish Union was
unusual in this respect when seen in the context of European history.
Christopher Smout, for instance, argued that 'unions between distinct
and established medieval kingdoms of some reputation, like England
and Scotland, to last for four hundred years (that is including the
Regal Union of 1603) is a rare thing'.[3] He then cites the example of
two well-known failed unions in western Europe, the ephemeral

connections between Spain and Portugal and Norway and Sweden, both of which came to an end in acrimonious divorce.

Indeed, the more closely one examines 1707 and its aftermath, the more unlikely seems the remarkable longevity of the Anglo-Scottish political association. The omens at that time were far from auspicious. Scotland's emergence as a nation out of miscellaneous tribal groupings in the medieval period was in large part the result of a centuries-old struggle to defend the kingdom from English aggression. Moreover, a mere fifty-odd years before the Treaty of Union, Scotland had been conquered and subjected to military dictatorship and annexation by the Cromwellian regime of the 1650s which left bitter memories. The prelude to 1707 itself was the 1703 legislation of the Scottish Parliament which in the key areas of foreign and dynastic policy suggested separation from England rather than union. The successful negotiations were carried out by a tiny patrician elite and resulted in a marriage of convenience passed through the Scottish Parliament in the teeth of both internal opposition and considerable external, popular hostility.

After 1707 the threat of 'the elephant' loomed closer in the form of the English constitutional principle of the absolute sovereignty of 'the Crown-in-Parliament'. Potentially this dictum was the most lethal threat to the new association. The old royal tradition of the Divine Right of Kings to rule without constitutional limit was transferred in the Glorious Revolution of 1688–9 to the English Parliament and later the British Parliament after 1707. Given the dramatically different levels of parliamentary representation, whether based on population levels or property values of the two nations, this constitutional assumption could imply the imposition of unacceptable policies by Westminster on Scotland. That this was not simply a theoretical possibility became brutally clear very quickly. In London, the High Church Tories, who replaced the Whigs in 1710, passed the Patronage Act 1712, re-establishing the legal right of local patrons (usually landowners) to appoint to vacant church offices. This decision did not simply outrage pious Presbyterians; it also opened up a running sore which poisoned church and state relations until the final crisis of the Disruption of 1843 and beyond. In addition, the Act confirmed unambiguously that the 1707 Treaty was not, as many Scots believed, an inviolate, fundamental and supreme law; rather it was one which could be altered by the whim of any electoral majority in Westminster. This interpretation was confirmed much later by the most influential constitutional expert of the Victorian era, Albert

Venn Dicey (1835–1922). Manifestly, this was the scenario for potential turbulence which became even more likely as taxation on such basic necessities as salt, linen, beer, soap and malt rose inexorably from 1710 when the anticipated post-union economic miracle failed to materialise. The deep frustration was symbolised by the motion in the House of Lords in June 1713 to repeal the Treaty of Union, an attempt at dissolution only narrowly defeated by a mere four proxy votes. Even more crucially, dissent and anger helped to fuel the Jacobite movement and was one reason why Scotland became the great hope of the exiled Stuarts in the early eighteenth century.

How the Union survived the Jacobite menace relates, of course, to the much broader question, which is mainly outside the scope of this chapter, of the reasons for Jacobite failure and disaster in 1746. There are several texts which deal with that fundamental issue which can really only be answered convincingly by taking a wider British and, indeed, European perspective.[4] But the febrile nature of anti-unionism should not obscure the fact that even in that volatile period the Union was gathering vital support. It came from two sources. First, just as enthusiastic Jacobites regarded 1707 as an effective recruiting sergeant, Presbyterian Scots (which meant the vast majority in the Lowlands) saw the Union increasingly as the best defence against the potential horrors of a Catholic Stuart restoration. The more menacing Jacobitism became, the more these fears were reinforced. It helped that anti-Jacobite feeling was often strongest in some of the most economically advanced areas of the economy. Glasgow's joyful relief when the news came of the happy deliverance at Culloden Moor was tangible. The town's newspaper, the *Glasgow Journal*, brought out a special large-print edition in celebration of Cumberland's victory to record 'the greatest rejoicings that have been at any time in the past'.[5]

A second factor was the effect which, in spite of public frustrations, the rewards of Union were already having before *c.* 1740 on the country's business and landed elites. The 'golden age' of the tobacco business, the huge prize of the Union settlement, is usually seen as a post-1740 phenomenon. In fact, recent evidence on the scale of smuggling and under-recording (an estimated average of 42 per cent of legal imports of tobacco leaf between 1715 and 1731) in the trade suggests that the good times could be pushed much further back. Even more crucially, the non-inheriting sons of the Scottish landed gentry, forced into other careers by primogeniture, were already moving in significant numbers into imperial and London jobs before mid-century.[6] The early emigration of these elites was noted everywhere from the frozen wastes of British North America (modern Canada) to the teeming cities of India. Later that link between elite careers, empire and Union was to be strengthened even further. It was, however, already a remarkably potent force in the first three to four decades after 1707 and, indeed, had become significant even before formal union became a reality.

Yet, Culloden and its brutal aftermath did not entirely end the tensions within the Union. True, the gravest threat to the relationship had been finally eliminated but, on the other hand, English suspicions of crypto-Jacobitism as a peculiarly Scottish disease lived on for some time. Scottish pride was offended by the Militia Act 1757 which created a volunteer force for defence of the realm against foreign attack in England and Wales but not in Scotland. The conclusion drawn north of the Border was that the treacherous Scots could not yet be trusted with the bearing of arms.[7] Scotophobia then reared its ugly head in the early 1760s, during the office of John, Earl of Bute, the first Scottish-born Prime Minister after the Union. His tenure in this exalted position was brief – ending in 1763 – but his influence endured through interest, networks and clientages. So too did the relentless personal attacks on him – his family name, Stuart, did not help – and Scots in general. During the 1760s the number of Scots holding state office rose dramatically and it was easy to suspect that Lord Bute was favouring his own kind. Paul Langford has noted recently that 'With the sole exception of the French, no other nationality [other than the Scots] was so despised and derided in the vast array of caricatures turned out by the London press'.[8] These cartoons were savagely racist in tone, portraying Scots as greedy mendicants growing rich on England's rich pastures. Bute himself was satirised in one ribald print after another as the well-endowed seducer of the mother of George III, which was explicit sexual symbolism for the intolerable penetration of England and the Empire by ragged swarms of Scots crossing the Border in search of places and pensions:

> Friend and favourite of France-a,
> Ev'ry day may you advance-a,
> And when dead by tomb be writon,
> 'Here lies one whom all must sh-t-on,
> Oh, the Great, the Great North Briton'[9]

Probably the turning point in these strained relations came to an extent during the American War of Independence and then, finally and even more emphatically, during the French Revolutionary and

Napoleonic Wars. The vital contrast here was with Ireland, the more awkward neighbour. Between 1776 and 1783 the Scots were enthusiastically loyal to the British crown. Even in the colonies more loyalists were apparently born in Scotland than in any other country. They became the hated enemies of the Patriot Party, denounced as natural supporters of tyranny because of Scottish support for the exiled Stuarts in 1745, a dynasty which was viewed as the very incarnation of absolute monarchy and Catholic autocracy by respectable Protestant colonists. At the same time, Irish politicians were seen to be behaving badly and attempting to extract advantage from England's travails.

That contrast between the two nations became even more glaring during the Napoleonic Wars, a conflict which ended the epic 'second Hundred Years War' with France for global imperial hegemony. Britain was comprehensively victorious and the foundation of *Pax Britannica* across the oceans of the world was well and truly established. Yet at the time it was a close run thing: from 1798 to 1805, Napoleon's all-conquering armies were encamped a few miles across the Channel. It was at this time that the Irish committed the ultimate betrayal as the rebellion of 1798 gave the French the real chance of an effective flank attack at the hour of England's greatest peril. The contrast with the Scots could not have been more dramatic. Already over-represented among the officer class in the field armies, 52,000 Scots also joined the ranks of the volunteers. With around 15 per cent of the British population, this amounted to 36 per cent of all the volunteer soldiery in 1797, 22 per cent in 1801 and 17 per cent in 1804.[10] Scottish loyalty and the Scottish contribution in blood to final victory had cemented the Union by 1815. If contemporary caricatures and cartoons are any guide, the 'venomous contempt' of the mid-eighteenth century became the 'innocent humour' of the Victorian era.[11]

Linda Colley makes great play of the shared Protestantism of the two nations as the ideological cement of the Union,[12] although there may have been just too many differences in church governance for this factor to be truly decisive.[13] Religious 'nationalism' was, after all, a basic factor in Scotland throughout this period. Presbyterians were, in the main, deeply critical of the subordination of the Christian churches to the British state and adhered in very large numbers to the 'Two Kingdoms' theory that Christ was supreme over the spiritual realm. Around a third of the members of the Church of Scotland had seceded over this issue by the 1830s and the related problem of patronage. The Disruption of 1843, when nearly 40 per cent of the ministers and a third of the congregations left the established Church, was the supreme assertion of spiritual independence from secular authority. It is arguable, then, that religion may have been more of a force for tension within the Union than a foundation of ultimate stability.

Perhaps more significant were two major influences on the Scottish governing classes: the first was material; the second more related to the world of ideas. Until well into the nineteenth century, Scotland was ruled by a tiny elite of landowners and their kindred in the law and commerce. Before the first Reform Act 1832 there were forty-five parliamentary seats in counties and fifteen in the burghs, each with a mere 2,600 and 1,500 voters, respectively. In all, only 0.2 per cent of the population of the country had the franchise, an extraordinarily small number even by the pre-democratic standards of the eighteenth century. Some among them were already gaining from rising rentals and mineral royalties from their estates as the Industrial Revolution in Scotland gathered pace. Even more critical for many others, however, were the vast increases in employment opportunities in the Empire through soldiering, trade, administration and the professions for the non-inheriting male offspring of this elite. This was an age of significant population increase and there were simply many more younger sons for whom careers had to be found commensurate with inherited social status. In that sense the Empire came as a godsend for the genteel but often impoverished landed gentry of Scotland. There was no barrier on entry placed on these Scots, even at the highest levels of colonial administration. By the end of the eighteenth century, not surprisingly, they were over-represented in almost every area of elite imperial employment. How important this was to the long-term stability of the Union is confirmed by comparison with Ireland in the 1790s and the provinces of the Austro-Hungarian Empire in the nineteenth century. Deep frustrations among the Irish Catholic gentry in the eighteenth century at the limited imperial prospects for their families helped to fuel Irish instability from the 1780s and was a significant influence helping to trigger the rebellion of 1798.[14] Similarly, ethnic discrimination against provincial elites in Austria-Hungary fed disaffection in central and eastern Europe. The Scottish gentry may have encountered prejudice and suspicion but this presented little practical obstacle to their remarkable imperial success. The terms of the 1707 Treaty had ensured that Scottish Presbyterians did not encounter any legal penalties or formal discrimination either in the domestic union state or its overseas territories.

Growing awareness of the material benefits of Union were paralleled by a developing consensus among the nation's intellectual leaders that progress and unionism were closely associated. In theory, of course, the stunning achievements of the Scottish Enlightenment could have built a new national confidence and even a platform for nationalist assertion. But almost to a man, the literati were wedded to the idea that the Union was the prime source of liberation from Scotland's dark past of religious obscurantism and feudal inertia. The rubbishing of Scotland's pre-Union history in the eighteenth century also fashioned a unionist intellectual agenda for the Victorian era. As Colin Kidd has suggested, standard nineteenth-century histories of the nation by authors such as John Hill Burton and P. F. Tytler embedded a tradition of portraying pre-1707 Scotland in a negative light.[15] Significantly, when the Royal Commission of 1876 suggested that chairs of history should be set up in the universities, they were filled by English-trained scholars who virtually ignored the Scottish past in their teaching and writings and focused on the glories of English constitutional history. Not until 1901 was the first professorship in Scottish history established when the Fraser Chair was endowed at Edinburgh in that year.

II

All this raised the possibility that even if the Union had promoted material progress, the 'elephant' still posed a mortal threat to the distinctive identity of the Scottish nation. Certainly, some leading thinkers of the early nineteenth century regarded this not simply as probable but inevitable. Sir John Sinclair, Henry Cockburn and Sir Walter Scott, among others, feared that assimilation with England was a real possibility and that Scotland faced the future as 'North Britain', a mere regional appendage of the British state. The Union had brought remarkable benefits but at the accelerating cost of anglicisation. As Scott put it, 'what makes Scotland Scotland is fast disappearing'. The Scots in this view were steadily becoming invisible as a people as their ancient traditions, identities and institutions were diluted by the corrosive effect of close association with the world's most powerful state.[16]

England was not the only threat to Scottishness. Between the 1760s and the 1850s Scotland experienced unprecedented economic growth and the fastest rate of urbanisation in western Europe. The argument made by several commentators at the time that this material revolution had severed the cultural and social links with an older Scotland seemed plausible and convincing. Economic modernity was creating a new order. In addition, the Enlightenment literati who subjected the ancient history of Scotland to rational enquiry and dismissed much of it as mythical, fanciful and beyond belief went with the grain of the times. As a result the nation was in danger of losing its connection with its ancient past. Even the three key national institutions of church, law and education which survived the Union and which have been hailed ever since as the transmitters of Scottish national identity from generation to generation were under acute pressure in the early Victorian era. The Presbyterian Church of Scotland played a pivotal role in Scottish society, watching over morality, administering much of the nation's schooling and its systems of welfare. Through the General Assembly it provided a surrogate parliament for a stateless nation. Now this great institution was fracturing rapidly as dissenting congregations multiplied in the first few decades of the nineteenth century until the old Church finally split in two in the Disruption. Education, too, was felt to be in a sorry state. George Lewis's devastating polemic, *Scotland: A half-educated nation*, 1836, caught the mood of the times as he argued that the country's former eminence in learning was being destroyed by urban growth, irreligion and Irish immigration. Many members of the Scottish legal establishment also lost confidence. Some, such as Henry Cockburn and Francis Jeffrey, denounced Scots law as backward in comparison with that of England, while the cream of the Glasgow merchant aristocracy asserted that further legal assimilation was a necessary step in order to reap all the economic benefits that the Union could provide.

We now know with the historian's supreme advantage of hindsight that all this pessimism proved to be groundless. Indeed, what is most remarkable is that so much of what we now regard as integral and accepted features of modern Scottish identity were created, invented, renewed or strengthened in the very period when the death of Scotland was widely predicted by many thinking Scots. The very threat of the annihilation of the historic identity triggered a reaction. Sir Walter Scott himself, who feared that Scotland might become invisible, helped to pioneer major collections of Scottish ballads and folk tales. Scottish history loomed large in the most popular working-class paper of the later nineteenth century, *The People's Journal*, which by 1875 had a circulation of 130,000 a week and a quarter of a million on the eve of the First World War. It contained frequent series on the Scottish past and also had a pioneering interest in folklore and social history that went far beyond the orthodoxy of kings, queens and national heroes. Presbyterian religious history attracted wide interest. Thomas McCrie's biographies of John Knox (1811) and Andrew Melville (1819) were best-sellers. The Reformation, the Covenanters and Presbyterian heroes were commemorated in the paintings of Sir George Harvey and immortalised in numerous monuments in stone erected in several Scottish towns.

Even more potent, however, were the mythical and semi-mythical stories and personalities, set in the times before industrialisation. Here again Scott had led the way followed closely by Jane Porter's enormously influential *The Scottish Chiefs* (1810) and the continuing massive popularity of the medieval accounts of Blind Harry and Barbour's *Bruce*. Through his Waverley novels and *Tales of a Grandfather*, Scott invested the Scottish past with a magical appeal and satisfied the powerful emotional needs for nostalgia in a society experiencing unprecedented change. He was a brilliant pioneer in the invention of tradition, a process which helped to develop a new set of national symbols and icons while at the same time renewing others of venerable antiquity in the contemporary image of Victorian Scotland. The tartan and kilt of the Highlands had, even before 1830, been appropriated by some as national dress. But its adoption was given further impetus by the well-publicised deeds of the kilted regiments in the Empire, the growing number of Caledonian societies in the emigrant communities abroad with their pipe bands and tartan dress and, not least, by Queen Victoria's love affair with the Highlands. The best-loved monarch of modern times built a residence at Balmoral on Deeside and, after 1848, spent the autumn of each year on holiday there. By comparison she visited Ireland only four times in her entire reign. The fact that Victoria showed such fascination with the Highlands and was sometimes even heard to proclaim herself a Jacobite at heart was found to have a major effect.[17] Highlandism had now been given wholehearted royal approval and tartan recognised as the sartorial badge of Scottish identity. It was no surprise when a company of radical volunteers was established to fight for Garibaldi in Italy, they were dressed in tartan shirts and bonnets topped with the Scottish thistle. At the same time, Scottish landscape painting developed a fascination with 'the land of the mountain and the flood' in the work of such artists as Horatio McCulloch (1805–67), with his pictures of lochs, corries and waterfalls, notably the archetypal and hugely popular *My Heart's in the Highlands* (1860).

The adoption of romantic Highland symbolism, paradoxically at the very time when crofting society itself was experiencing the terrible agony of clearance and dispossession, was only one element in the reinvention of Scotland. The historic building tradition of castles, keeps, towers and fortifications which had died out in the later seventeenth century was rehabilitated in the Victorian period in the architectural style which became known as Scotch Baronial. A key influence here was Robert Billings (1813–74) whose multi-volume, *Baronial and Ecclesiastical Antiquities of Scotland*, published between 1848 and 1852, was the primary source for the movement. Soon turrets, battlements and towers were appearing everywhere in rich profusion, first in country houses (Queen Victoria led the way with Balmoral Castle), and then on urban sheriff courts, municipal offices and infirmaries.

Above all, the cult of national heroes became one of the most popular ways of linking urban Scotland with its history. Pre-eminent in this respect were Robert Burns and William Wallace. The modern Burns cult was born in this period. In one Burns festival in 1844 an estimated 80,000 were in attendance, and of this multitude 2,000 sat down to eat lunch, accompanied by numerous toasts to the bard. Burns' standing was reflected in the countless attempts at imitations of his verse which dominated the 'poetry corners' of local newspapers throughout Scotland. However, the historic Burns and his remarkable literary achievement were also moulded to suit the political tastes of a Victorian middle-class readership. He was depicted as anti-aristocratic and as a man who had succeeded by his own individual talent rather than through inherited privilege or noble birth. Burns became the apotheosis of 'the lad o' pairts', a key element in the most influential Victorian Scottish myths, that personal ability alone was enough to achieve success in life. But he was also praised because he linked the Scots with their rural past – it was often said that the blood of the Ayrshire Covenanters flowed in his veins – and preserved the ancient vernacular language by his genius.

The cult of William Wallace in the nineteenth century was equally complex and bears little relation to the raw nationalism of Hollywood's *Braveheart* of the 1990s. There can be little doubt that Wallace was one of the supreme Victorian icons. Magnificent statues to the hero of the Wars of Independence were erected overlooking the Tweed in Lanark, but these paled before the grandest of such projects, the 220-foot high tower of the National Wallace Monument, built near Stirling between 1859 and 1869. This colossal edifice overlooked the country where the Scots at Stirling Bridge and Bannockburn had fought their most decisive battles against the English in the fourteenth century. Wallace was not only remembered in statuary and monuments. Blind Harry's fifteenth-century epic, *The Wallace*, which was vehemently anti-English in language and tone, maintained its popularity, while tales of Bruce and Wallace were always familiar features in the local press. The Wallace cult of that period was not, however, designed to threaten the Union or inspire political nationalism, though the membership of the National Association for the Vindication of Scottish Rights were among the most enthusiastic supporters of the proposal for a national monument. Rather, the cult reminded the Scots of their own history in which the Union had been achieved *because* of Wallace's struggle for freedom. Wallace had ensured that the Scottish people had never been conquered. As a result of their own courageous fight for independence in medieval times, a fruitful union between equal partners had become possible in 1707. In addition, Wallace could appeal to a Victorian Scotland profoundly divided across class lines. To middle-class liberals, he had saved the nation when it had been betrayed by the aristocracy which still held power in the nineteenth century and which remained the reactionary enemy of many of the urban bourgeoisie throughout the Victorian era. For working-class Chartists, who often passionately sang 'Scots wha hae' at their meetings, he represented the spirit of the common man striving for freedom against oppression. The national devotion to Wallace demonstrated that pride in Scottish nationhood and loyalty to Union and empire could be reconciled.

A set of influences peculiar to the nineteenth century helped to fashion all these symbols of Scottish identity. But to a greater or lesser extent many of them harked back to an older Scotland. The pessimistic commentators of the early Victorian era underestimated the power of the past over a rapidly changing present. The inventors of tradition, the novelists, poets, song-writers, painters and architects, were not working in a vacuum. They were addressing an audience with a social memory moulded by inherited myth and story. Between the thirteenth century and 1707 Scotland had been a sovereign state with its own administrative, legal and ecclesiastical apparatus. There was also, unlike Wales, a clearly territorial Scotland which had been preserved during the medieval Wars of Independence. The nation was unified with the kingdom of England in 1603 and with the English state in 1707, but the distinctiveness of Scotland endured because the crucial forms of institutional and social identity proved much more robust than the pessimists had predicted.

The English factor was also relevant. With security on the northern border firmly established and underpinned by the proven loyalty of the Scots, Westminster could virtually afford to let Scotland go its own way within the parameters of the Union. Unlike English policy in Ireland, there was no army of occupation or extensive colonial bureaucracy. Instead, the 'elephant' reverted to a posture of benign neglect. Only in the Disruption crisis of 1843 did it stir. Indeed, from 1827 until 1885, there was no minister or department with defined responsibility for Scotland. Contrary to the assimilationist interpretation, most of the actual day-to-day business of governing Scotland remained in Scottish hands for much of the nineteenth century. Not until the passing of the Education Act 1872, the extension of the franchise to the working class on a larger scale and the creation of the Scottish Office in 1885 was there a decisive movement towards a more centralised state. Before then the United Kingdom was probably more decentralised than any other country in Europe. As in the eighteenth century, Parliament in London rarely intervened on Scottish issues unless invited to do so, and the Lord Advocate in Edinburgh continued to control such key areas as law enforcement and policing. In the second half of the twentieth century the enormous influence of the state in education, health, welfare and economic management was taken for granted. In the nineteenth century government intervention was, however, limited in the extreme.

Below the parliamentary level the routine of government and administration was devolved to town councils and supervisory boards which grew up from the 1840s. The Scottish Board of Supervision ran the Poor Law from 1845, and the Prisons Board was set up in 1838. These two were followed in due course by others for public health, lunatic asylums (1857) and education (1872). Scots lawyers staffed this new bureaucracy and its inspectors were Scots doctors, surveyors and architects. Along with these, the Scottish Burgh Reform Act 1833 created a new and powerful local state, run by the Scottish middle classes and reflecting their political religious values. It was this, rather than a distant and usually indifferent Westminster authority, that in effect routinely governed Scotland. The middle classes had, therefore, no reason to seek parliamentary independence or to adopt a nationalism which was hostile to the British state. They enthusiastically supported Kossuth in Hungary and Garibaldi in Italy in their struggles for national unity, but they did not feel similarly oppressed or need a national parliament to achieve what the middle classes in Scotland already possessed, namely liberty, economic prosperity and cultural integrity, the very advantages for which European nationalists had yearned for so long.[18]

III

On the eve of the First World War, the Anglo-Scottish Union must have seemed a rock of stability in an uncertain world. It was such a fact of life that no one of any influence questioned its future. If truth be told, the Scots had been remarkably fortunate. Rightly or wrongly, they assumed that their global economic eminence was rooted in the Union. Nevertheless, that wealth had not come at the expense of either cultural dependency or loss of identity. The old saying, 'having one's cake and eating it at the same time', does come to mind!

However, between 1914 and the 1950s, this almost smug relationship was assailed to an extent unknown since the eighteenth century. Despite final victory, the First World War was a human catastrophe on an enormous scale for Scotland. At the start of the conflict national euphoria was the mood, but by 1918 this had degenerated into dark pessimism. One historian has controversially suggested that the Scots regiments on a per capita basis, suffered most from the carnage on the Western Front. The Serbs and the Turks did have higher per capita mortality rates but this was mainly as a result of disease rather than losses in battle.[19] Whether this particular verdict is reliable or not the slaughter of the nation's young men on such a scale was entirely unprecedented. This catastrophe was then followed by the collapse of the markets for Scottish heavy industry in the late 1920s and thereafter, together with a remarkably high level of emigration which, for the first time since census records began, caused an actual fall in the Scottish population. Edwin Muir eloquently captured the crisis of national confidence in his *Scottish Journey* of 1935: 'Scotland is gradually being emptied of its population, its spirit, its wealth, industry, art, intellect and innate character', while another commentator, George Malcolm Thomson, was even gloomier: 'The first fact about the Scot is that he is a man eclipsed. The Scots are a dying race'.[20]

Yet despite all this, the Union remained impregnable. The Conservative and Unionist Party in Scotland was hugely popular between the wars, winning five of the seven General Elections over that period. During the long drawn-out economic crisis of these years, Scottish voters preferred the secure umbrella of the British state to any nationalist adventure. The foundation of the SNP in 1934 showed that not all Scots were in the unionist camp but its successive failures at the polls demonstrated conclusively that the vast majority were. Indeed, the emergence of the SNP came about in large part because of the growing indifference to Home Rule on the part of the more established Liberal and Labour parties. The outbreak of the Second World War further strengthened British identity. For a time plucky Britain and its Empire stood alone against an evil foe. Every nook and cranny of life was affected as the nation geared up for total war. The age-old distinction between combatants and non-combatants faded as the civilian population on the home front struggled against enemy bombers, food shortages and, until the end of 1941, the fear of invasion. The legacy of Britain united in a good cause endured in the folk memory of the post-1945 generation through the extraordinary popularity (and longevity) of war comics, books and films.

This was not the only vital factor buttressing Britishness. The foundation of the welfare state, promising cradle to grave security and the commitment to full employment in the post-war world, had enormous appeal for Scots who had suffered the full impact of market failure in the 1930s, as evidenced by serious unemployment levels and appalling housing conditions. With free trade, the actual impact of the Union in the nineteenth century was probably broadly neutral. Only from the 1950s with welfarism and nationalisation of industry did it once again have a marked effect on Scotland. Even the beginnings of the end of Empire with the independence of India and Pakistan did not disturb the Union connection. A new bond had been formed. As living standards finally started to improve in the 1950s and the years of austerity faded into the past, unionism in Scotland seemed unchallenged. Indeed, in 1950 Labour dropped its long-standing manifesto commitment to Scottish self-government and the SNP continued to stagnate in political irrelevance. The Unionists achieved just over half of the popular vote in 1955, a unique and remarkable achievement in Scottish electoral history.

However, this political consensus did not mean that 'Scottishness' had in any sense evaporated. On the contrary, the mass interest in the Scottish Covenant of 1949, advocating a parliament in Edinburgh within the Union and attracting nearly two million signatures, suggested that Scotland's sense of itself remained robust. Moreover, by the later 1950s all was not well with the Scottish economy. The long period of Britain's post-war relative decline against international competitors, which lasted from the 1960s to the 1990s, had begun.

The balance between 'Scottishness' and 'Britishness' now shifted. The rise of the SNP, the new and pragmatic interest in devolution by Westminster and a fresh vitality in Scottish culture were all signs of the times. A key decade was the 1980s when the English 'elephant', for the first time since the eighteenth century, moved to the Scottish side of the 'bed', with the imposition of hugely unpopular social and economic policies by the Thatcher governments. The Scots had not voted for Tory radicalism and many began to feel that they were now suffering from an electoral dictatorship. That experience put more steel into the Scottish electorate and their politicians. Any ambiguity about the relevance of a Scottish Parliament to the future of the nation quickly receded.

More than half a century on from the high noon of unionism in the 1950s the issue now is whether the time-honoured connection between Scotland and England will survive for much longer in the new millennium. Scottish identity has become stronger and more confident. In 2004, around three-quarters of Scots felt 'exclusively' or 'mainly' Scottish, a significantly higher proportion than the equivalent measures in England and Wales. These 'Scottish' loyalties are especially common among the younger generation. But that need not mean that political independence is inevitable. It may be yet another manifestation of the Union's historic capacity not only for flexibility but for giving full and easy scope for the Welsh, English and Scots to express their cultural and ethnic identities within a UK framework. Perhaps inevitably, however, most recent comment both in the media and among academic analysts has been about the reasons for the decline of 'Britishness' over the last half century. The obvious check list might include the waning of protestantism (for some writers a key ideological British resource for earlier generations), the end of Empire and Britain's subsequent fall for a time to the status of a second-rate power, the huge and increasing importance of Europe and the parallel decline in the authority of the British state and the ebbing of respect for the institution of monarchy. Again, since the end of the Second World War and the collapse of the Soviet threat, there is the loss of a clear 'other' which can help to sustain British national solidarity against a common foe.

However, whether all this means that a political divorce is likely in the short-term is less certain. Three hundred years of union have resulted in multiple familial, personal, economic and cultural connections between the two nations. Many hundreds of thousands of Scots have long migrated to England. Less well known is the continuous movement in modern times from England to Scotland. Between 1841 and 1911 a quarter of a million English and Welsh men, women and children came north. At the last census (2001) there were over 400,000 English-born residents in Scotland, by far the nation's largest immigrant group. Not so long ago, it was possible to speak with concern about the 'Englishing' of Scotland. More common nowadays is reference to the 'Scottish Raj' in English politics, media and London's financial institutions. The story about the Midlands MP who asked, why should the Scots need a parliament when 'they are running ours', may be apocryphal but still strikes a chord. The Scots have felt themselves to be provincials from time to time and have also often been the target of some English humour, but such minor irritations have never really prevented them achieving access to the highest positions in politics, business or academe south of the Border.

In addition, the economic crises of the 1970s through to the 1980s, which undermined confidence in the British state, have at present (2008) disappeared. Balance of payments problems, hyperinflation and trade union militancy have, for the last decade or so, gone from the UK. Since emerging from the recession of the early 1990s, Britain has thrived and most Scots have shared in the benefits. According to the International Monetary Fund, the growth of GDP per person in the UK was both stronger and less variable than that of other rich nations in the G7 over that period.[21] Not surprisingly, therefore, as John Curtice shows below, most Scots remain committed to the Union.

However, these good times have not led to a final stability in the relationship. As Charlie Jeffery argues in this book, the devolution settlement is not entirely fit for purpose and has too many anomalies, not least the notorious West Lothian Question, to provide a permanent and harmonious consensus on each side of the Border. Indeed, one of the novel developments of the past few years has been the rise of English nationalism, in part fuelled by perceptions in the south of mendicant Scots being subsidised by the English through the 'unfair' generosity of the Barnett Formula.

It was a profound historical irony that in the very month of the 300th anniversary of the Union a minority SNP administration first took power in Edinburgh. The pundits produced a variety of reasons for the historic success of the nationalists: these ranged from the unpopularity of the Iraq war to the mid-term malaise of the Labour government. Whatever the fundamental influences, however, there can be little doubt that the SNP victory ushered a new period of volatility in the Union, making speculation about its long-term future even more hazardous. However, research published by the Institute of Public Policy Research North in autumn 2007 cast doubt on the belief that the SNP triumph and the party's electoral popularity since May 2007, had brought the break-up of the United Kingdom much closer.[23] The Institute's findings suggested that around three in every ten Scots supported independence and that figure had hardly moved from the levels which existed even before devolution. Indeed, before the Scottish elections in 2007, only 63 per cent of those who intended to vote SNP said they supported its core policy of independence. During the course of the election campaign itself, the numbers favouring independence declined. In the event the electorate voted for unionist parties by a considerable majority and, to a large extent, the SNP's success came not from a collapse of Labour support, which fell only slightly, but from the failure of smaller parties like the Socialists and the Greens to make the kind of impact in 2007 that they had achieved in previous contests. What the research did reveal was a widespread desire in both Scotland and England for changes to be made in the devolution settlement. English voters want such anomalies as the Barnett Formula and the West Lothian Question to be addressed by Westminster, while a majority of Scots wish for more powers for the Holyrood Parliament within the framework of the Union. These results tend to suggest that in its tercentenary year the Union is far from stable but may still have much more resilience than media speculation in the spring of 2007 suggested.

Notes

1 This is a modified version of an essay which first appeared in *Scottish Affairs*, No. 57, Autumn 2006, pp. 1–18. The essay has been included here following advice to Edinburgh University Press from external academic assessors who suggested it would be a useful introductory overview of the subject of the book.

2 Quoted in I. G .C. Hutchison, 'Anglo-Scottish political relations in the nineteenth century, c. 1815–1914', in T. C. Smout (ed.), *Anglo-Scottish Relations from 1600 to 1900* (Oxford: Oxford University Press, 2005), p. 264.

3 T. C. Smout, 'Introduction', in Smout (ed.), *Anglo-Scottish Relations*, p. 2.

4 The most recent study is Christopher Duffy, *The 45* (London: Cassell, 2003).

5 *Glasgow Journal*, 28 April 1746.

6 R. C. Nash, 'The English and Scottish tobacco trades in the seventeenth and eighteenth centuries: legal and illegal Trade', *Economic History Review*, 2nd series, XXV, 1982, pp. 354–72; T. M. Devine, *Scotland's Empire 1600–1815* (London: Allen Lane. Penguin Press, 2003).

7 John Robertson, *The Scottish Enlightenment and the Militia Issue* (Edinburgh: John Donald, 1985).

8 Paul Langford, 'South Britons reception of North Britons, 1701–1820', in Smout (ed.), *Anglo-Scottish Relations*, p. 148.

9 Quoted in Douglas J. Hamilton, 'Patronage and profit: Scottish networks in the British West Indies, c. 1763–1807', unpublished Ph.D. thesis, University of Aberdeen, 1999, p. 208.

10 J. M. Cookson, *The British Armed Nation 1793–1815* (Oxford: Oxford University Press, 1997), p. 128.

11 Langford, 'South Britons', p. 148.

12 Linda Colley, *Britons* (New Haven: Yale University Press, 1992).

13 Richard J. Finlay, 'Keeping the covenant: Scottish national identity', in T. M. Devine and J. R. Young (eds), *Eighteenth Century Scotland. New Perspectives* (East Linton: Tuckwell Press, 1999), pp. 122–44.

14 L. M. Cullen, 'Scotland and Ireland, 1600–1815', in R. A. Houston and I. D. Whyte (eds), *Scottish Society, 1500–1800* (Cambridge: Cambridge University Press, 1989), pp. 241–2.

15 Colin Kidd, *Subverting Scotland's Past* (Cambridge: Cambridge University Press, 1993), p. 274.

16 For a more detailed discussion of these issues see T. M. Devine, 'The invention of Scotland', in D. Dickson, S. Duffy, C. O'Hanle and I. C. Ross (eds), *Ireland and Scotland. Nation, Region, Identity* (Dublin: Centre for Irish and Scottish Studies, 2001), pp. 18–25.

17 Richard J. Finlay, 'Queen Victoria and the cult of Scottish monarchy', in E. J. Cowan and R. F. Finlay (eds), *Scottish History. The Power of the Past* (Edinburgh: Edinburgh University Press, 2002), pp. 209–24.

18 G. Morton, *Unionist-nationalism* (East Linton: Tuckwell Press, 1999).

19 Niall Ferguson, *The Pity of War* (Harmondsworth: Allen Lane. Penguin Press, 1999), p. 298.

20 G. M. Thomson, *Caledonia or the Future of the Scots* (London: Kegan Paul, 1927), pp.18–19. For a recent survey of the problems see N. J. Evans, 'The emigration of skilled male workers from Clydeside during the interwar period', *International Journal of Maritime History*, XVII, 2006, pp. 255–80.

21 *The Economist*, 25 April 2006.

22 David McCrone, 'W(h)ither the Union? Anglo-Scottish relations in the twenty-first century', in W. L. Miller (ed.), *Anglo-Scottish Relations from 1900 to Devolution and Beyond* (Oxford: Oxford University Press, 2005), pp. 203–17.

23 As reported in *The Times*, 11 September 2007.

PART ONE
FOUNDATIONS

2

THE MAKING OF THE UNION OF
1707: HISTORY WITH A HISTORY

Christopher A. Whatley

Why Scottish politicians voted in the winter of 1706–7 to abandon their own parliament and the sovereignty that this enshrined is a question that has been the subject of discussion and, periodically, intense debate for the past three centuries. Within weeks of the decision being taken, bundles of pamphlets and other printed materials, the authors of which had harangued their readers with arguments for and against union in the preceding eighteen months or so, were being sold as job lots. Thus, even at this early stage, their vendors believed – or hoped – that interest in the issues would continue. It did. For some years the future of the Union hung in the balance, due largely to its failure to deliver the material benefits its promoters had promised. Presbyterians, too, were incensed that guarantees given in 1706 for the security of the Kirk were ignored in 1712 when Westminster approved the Toleration and Patronage Acts.[1]

By 1709 Daniel Defoe had brought out his *History of the Union*, which drew on many of his pamphlets and other contributions to public debate in the years preceding 1707. Five years later the Jacobite George Lockhart of Carnwath's *Memoirs* appeared in print – in effect a history of the Union.[2] In an appendix were listed the thirty-two recipients of the £20,000 that had been sent from London in 1706 – allegedly to ease passage of the Union through the Scottish Parliament. Responses to Lockhart at the time were often hostile. Some unionist politicians, whose reputations he had tarnished, were outraged – in at least one case Lockhart's charges had exposed the victim's duplicity.[3] To counter what he judged were several 'erroneous' claims made by Lockhart, expressed in the heat of the moment, the union-supporting Sir John Clerk embarked on a line-by-line critique of the *Memoirs*, and over a period of four decades wrote – in Latin – an alternative history.[4] This, however, was not published in English until 1993, by which time Lockhart's interpretation of how the Union had been achieved had established a head start of almost three centuries. In the view of some historians Lockhart is a bedrock source for studying the politics and politicians of the Union era. Yet Clerk had been witness to the same events as Lockhart, and was as familiar with the leading politicians of the day. Hitherto, however, posterity has been inclined to believe Lockhart's version of events, even though he too had an axe to grind. The mud has stuck.

By the end of the eighteenth century, however, the Union was generally regarded as having been beneficial – for British commerce, including Scotland's, and in the united nations' long-lasting struggle for ascendancy with France. Under the sway of Enlightenment historians such as William Robertson, pre-Union Scotland was condemned as feudal and backward.[5] Union in this Whig interpretation of Scotland's modern history was a blessing: the means by which the Scots had managed to maintain their progress from barbarism to eighteenth-century civility; an interpretation which has little support today. Scottish achievements – intellectual, cultural and economic – prior to 1707 were clearly substantial. Recent investigations have revealed that the unruliness and barbarity of the Scots, even of the much-maligned Highlanders, has been exaggerated to the point of caricature.[6]

About the Union, however, there were both caveats and critics. Even before the terms of the 1707 Treaty were settled, the seeds of an anti-London government, anti-union critique had been sown. It was nourished by widespread dissatisfaction about Scotland's treatment within the regal union, and the age-old, part visceral, hostility within Scottish society to England. Appropriated for the anti-union cause were heroic figures from Scotland's past, Wallace and the 'valiant' Bruce, while Scotland was portrayed as a freedom-loving, conquest-resisting, martial nation, perhaps the oldest in Europe. In a speech against the proposed union late in 1706 the duke of Atholl ingeniously adapted the words of the 1320 Declaration of Arbroath, to announce that as long as there were 'one hundred Scots alive, we will never enter into a treaty so dishonourable and entirely subversive as this one is'.[7] Post-1707 the critique was sustained by Jacobites and their publishers, and romanticised in song and in the work of influential national poets such as Allan Ramsay, Robert Fergusson and Robert Burns.[8] Although not always visible under the verdant canopy of Britishness and Empire that flourished in the later eighteenth century and well into the nineteenth, the roots of the anti-union critique drove deep, sustaining the Stuart-sympathising strand of Scotland's political culture.[9] It had little purchase against the dominance of a national identity in which protestantism, as assured by the

Union, reigned more or less supreme for well over two centuries. Even so, the critique's tap root could be drawn on by opponents of the Union as the opportunity arose.

Yet one hundred years ago, at its bicentenary, it appears that the Union was acceptable to most Scots. The Union had survived Westminster's decision early in the nineteenth century to administer Scotland from the Home Office, and the offence caused by English indifference to Scotland's place within it, and the Scots' contribution to British success at home and abroad.[10] It was even applauded by historians who felt able to portray the leading politicians who had negotiated it as far-sighted statesmen.[11] This was going too far, but there is another extreme. Over the past half century, a small but influential group of historians in Scotland has drawn very different conclusions, denouncing Scotland's leading politicians of the Union period as a parcel of cowardly rogues, bereft of any sense of patriotic duty and lacking any kind of moral compass.[12]

This is a highly partisan perspective. It owes something to the changed political climate in post-1945 Scotland, and the emergence of stronger nationalist sentiment which influenced the thinking of Scottish historians in the 1960s and beyond.[13] Although now substantially discredited in its application to English politics in the eighteenth century, Sir Lewis Namier's ultra-cynical assessment in 1929 of the motives that took men into parliament in the early eighteenth century was clearly influential in shaping historians' views of the forces that motivated Scottish politicians. The historical roots of the cynicism concerning pro-union parliamentarians in Scotland, however, lie in the campaign led by the Country opposition that emerged in the Scottish Parliament in the later 1690s, alluded to above. Hi-jacking the 'national' interest and fanning and directing the flames of public anger in the wake of the retreat from Darien, the Country Party attacked government ministers in Scotland as self-interested pragmatists, unscrupulously venal, and Anglophile to boot.[14]

Ministers' failure to join with the opposition in demanding from William III recognition of the legitimacy of the Company of Scotland's colony at Darien, seriously undermined their reputations.[15] Union in the eyes of their critics was the final act of treachery. For the more extreme proponents of this school of thought, the Union in 1707 represented *England's* moment of triumph, conquest of Scotland, the attainment of a goal that had driven the English nation – the great Satan – since the time of Edward I. For Scotland on the other hand, the Union represented national humiliation and ignominious defeat. In interpreting the Union this way, it has been easy for Scots who were so minded to blame all Scotland's ills on England and the English connection.

Explaining why the Union that created the United Kingdom of Great Britain in one parliament was arrived at in 1707 is in one sense straightforward. It was the monarch's will, and in the eyes of her many contemporaries, Queen Anne's triumph. That the Scottish commissioners who met with their English counterparts in the spring and early summer of 1706 to settle the broad terms of the Union felt they were acting in the Queen's service is exemplified by what they brought north with them – a specially commissioned portrait of Queen Anne, freshly painted by one of the leading court painters of the day, Sir Godfrey Kneller.[16]

Union had been advocated by King William as a means of settling growing Anglo-Scottish tensions. Amongst their causes was the succession. Following the premature death of Queen Anne's last surviving child (the duke of Gloucester) in 1700, Westminster had hurriedly, and without consulting the Scots, passed the Act of Succession in 1701. This was designed to block any attempt by the son of the exiled James VII to reclaim the throne, a serious threat following Louis XIV's recognition of the 'Old' Pretender, James Edward Francis Stuart, as 'James VIII' on the death of his father. The Scottish Parliament's passing of the Act of Security in 1703, which declared the right of Scots to choose Anne's successor, served to galvanise the Queen's belief that union was a political necessity. (There is a suggestion that Anne had welcomed and approved the Act as it served to arouse English ire, and encouraged English politicians to look more favourably on union – with significant commercial concessions – as a means of settling matters with the Scots, who were becoming increasingly difficult to manage.[17]) It was not until 1705, however, that English Whigs began to push more determinedly for such an outcome, partly for party political gain but also in the hope that this would bury the bone of contention between the two nations that the succession issue had become.[18] At risk was the Revolution settlement of 1688–9, which had seen the removal of James VII and the crowning in his stead of William of Orange. The Scottish Parliament had dug its heels in from the general election of 1702. During impassioned debates in which the voice of the federalist Andrew Fletcher was one of the most prominent, commissioners demanded concessions in return for their agreement to the terms of the succession. The Scots' demands included limitations on the powers of the crown, the right of the Scottish Parliament to be consulted over the declaration of war and making peace, trading rights, and compensation for the losses incurred by investors in the Company of Scotland. The other key consideration south of the border was the highly unpredictable outcome of the ongoing War of the Spanish Succession (1702–13), which was being waged over the future of the continent of Europe and the colonial possessions of its constituent states. The commander-in-chief of the British forces, the duke of Marlborough, was anxious to avoid any conflict at home on England's northern border, instigated either by the Scots or by the French as a diversionary tactic.

Notwithstanding the declarations of independence and national purpose that marked this period in Scottish parliamentary history, the truth is that the opposition was bolstered by a sizeable grouping of 'cavaliers' – Jacobite MPs – who had been returned in the general election of 1702. It was the Jacobites who fought hardest within the Scottish Parliament to resist – and wreck – any agreement with England over the succession, through union or otherwise. It was the Jacobites who cried most loudly of treachery. As noted already, it is from the pens of men such as the militant Jacobite George Lockhart of Carnwath, pathologically obsessive in his hatred of Hanover and the Union, that much of the picture of a nation shamed and betrayed has been drawn.[19] For Jacobites, the Union was anathema to be prevented at all costs. Under the terms of the Union the Scots agreed that after the death of the Queen, and 'in default of Issue of her Majesty', she would be succeeded by the Protestant Princess Sophia, electress and duchess dowager of Hanover. Henceforth, 'all Papists, and Persons marrying Papists' were debarred from the imperial British crown – a clause which ruled out the Old Pretender. With the treaty inaugurated, the Jacobites' aim then was to break it by musket and sword, or fatally weaken the Union by the acid drip of a critique that was designed to undermine its legitimacy. Otherwise their cause would be lost, at least for the foreseeable future.[20] They had gloried as relations between the nations worsened in 1703 and 1704, and might even have descended into open conflict.[21] We should, however, be clear that whatever their protestations, the Jacobites' interests were dynastic, and not national, even though they tried hard – not without considerable and lasting success – to conflate the two causes. Queen Anne and her advisers had good reason to fear that such was the strength of anti-English feeling in Scotland in the early 1700s that the union of the crowns might be breached, and the recent Revolution settlement of 1688–9 overturned.

The consequence was that in February 1705 Westminster passed the much resented Aliens Act. The Act threatened, among other things, to block Scottish exports to England if the Scots refused to accept the Hanoverian succession or to begin to treat for a union. This induced a further hostile response in Scotland, with the nadir in relations between the two countries being reached in April 1705 when the English captain Green and two of his crewmen were hanged in front of a braying Anglophobe mob on Leith sands.[22] But this was as bad as it got. The boil lanced, the fever cooled. Shocked, appalled even, thoughtful politicians from both sides of the border recognised the dangers that would result for both nations if the situation was allowed to deteriorate further.

For if it had, there was a strong likelihood that there would be only one winner – Catholic France, led by Louis XIV – whose aim was European hegemony. Nothing in the British constitution, John Clerk reflected some years later, 'was in all ages more terrible to France than a Union of Scotland and England'.[23] It was for this reason that funds from France were channelled into Scotland to stoke the opposition to a measure that would strengthen the existing but temporarily weakened British regal union. Some Scots believed that the concept of Great Britain was more than just a form of words. Even the Country opposition leader the duke of Hamilton could reflect in 1704 that, 'they are not good Brittains who would make a treaty difficult', and hoped the nations would not draw farther apart over the succession – in which cause he was then attempting to secure a prominent role.[24] Scots, too, celebrated the duke of Marlborough's victories on the battlefields of Europe – not least as Scottish soldiers even prior to 1707 were playing a valiant part in the allies' campaign, and had no need for union to bring them into the British camp. Indeed, with very few exceptions, members of the Scottish Parliament who had seen action in the British army were rock solid supporters of the Articles of Union.[25]

What should be emphasised, however, is that serious interest in union in England was relatively new, the period of the Cromwellian occupation excepted, and few in either country wished to repeat that experiment. Discussions about union instigated by King William had petered out. Tories in particular were loath to share the spoils of their commercial success with down-at-heel Scots Presbyterians. When the talks ended, it was the Scottish commissioners who had been disappointed, although several of them were also incensed at the offhand treatment they had received at the hands of their English counterparts. But the regret was genuine. Union had much to offer.

Hidden from history, concealed behind the thick plaque of misinterpretation that has formed over the past 300 years – and especially in recent decades – is a body of evidence that is of fundamental importance for our understanding of the making of the Union of 1707. Currently, in many minds, this rests on a number of (mainly) nationalist shibboleths. One of these, as noted already, is the claim that the drive for union came from England alone. To this is sometimes added the claim that had the Scots proved difficult, waiting offstage was an English army of occupation.[26] Another is that the terms of the treaty (including the form of union) were imposed on the Scots, with minimum consultation, and then settled without reference to public opinion in Scotland.

Uncomfortable though it may be for those who are inclined to such simplistic, faintly Anglophobic and largely parochial explanations for the Union, the fact is that there were Scots too who sought union with England. A fresh wave of such calls followed in the wake of the 'Glorious' Revolution – a pivotal event in the history of the Union of 1707. It was not a federal union that was advocated, but what was called a 'complete' or 'entire' union, that is, a union that incorporated the parliaments of Scotland and England.[27] Indeed, so interested in such a union were the Scots who petitioned the new king in 1689 about it, that a full complement of commissioners was appointed by the Convention of Estates that met in Edinburgh to secure it. Three of these men, the future earls of Seafield and Stair, along with Adam Cockburn of Ormiston, were to be union commissioners again in 1702, as well as in 1706. Indeed, within the Scottish Parliament as a whole, there was solid core of pro-Union support which can be tracked back to 1689 and through key votes in 1703 and 1706.[28] Although the nation was divided over union, supporters were to be found in most parts of Scotland: from the Borders in the south, variously throughout the central lowlands, through Argyll in the west, across to Moray in the northeast and northwards as far as Caithness and Sutherland. In Orkney and Shetland, both shire and burgh commissioners (members of parliament) were pro-Union.

The evidence adduced above turns on its head the often made but erroneous assertion that the Scottish union commissioners in London in the spring of 1706 were shocked or even surprised when their English counterparts proposed an incorporating union. It also demonstrates that at least some of the men who voted for union in the Scottish Parliament in 1706–7 were far from being last-minute converts, brought round by English bullying and bribes. No doubt many, probably most, men entered Parliament with hopes of some kind of preferment and personal pecuniary advantage. While political management, including promises of posts and pensions and promotions, helped to secure pro-Union votes, such inducements, including cash bribes, persuaded only a handful of men to change sides. (Lockhart's list of beneficiaries of Queen Anne's largesse even includes men who were not members of parliament and, in fact, most of the payments were of salary arrears.) The longer a man had been in the Scottish Parliament, the more likely it was that he would vote for incorporation. Almost half of the commissioners in the Union Parliament had been elected or had entered Parliament prior to the end of 1702; of these, nearly two-thirds voted in favour of most of the Articles of Union. Significantly, the same degree of long-standing commitment to union is to be found among its most active supporters outside Parliament. One of these was the Revd William Carstares, one time chaplain to William of Orange and from 1704 principal of the 'college' in Edinburgh. Carstares' role in dampening down Church of Scotland opposition to the Union was critical.[29]

In their support for the measure such individuals were not only consistent, but persistent. They were patriotic too. In this last respect – love of and concern for Scotland – many unionists had as strong a claim as the Jacobites and other opponents of incorporation who were rarely reticent about playing the patriotic card. Actions offer confirmation of this, and Sir David Dalrymple of Hailes provides a telling example. Dalrymple had confronted Lockhart directly over the contents of his *Memoirs*. In contrast to Lockhart, Dalrymple was an active supporter of the Revolution, and backed the Hanoverian succession. He was an advocate for and architect of union (he was a union commissioner in 1702 and 1706, as was his brother Hugh), but not at any price. He had left the 1702 union negotiations in disgust, determined that the Scots should not again be subject to the same derisory treatment. As a Westminster MP after 1707 he earned a reputation as one of the stoutest defenders of Scotland's interests.[30] Relatively few members of the Scottish Parliament were actually the ciphers and time-servers portrayed by historians of the second half of the twentieth century.

Too much was at stake for it to be otherwise. In Scotland, no less than in London, a much aired topic was the course of the war in Europe. Its reverberations were felt even in the furthest corners of the nation, as in 1703 when the Dutch fleet lying off Shetland suffered catastrophic damage at French hands. At issue were: religion – broadly the contest between protestantism and catholicism, resurgent under the counter-Reformation; politics – constitutional monarchies and meaningful parliaments in an age of monarchical absolutism; and economic success, supported by mercantilist-minded states. For Britain and her allies it was France who stood on the wrong side on all three issues, and which posed the greatest challenge. Capping the French threat was Louis XIV's drive for universal monarchy and the dangers this posed for English – and British – national integrity.[31] Often overlooked is how fearful of France many *Scots* were. France was a formidable enemy, remarkable 'for its extent of Country, vastness of Treasure, number of Forces by Sea and Land, Bravery of Officers', and the 'Wisdom and steady Council of its State-Ministers'. That a united British kingdom would be better able to counter French might was a factor that led the writer of these words, William Seton of Pitmedden, younger, to advocate incorporating union – some four years prior to his seeking the pension that it has been alleged caused him to come in behind the Court.[32] Similarly, the strategic aims around which the Scottish union commissioners united in 1706 as they gathered in London, were, first and foremost, to disappoint the 'designs of our enemies', defend protestantism and advance the riches and trade of Britain.[33]

All this is crucial if we are to comprehend in full, and free of partisan bias, the pathways that led to union in 1707. Several of the leading proponents of union in the Scottish Parliament in 1706–7 had under the later Stuarts during the 1670s and 1680s either themselves endured at first hand, or seen their countrymen, co-religionists and political allies suffer economic privation or forfeiture of their estates. Some had paid an even higher price for their faith and political agenda: imprisonment – often on the Bass Rock, and torture, including the application of the thumbikins, bone-crushing devices which were used expressly on Presbyterian dissidents. Carstares had been one of these. Several were executed. Many hundreds had fled into exile, most to the Low Countries, where they had met, caballed and committed themselves to William of Orange and the Revolution which they were in no doubt had been truly glorious.[34] Their conviction was that a Britain conjoined in an incorporating union would be better able to defend the political and religious gains of the Revolution from the twin threat posed by France under Louis XIV and the Church of Rome. This, however, was a perspective adopted by a minority of Presbyterians – largely those who looked beyond Scotland, and to the European dynastic and confessional environment discussed earlier. Presbyterianism had only been re-established formally as the national church in 1690, and in practice was faced with an uphill struggle to replace episcopalianism in the parishes. Insecure therefore, and fearing domination by the Church of England within an incorporating union, more zealous churchmen and their flocks were initially hostile. Others viewed such a union as a breach of the Scots' covenant with God to create a pan-British Presbyterian Church. Perhaps as many as tens of thousands of Scots – the heirs of the covenanters in the southwest and some central districts – continued in their opposition up to and even beyond 1707, although there was some softening with the recognition that France continued to be a powerful enemy and sponsor of militant Jacobitism.[35]

Lockhart used epithets such as 'zealous Revolutioner', and 'bigoted' Presbyterian to describe his unionist enemies – terms which at least have the merit of according those to whom they applied a vestige of political ideology. Paradoxically, it is the same language that exposes the links between the Revolution, the Hanoverian succession and union. The instigator of what Lockhart termed Scotland's 'ruine' (for which we should read the blocked interest of the male Stuart line), was James Dalrymple, earl of Stair – elder brother of the aforementioned David. It was Stair in Lockhart's eyes, who had carried 'underhand' the Revolution in Scotland, allowed England to rule 'Arbitrarily' over Scottish affairs and to destroy the nation's trade. But Stair's most heinous crime was to have been at the 'Bottom of the Union'. So, Lockhart raged, 'may [he] be Stiled the Judas of his Country'.[36] Yet notwithstanding the aptness of some of Lockhart's characterisations of politicians with whom he was familiar, the irony is that men like the 'Morose, Proud and Severe' George Baillie of Jerviswood and his circle of borders lairds who formed the core of the small new party, or *Squadrone Volante*, were moderates in matters of religion, and relatively relaxed in their lifestyles.[37] In the pro-Union camp there were even a few Episcopalians. It was among the Presbyterian opponents of union that were to be found the fundamentalists and more zealous of Scotland's early modern divines and their followers.

Unionists in Scotland may have been personally ambitious, but they were also committed to a secure, prosperous, urbane Scotland. They tended to be economic modernisers – exemplified by David Melville, third earl of Leven, an émigré and a soldier who was a major shareholder in and governor of the Bank of Scotland from 1697 until his death in 1728.[38] Men such as Leven had seen at first hand the economically robust, politically liberal example of the Netherlands and visualised what Scotland could be, but how far short of the ideal Scotland really was. The recognition that Scotland was experiencing relative decline was uncomfortable for many whatever their political allegiance and demanded rectification.[39] To turn around the ailing Scottish economy, the Scottish Parliament and privy council had after the Revolution approved an ambitious raft of legislation designed to promote trade and industry.[40] However, and notwithstanding the undoubted economic achievements of individual Scots at home and within their commercial networks overseas, the brutal truth for those concerned to create a robust Scottish *state* wielding influence on the world stage, is that such measures bore little fruit.[41] 'Scotland' was on the verge of bankruptcy, and barely viable as an independent entity.[42] Cash was in desperately short supply.[43] Europe was a continent of expanding nation-states, their trade and infant manufacturing industries backed by conquest and high tariffs, respectively. With a weakly developed state machine, including a navy which boasted only three armed vessels on the eve of the Union, Scottish overseas merchants as well as those plying coastal waters were vulnerable to enemy attack in the era of muscular mercantilism.[44] All this provided another reason why some Scots looked to Westminster, and why they were prepared to sacrifice their parliamentary independence.

There were, however, unionists who were profoundly troubled by what was to be lost – above all, Scottish sovereignty. This was an issue which, with justification, the opposition exploited to the full. Yet, as John Clerk reflected later: 'As to this sovereignty . . . I could never conceive of what it consisted', effective as it was only within Scotland. Where it mattered, on the high seas, it was of little consequence. As to 'Independency', Clerk went on, 'it was at best a meer shadow and an empty name' within the regal union.[45] A similar point was made in an address in Parliament delivered by the young earl of Roxburghe, one of the leading figures in the *Squadrone Volante* whose votes held the balance in the Scottish Parliament. On 3 November 1706, Roxburghe remarked that he had 'heard a great many fine speeches against this union . . . but one thing I observe, that there is no remedy proposed by them, for our present ill circumstances we now lie under . . . How is it my lord to remedy these evils, I know no way but this union'.[46]

Roxburghe was not alone. *Squadrone* men had sided with the country party opposition in the aftermath of Darien, and contributed to the outpouring of patriotic anti-Court ardour that marked the proceedings of the Scottish Parliament between 1703 and 1705. Yet in April 1706, as rumours of the terms of the treaty filtered north, these very same men were turning towards union, not only as it would secure the Revolution and the Hanoverian succession by removing Anglo-Scottish tensions and acting as a bulwark against France. Also important was the fact that the Company of Scotland investors were now to be compensated. In 1702 the complicated financial package – the Equivalent – which was worth almost £400,000, (£55.5 million at 2006 prices) had not been available in the form arrived at in 1706. Other figures were bandied about, but £400,000 which was 2.6 times the cash actually raised by the seriously under-capitalised Company of Scotland, offered a welcome injection of liquidity to a cash-parched economy.[47] The significance of compensation for Company of Scotland subscribers in easing the passage of the Union should not be overestimated, however, even within the *Squadrone*. Roxburghe, for instance, had no direct interest in the company. Among members of parliament generally, more non-stockholders voted in favour than did those who held company stock.[48]

Union also secured the union of trade that many Scots had long sought. Even if this was restricted to the Atlantic and blocked Scottish ambitions for direct involvement in the Far East, the fact is that this article of the treaty attracted more opposition votes than any other in its favour. In addition, Scottish merchant ships could now call on the Royal Navy and the convoy system to provide protection on the high seas from French and other privateers – as they had begun to do as the Union negotiations got under way.[49]

There were, however, other reasons why the articles were approved. Contrary to what has so often been alleged of them, a number of the Scots commissioners who went to London in the spring of 1706 to hammer out the broad terms of a union did so determined to represent what they understood to be the will of the Scottish Parliament, and to return north if they were unable to obtain the guarantees they sought.[50] Critical was the retention of what were called the 'Fundamentals': these included the legal system and the law courts, and the uniquely Scottish, Convention of Royal Burghs. Scotland's civil society thereby remained intact, distinct from and not subordinate to England.

Once back in Scotland, far from being impervious to public opinion, court politicians responded by making adjustments to the articles. First though, the Church of Scotland was secured by a separate Act – a step that finally cleared away mainstream Presbyterian reservations about incorporation. Politicians, too, were aware of how potent a symbol of Scottish nationhood the honours of Scotland were, which not even Cromwell's forces had been able to seize. Outrage would have resulted had these gone south, and rumours swept Edinburgh that this was what was intended. Inserted into the treaty, therefore, was the undertaking that the Scottish crown and sword and sceptre of state would forever remain in Scotland – as they have. Similar steps were taken to secure the independent nation's memory – its written records – which were also to be retained in Scotland. Several of the Articles dealing with economic matters, including taxation, were amended in response to demands for protection for particular industries and interests.[51]

Scottish politicians who sought union in 1706–7 and approved its terms were not a parcel of rogues. Rather they were men who, in the immensely difficult circumstances of the time, believed they were making the right choice for Scotland. They stood their ground against the swell-tide of popular opposition when it might have been easier to do otherwise. The background was near global war, and a new political settlement in Britain that international instability was putting at risk. Union was achieved at an historical moment that suited England, but the monarch who pushed it through, Anne, was queen of Scots too – and increasingly popular as better news from the European theatre of war began to filter back to Scotland after the allies' victory at Blenheim in 1704. In some respects union was settled on England's terms, but much was conceded to satisfy the Scots. Union also served what its Scottish supporters reckoned were Scotland's strategic interests. Although those who pushed for and agreed the terms of the Union were realists, they also had a particular confessional, dynastic and material vision for the nation – much of which was realised. The Treaty of 1707 was not a union of conquest, or of social and cultural hegemony, as were some unions elsewhere in early modern Europe. Scots – whether for or against the Union – have made sure of this by rising to the defence of and maintaining with varying degrees of success Scotland's language, its pre-Union history and heritage and its institutions. Experience was to show that the parliamentary union was capable of adaptation as circumstances demanded. But a union that was forged partly on the basis of confessional preference looks increasingly anachronistic for a society striving to free itself of outdated religious prejudices. Other contexts which earlier sustained the case for incorporation have also changed. Whatever choice Scots make about their constitutional future, this should be based not on the part party-driven, anti-Union critique of 1707, with its stray hints of Anglophobia – echoes of which are still be to heard in some quarters – but on an assessment of world conditions now and the nation's needs for the twenty-first century.

Notes

1 See C. A. Whatley, *The Scots and the Union* (Edinburgh: Edinburgh University Press, 2006, 2007), pp. 322–46.

2 *Memoirs Concerning the Affairs of Scotland From Queen Anne's Accession to the Throne To The Commencement of the Union of the Two Kingdoms of Scotland and England in May 1707* (London, 1714).

3 C. A. Whatley and D. J. Patrick, 'Contesting interpretations of the Union of 1707: the abuse and use of George Lockhart of Carnwath's Memoirs', *Journal of Scottish Historical Studies*, 21, 1 (2007), pp. 27–30.

4 National Archives of Scotland [NAS], Clerk of Penicuik MSS, GD 18/6080, *Memoirs Concerning the Affairs of Scotland*, with MS annotations by Sir John Clerk; D. Duncan (ed.), *History of the Union of Scotland and England by Sir John Clerk of Penicuik* (Edinburgh: Scottish History Society, 1993).

5 C. Kidd, *Subverting Scotland's Past: Scottish Whig Historians and the Creation of an Anglo-British Identity, 1689–c.1830* (Cambridge: Cambridge University Press, 1993), pp. 180–4.

6 A. I. Macinnes, *Clanship, Commerce and the House of Stuart, 1603–1788* (East Linton: Tuckwell Press, 1996), p. 31.

7 W. Ferguson, *The Identity of the Scottish Nation: An Historic Quest* (Edinburgh: Edinburgh University Press, 1998), p. 151; Whatley, *Scots*, p. 297.

8 W. Donaldson, *The Jacobite Song: Political Myth and National Identity* (Aberdeen: Aberdeen University Press, 1988); M. G. H. Pittock, *Inventing and Resisting Britain: Cultural Identities in Britain and Ireland, 1685–1789* (Houndmills: Macmillan, 1997), p. 32.

9 See M. G. H. Pittock, *The Invention of Scotland: The Stuart Myth and the Scottish Identity, 1638 to the Present* (London: Routledge, 1991).

10 See T. M. Devine, *Scotland's Empire, 1600–1815* (London: Allen Lane, 2003).

11 See, for example, P. Hume Brown (ed.), *The Union of 1707: A Survey of Events* (Glasgow: George Outram, 1907), and A. V. Dicey and R. S. Rait, *Thoughts on the Union Between England and Scotland* (London: Macmillan, 1920).

12 Most recently exemplified in P. H. Scott, *The Union: Why and How?* (Edinburgh: Saltire Society, 2006).

13 The prime example is William Ferguson's masterly *Scotland's Relations with England: A Survey to 1707* (Edinburgh: John Donald, 1977); see

too P. H. Scott, *Andrew Fletcher and the Treaty of Union* (Edinburgh: John Donald, 1992).

14 On the emergence of the country opposition, see K. Bowie, *Scottish Public Opinion and the Anglo-Scottish Union, 1699–1707* (Woodbridge: Boydell Press, 2007), pp. 27–44; on politics the classic texts are P. W. J. Riley's, *King William and the Scottish Politicians* (Edinburgh: John Donald, 1979), and *The Union of England and Scotland* (Manchester: Manchester University Press, 1978).

15 See D. W. Hayton, *The House of Commons, 1690–1715* (Cambridge: Cambridge University Press, 2002), p. 505.

16 *Edinburgh Courant*, 22 July 1706.

17 Whatley, *Scots*, pp. 215–16.

18 C. A. Whatley, *Bought and Sold for English Gold? Explaining the Union of 1707* (East Linton: Tuckwell Press, 2001), p. 51.

19 D. Szechi, *George Lockhart of Carnwath, 1689–1727: A Study in Jacobitism* (East Linton: Tuckwell Press, 2002), pp. 157–81.

20 For an account that captures the intensity of the Jacobites' commitment to the overthrow of the existing political order, see D. Szechi, *1715: The Great Jacobite Rebellion* (New Haven: Yale University Press, 2006).

21 Whatley, *Scots*, p. 212.

22 For a recent account see E. J. Graham, *Seawolves: Pirates and The Scots* (Edinburgh: Birlinn, 2005), pp. 153–90.

23 NAS, GD 18/6080, *Memoirs*, p. 222.

24 Whatley, *Scots*, p. 85.

25 K. M. Brown, 'From Scottish lords to British officers: state building, elite integration and the British army in the seventeenth century', in N. Macdougall (ed.), *Scotland and War, AD 79–1918* (Edinburgh: John Donald, 1991), p. 152.

26 In 1705 English troops had been sent north to resist any incursions *from* Scotland. In 1706 a military presence had been requested by Scottish ministers, largely to quell public disorders that looked as though they might get out of hand.

27 Duncan, *History*, p. 131.

28 I. MacLean and A. McMillan, *State of the Union: Unionism and the Alternatives in the United Kingdom since 1707* (Oxford: Oxford University Press, 2005), pp. 28–9.

29 A. I. Dunlop, *William Carstares and The Kirk By Law Established* (Edinburgh: Saint Andrew Press, 1967), p. 115.

30 E. Cruickshanks, S. Handley and D. W. Hayton (eds), *The House of Commons, 1690–1715* (Cambridge: Cambridge University Press, 2004), 4 vols, IV, pp. 825–33.

31 S. Pincus, 'The English debate over universal monarchy', in J. Robertson (ed.), *A Union for Empire: Political Thought and the Union of 1707* (Cambridge: Cambridge: University Press, 1995), pp. 50–62.

32 *The Interest of Scotland in Three Essays* (London, 1702), p. 59; Scott, *Andrew Fletcher*, p. 119.

33 Whatley, *Scots*, p. 235.

34 See G. Gardner, *The Scottish Exile Community in the Netherlands, 1660–1690* (East Linton: Tuckwell Press, 2004); for the contemporaneous sense of what the Revolution meant for Scottish protestants, see Revd R. Wodrow, *The History of the Sufferings of the Church of Scotland from the Restoration to the Revolution* (Glasgow: Blackie, Fullarton, 1828 edn).

35 Whatley, *Scots*, p. 368.

36 Lockhart, *Memoirs*, pp. 95–8.

37 Whatley and Patrick, 'Contesting interpretations', pp. 41–4.

38 R. Saville, *Bank of Scotland: A History, 1695–1995* (Edinburgh: Edinburgh University Press, 1996), p. 827; Whatley, *Scots*, p. 301.

39 C. A. Whatley, 'Taking stock: Scotland at the end of the seventeenth century', in T. C. Smout (ed.), *Anglo-Scottish Relations from 1603 to 1900* (Oxford: Oxford University Press, 2005), pp. 105–6.

40 R. Saville, 'Scottish modernisation prior to the Industrial Revolution', in T. M. Devine and J. R. Young (eds), *Eighteenth Century Scotland: New Perspectives* (East Linton: Tuckwell Press, 1999), pp. 6–14.

41 See S. Murdoch, 'Scotland and Europe', in Bob Harris and A. R. Macdonald (eds), *Scotland: The Making and Unmaking of the Nation, c. 1100–1707* (Dundee: Dundee University Press, 2007), pp. 126–44.

42 Whatley, 'Taking stock', pp. 106–7.

43 Whatley, *Scots*, pp. 184–202.

44 E. J. Graham, *A Maritime History of Scotland, 1650–1790* (East Linton: Tuckwell Press, 2002), pp. 89–93.

45 Duncan, *History*, pp. 199–200.

46 National Archives of Scotland, Hamilton MSS, GD 406/M9/266, Parliamentary Minutes, 1706–7, f.33.

47 D. Watt, *The Price of Scotland: Darien, Union and the Wealth of Nations* (Edinburgh: Luath Press, 2007), p. 221.

48 McLean and McMillan, *State*, p. 43.

49 Whatley, *Scots*, pp. 360–1.

50 *Ibid.*, pp. 238–9.

51 MacLean and MacMillan, *State*, pp. 37–8.

3

POPULAR RESISTANCE, RELIGION AND THE UNION OF 1707

Karin Bowie

From October 1706 to January 1707, the Scottish Parliament voted, article by article, to ratify a treaty to incorporate the kingdoms of Scotland and England into a new British kingdom. As it did so, dozens of petitions against the treaty rained down on Parliament, riots erupted in the streets of Edinburgh and Glasgow and angry demonstrators burned the treaty in towns like Dumfries and Stirling. From 1707 to the present, many histories of the making of the Union have highlighted this popular resistance to it. In more extreme accounts, popular protest has been linked with evidence of political management to create a story of corruption and treachery, in which a self-serving parliament sold out the Scottish people for personal gain.[1] In recent years, some historians have challenged these accounts, providing evidence of other factors, particularly religion, which operated alongside political management in determining parliamentary votes for union.[2] The idea of a helplessly betrayed people can also be questioned. A closer look at the sources suggests a more nuanced picture, one that helps us to better understand why the Union was made in 1707 and remained in place thereafter. In popular as well as parliamentary politics, religious differences were a key factor in the making of the Union in Scotland.

Divergences in Scottish religious culture underpinned clear divisions of opinion appearing in the surviving evidence of public debates and popular protests on the Union treaty. These sources suggest that many parliamentary votes for union reflected the views of a religiously moderate camp that favoured, or at least accepted, incorporation. On the anti-union side, both the parliamentary opposition and a wider body of anti-incorporation opinion were dominated, and fractured, by the hardline religious commitments of covenanting Presbyterianism and Jacobite Episcopalianism. From the national to the local level, adherence to competing covenanting and Jacobite visions of the Scottish Church and monarchy informed popular opinion and actions against the treaty. Despite the appearance of popular unity in the anti-incorporation camp, covenanting Presbyterians and Jacobite Episcopalians formed two ultimately incompatible wings in this camp. Hampered by their differences, protesters managed to intimidate the government into offering concessions on the treaty but could not block the union. As more aggressive resistance faltered, the government marshalled the often lukewarm support of a majority of parliamentarians in favour of an amended treaty.

It is difficult to assess popular or public opinion in pre-modern times, with no mass media to supply news and commentary or opinion polls to take the pulse of a nation. Nevertheless, Scotland in the early eighteenth century experienced notable advances in the publicity of its national affairs, with pamphlets and mass petitions accompanying strident debates on the Anglo-Scottish union not just in Parliament but the General Assembly and the Convention of Royal Burghs. Politics, according to one pamphlet author writing in 1700, was not just for nobles and MPs but all citizens. This author urged his readers to ensure that Parliament made good laws by being 'diligent, in putting the Members of Parliament in mind of their Duty'.[3] Devices like petitions allowed ordinary people in the localities to lay their grievances before Parliament, usually in campaigns initiated by leaders in the parliamentary opposition, known as the Country Party.

Popular political engagement relied on information supplied by pamphlets, newspapers, letters and oral exchanges between Edinburgh and provincial communities. By 1700, Scotland enjoyed strong levels of reading literacy, especially in its towns.[4] Augmented by oral communications, this supported the spread of news and arguments throughout the Lowlands. Many of the political pamphlets of the day have survived, providing evidence of the range of opinions expressed on the Union question. While public opinion cannot be extrapolated from a single pamphlet, an accumulation of pamphlets on particular issues can indicate hot topics and shared ideas, especially where tracts by private authors joined those of known political figures or paid writers. Alongside this, petitions and crowd protests emanating from local areas can give a more direct reading on the opinions of at least some groups and regions. While recognising that party organisers influenced petitions, the expression of particular views in these texts can point us to the strength of certain opinions at the local level. Views expressed in petitions can also be corroborated by other protest activities, such as riots or organised demonstrations. These do not suggest that everyone in a given locality held a particular opinion, but they indicate that enough people held it to allow protestors to feel justified in expressing their views. Here the type of protest, the degree of participation in it and whether or not the authorities responded can provide important clues to the potency of local feeling.

By interpreting these diverse sources in conjunction with an understanding of religious traditions in Scotland, we can begin to piece together a picture of popular opinion on the union question. It should be stressed that this picture is almost entirely a Lowland view. There are few records of tracts, petitions or crowd protests from Gaelic-speaking areas, while surviving Gaelic poetry offers only fragmentary glimpses of opinion outside the Lowlands. Additionally, the picture is skewed towards Scotland's middling sorts – literate lairds, tenant farmers, burgesses and clergy – who read and circulated pamphlets and newspapers and helped to organise and sign local petitions. Nevertheless, broad social diversity can be found in many petitions, with the signatures of illiterate persons being provided by notaries or parish elders, and in a variety of crowd activities. This allows us to reconstruct at least a tentative picture of popular opinion, or, more precisely, the varying opinions of those Lowland Scots who were able and willing to engage with national affairs.

New research has made it clear that parliamentary votes for the Treaty of Union rested on a core commitment to the Revolution of 1688–9 and a desire to secure Scotland from a return of the Catholic Stuarts ousted in the Revolution. Many also wished to maintain the Presbyterian Church, which had been re-established in the Revolution settlement with the removal of the Stuarts and the Episcopalian Church. Lastly, some hoped that the Union treaty's economic concessions, including free trade with England and its colonies, would allow the Scottish economy to recover from a deep recession dating from the 1690s.[5] The evidence of the public debates on union suggests that this parliamentary support for the treaty reflected opinions held by a wider, though still limited, constituency.

Unionism appealed most to those who were moderate in their religious commitments. This encompassed Presbyterians and Episcopalians who thought it was more important to protect protestantism from a perceived French Catholic threat than to convert other Protestants to their particular form of church government. The Presbyterians in this group represented a new generation ready to accept the establishment of Episcopacy in England alongside a firm and secure Presbyterian Church in Scotland. This meant that they

had relinquished the requirements of the 1643 Solemn League and
Covenant, which demanded the further reformation of England along
Presbyterian lines. Similarly, moderate Episcopalians rejected
Jacobitism and the idea that the Stuarts must return to restore
Episcopacy to Scotland. They looked to incorporation with
Episcopalian England as the best means to secure toleration for their
meeting-houses.[6]

Surviving pamphlets reveal the thoughts of moderate Presbyterians
who, often grudgingly, supported incorporation. Faced with the question of whether Catholic France or Episcopalian England posed a
greater threat to Presbyterian Scotland, these writers pointed to
France and its support of the Stuarts, though they still sought to
ensure that the terms of union would prevent English domination of
Scotland. Writing early in the session, the advocate John Spotiswoode
indicated his fear of 'the Tyrant of France, that Grand Enemy of
Christendom' and advocated a 'well ballanc'd Union' between
Scotland and England to meet this threat. To achieve such a union, he
advised Parliament to amend the treaty to better secure the Scottish
Church from English encroachment.[7] After an Act to this effect was
passed in November 1706, another advocate, Francis Grant, found
himself able to support the treaty. In a tract published late in the
1706–7 session, Grant expressed regret that circumstances would not
allow Scotland to maintain its own parliament, but saw the treaty as
'the only remaining Remedy of all our Incumbent and Imminent
Disasters'. Incorporation would confirm the Revolution monarchy
and improve trade while providing the Presbyterian Church with 'a
better Fence than ever was in this or any other Nation'.[8]

As these tracts suggest, unionists were aware of the dangers of
English power in union, but saw advantages for Scotland with appropriate safeguards. These advantages included the resolution of severe
economic problems blamed by observers on the existing Anglo-
Scottish union. Since 1603, Scotland and England had been joined in a
union of crowns under one monarch. This connection had been under
attack in recent years as the failure of a Scottish colony at Darien in
South America, combined with restrictions on trade resulting from
repeated British wars with France, highlighted Scotland's subordinate
position in the union. In pamphlets and parliamentary speeches,
heated demands were made for constitutional reforms to reduce
English hegemony in the existing union. With few proposing complete
separation, most argued for economic and constitutional concessions
within a confederal or federal union. In essence, federalists demanded

a union of crowns with free trade and a more powerful Scottish Parliament. Others, not expecting England to concede free trade without an entire union, turned to incorporation.

A small stream of pamphlets expressed the incorporationist position in Scotland from 1700, marked by a resigned acceptance of Scotland's weakened position after a century in the union of crowns. In 1700, William Seton of Pitmedden concluded that 'there is a Necessity for Scotland, either to unite with England, or separat from it' due to 'the Experience of 97 years' in the union of crowns. Seton concluded in favour of incorporation and called on the 1700–1 Parliament to petition the King for a closer union. The same pamphlet also indicated Seton's religious moderation as he urged his fellow Scots to set aside disputes between forms of protestantism to focus on the greater threat of expansionary catholicism.[9] Similarly, an anonymous manuscript tract of 1702 stated that 'Priest Craft never yet made any Natione either Rich, Wise or Strong' but 'the Hony Lys in the Trade'. The author advocated 'a free and Common Trade' with England, hoping that 'having once got in a foot we may possibly scrue into the bowels of their hive'. As he saw it, the loss of the Scottish kingdom was no loss when set against expected gains.[10] As the Scottish Parliament turned to consider union in 1706, Seton, now a member for Aberdeenshire, urged Parliament to accept the treaty as the best possible path to prosperity for Scotland.[11] Before the session opened, backing was reported from some merchants, 'especially in Glasgow', who expected the treaty to yield 'vast wealth by liberty of Trading in the West Indies'.[12]

Though these supporters of union were willing to give up the Scottish kingdom, few aspired to replace Scotland with Britain.[13] Only Daniel Defoe, the English writer sent to Edinburgh to write propaganda for union, and one prominent Scot, the politician George Mackenzie, earl of Cromarty, made any real attempt to build a sense of national identification with 'Britain'. Unionist writers and speakers made reference to a Protestant Britain, but they concentrated on Scotland, its troubles and the anticipated benefits of incorporation for the Scots. Incorporation was not celebrated as an end in itself, but as a means to particular ends for Scotland. As Seton put it, 'I wish nothing more than the Prosperity and Wellfare of my Country, and know no better means to procure the same, than by Uniting on such Honourable and Advantageous terms'.[14] Unionists like Seton stressed the patriotism of their position, a claim that rested on a definition of Scotland as a people and a national church, not as a sovereign kingdom. When the treaty was ratified in January 1707, unionist speakers congratulated 'all Scotsmen, who may now at last pursue true honour and dignity and true freedom, freedom that is substantial, not a shifting shadow or an empty ghost', claiming that 'Scotland, guided by us, has been led from the political wilderness on to the only true road to happiness and prosperity'.[15] For these unionists, it was more important to aid the Scots by preserving their Presbyterian Church and improving their prosperity than by retaining what they saw as the profitless constitutional structure of the Scottish kingdom.[16]

Yet while seeing advantages in closer union, many unionists still expressed a cautious and conditional approach to the treaty. It has often been noted that there were no petitions or demonstrations in favour of the treaty but many against. In part this reflected the oppositional nature of petitions and protests in early modern Scottish politics. By definition, petitions were less likely to be generated in favour of government policy. It also suggests the limited and unimpassioned nature of Scottish support for incorporation. Though some propagandists like Defoe attempted to paint glowing pictures of life after union, others like Seton admitted that incorporation might not be much better than Scotland's current state. All he could promise was that it could be no worse.[17]

An attempt to generate petitions in favour of the treaty demonstrated the conditional nature of Scottish unionism. The burgh council of Ayr submitted an address to Parliament stating that they were 'fullie satisfied that ane union with England is very desyreable and hes bein much wished for', but still expressed reservations about the terms of union and asked for 'rectificationes' on 'dewties and publict Taxes' in the treaty. This petition indicated the position of many, like the author John Spotiswoode, who did not hold a dogmatic objection to incorporation but wished for improved terms and safeguards. Government ministers soon realised the futility of organising further petitions, especially when the Ayr petition was firmly refuted by a competing address signed by over 1,000 'merchants, Deacons of trads and other Inhabitants' of Ayr. Support among expatriate Scots in London appeared more readily, with some proposing to send up an address to Parliament in favour of the treaty. The earl of Mar expressed interest in using this for private lobbying among members of parliament, but the project was quashed in London for fear that opinions from the south would 'irritat the discontented' in Scotland.[18]

If only a few Scots were enthusiastic enough to petition in support of the treaty, more were ready to acquiesce for fear of something worse. Some expected that rejection of the treaty would lead the English to renew the 1705 Aliens Act, with its threat of economic sanctions. In the burgh of Montrose, the magistrates asked the town's representative to support incorporation lest the English retaliate against their linen trade.[19] John Spotiswoode also warned of the dangers of English resentment in his tract: were Parliament to throw out the treaty, 'who can think that a Nation so Powerful, so High, and so Renown'd and Victorious, can put up [with] such an Affront?'.[20] War between England and Scotland had been mooted in pamphlets in 1705 and remained in the air in 1706–7. Support for the treaty also turned on fears of civil disorder within Scotland. A perilous state of mayhem seemed imminent as riots broke out in Edinburgh and Glasgow in October and November 1706 and rumours spread of preparations for an armed march on Parliament. Concern for bloody unrest and a possible Jacobite coup underpinned clerical support for a letter issued by the Commission of the General Assembly early in December 1706 asking clergy to help calm the people in the parishes. At the same time, the movement of royal troops to the English border and Northern Ireland in November, though intended to put down any insurrection against Parliament, served to emphasise England's martial power.[21]

If ratification relied on a combination of feared consequences and anticipated gains, it also rested on the opposition's failure to destabilise the 1706–7 parliamentary session. In May 1700 the opposition had used mass petitioning to disrupt Parliament and had walked out in protest in 1702, setting potential precedents for 1706–7. Anti-unionists succeeded in organising remarkable levels of popular petitioning and crowd protests against the treaty, accompanied by the publication of large numbers of anti-union pamphlets. These included eighty petitions from shires, burghs and parishes, riots in Edinburgh and Glasgow and demonstrations in Glasgow, Dumfries and Stirling. Nevertheless, it proved impossible to launch sufficiently aggressive action against Parliament as fundamental differences within the anti-union camp eroded its unity. Presbyterian and Jacobite anti-unionists shared a generic sense of patriotism to the Scottish kingdom and could agree on certain arguments, such as those against higher customs and excise taxes in economic union or the paucity of Scotland's representation in the new British Parliament, but they could not concur on alternatives to the treaty. Though the personal ambitions of the nobles who led these groups contributed to their problems, ideological incompatibility played a major role in reducing the effectiveness of popular resistance. Jacobite Episcopalians and covenanting Presbyterians both protested the loss of the Scottish kingdom, but disagreed on the nature of the kingdom they hoped to save.

For hardline Presbyterians, the National Covenant of 1638 and Solemn League and Covenant of 1643 required them to defend what they saw as a covenanted Presbyterian Church and kingdom. The treaty offended their covenanting principles by erasing the Scottish kingdom and replacing the Scottish Parliament with a British assembly in which English bishops would sit. More pragmatically, Anglicans would have a clear majority in the new Parliament. While moderates highlighted the problem of Catholic France, covenanting Presbyterians saw not just France but England and its Anglican Tories as an immediate threat to the Revolution and, therefore, the Presbyterian Church. They expected the Tories to disestablish the Presbyterian Church or at least give toleration to Scottish Episcopalians in union. Toleration in turn was expected to encourage Jacobitism, a connection recently reinforced in 1703 during a public uproar over toleration proposals.[22] As a result, anti-union Presbyterians argued that incorporation would undermine the Revolution, not preserve it as the unionists suggested. The Hebronites, a body of extreme Presbyterians in the southwest, stressed 'hou easie an access throw this and the great ferment of the Nation, it may make for the pretended K. James the 8ᵗ to come to the Throne, at least we cannot understand how this Union can put a barr therupon'.[23]

Fuelled by anxieties about the English and the security of the Revolution, many Presbyterians protested against the treaty during the 1706–7 session. Most of the eighty addresses delivered to the Scottish Parliament from ordinary people in the shires, burghs, parishes and presbyteries contained an explicitly Presbyterian message.[24] Though Jacobite and Presbyterian political leaders in Edinburgh collaborated on a petition text that barely mentioned the national church, many addressers rewrote this to emphasise what they saw as the endangerment of their covenanted Presbyterian Church. The parish of Clackmannan added its fear that incorporation 'may prove destructive to the present Church government', while several Lanarkshire parishes expressed their dismay at the prospect of being subject to 'the English and there Prelats in a Brittish Parliament'. A number of localities prepared their own petitions, including the town and parish of Culross and three neighbouring parishes. These Fife parishioners joined together to declare the treaty 'inconsistent with the knowen presbiterian principles of this Church and Covenants by which we are bound'. They begged Parliament 'that yow would not Incorporat this Nation with England, so as to extinguish Our Soveraignity and parliaments; without the continuing of which: we are in feares to be exposed to new sufferings upon Accompt of Religion'. At the same time, they also asked Parliament to protect the kingdom and Church by securing the Protestant succession against 'Popish pretenders'.[25]

While incorporationists felt able to solve the problem of the Protestant succession by joining with England in a British union, anti-incorporationists like those in Culross did not. Distrust of England also appeared in economic matters with widespread complaints on the imposition of higher English customs and excise rates and the likely domination of British trade by the English through their control of parliamentary regulation. The Culross petition protested against the prospect of 'new and heavie Taxes' and the 'hasard of being exposed to Additional burdens' imposed by 'the English in a British parliament, who cannot know how to Adjust and proportion Taxes upon the people of this Nation, so well as a Scots parliament'. This petition echoed that of the Convention of Royal Burghs, which had complained of 'the English taxes' and stressed the risks posed by 'the English in a Brittish parliament' in which Scotland would have only a 'mean representatione'. The town of Cupar rewrote this text to make the point even more clear: by the treaty, 'all that is dear to us' would be 'unavoidably Exposed and in danger of being Incroached on[,] Altered or intirely Extirpat and Ruined by the English in a British Parliament'.[26]

While accepting the British union of crowns, covenanting Presbyterians rejected closer union on terms other than those of the 1643 Solemn League and Covenant. Public demands in recent years for a renegotiation of the terms of the union of crowns had led many to expect that a form of federal union would be agreed between Scotland and England. In their petition against incorporation, the town and parish of Lanark expressed their hope that 'such ane Union may be carried on and concluded, as may be Honourable and Safe, and make both Nations happy'. This meant a union that maintained, in Lanark's words, 'the soveraignity and independency of this Kingdom and the being and continuance of our parliament (where the Nation is fully represented)' as well as 'our Glorious work of

Reformation and established Church Government according to the vowes of God upon us'.[27] Many Presbyterians saw anything less as a shameful conquest by a neighbour who had long been trying to dominate Scotland. The parish of Cambuslang made this explicit in its plea for a union that preserved the Presbyterian Church, the rights and liberties of which 'England hath still been attempting to robb us, since the Union of the two crowns'.[28]

At a superficial level, distrust of the English and rejection of incorporation provided a shared platform for covenanting Presbyterians and Jacobite Episcopalians as both groups sought to defend the Scottish kingdom. The Jacobites, however, envisioned the Scottish kingdom not as a covenanted Presbyterian realm but as an Episcopalian kingdom ruled by hereditary Stuart monarchs.[29] For them, the union threatened their hopes of overturning the Revolution of 1688–9 and reinstating the Anglo-Scottish union and Episcopalian Church as established in the Restoration period. Therefore, though they wished to prevent incorporation, they could not support the strongest political alternative, a settlement of the open Scottish succession on the Protestant heir already named by England, Sophia of Hanover. This meant that the opposition faced serious difficulties in cooperating to defeat the treaty, as they could only join together in generalised political and economic complaints.

In public debates on the Anglo-Scottish union before 1706–7, opposition writers and speakers had promulgated a secularised form of Scottish patriotism that focused on the kingdom's martial honour, ancient crown and historical resistance to English aggrandisement. This drew on popular resentment of England, aggravated by recent events, and provided a veneer of unity for opposition factions cooperating in attacks on the government. In 1704, as a Jacobite–Presbyterian coalition resisted the settlement of the succession, an Aberdeenshire laird, William Forbes of Disblair, celebrated Scottish self-assertion in his poem *The Scots genius reviving*:

> Rous'd from a Lethargy of hundred Years
> At last her Martial Head Old Scotia Rears
> Despite the attempts of the English to take her crown:
> It proves to[o] closly fix'd to Scotland's Head

Disblair followed this in 1705 with a poem attacking English attempts to pressure Scotland into union, *Pill for pork-eaters: or, a Scots lancet for an English swelling*. The poem called for unity in the name of old Scotland, with no mention of the kingdom's church:

Let our Chiefs all Factious Broils oppose,
And join together in our Common Cause.
Insulting England to her Cost shall know,
What brave united Scots-men then can do.[30]

Faced with the Treaty of Union in 1706, Presbyterians and Jacobites tried to make common cause for the ancient Scottish kingdom. Both groups could support anti-English expressions like that found in a 1706 broadside warning the Scots not to let go of their sovereignty lest they 'All be Slaves'.[31] Some Presbyterians and Jacobites managed to work together in the 1706–7 petitioning campaign, using a shared text that minimised their religious differences while entreating Parliament to preserve the Scottish kingdom and Parliament 'which have been so valiantly maintained by our heroick ancestors for the space of two thousand years'.[32] Anti-unionists of any stripe could join in riots in which government figures were targeted or demonstrations in which the Articles of Union were burned. A march of the trades in Glasgow in early November brought together the town's artisans with a simple anti-incorporation message, the men having papers pinned to their hats saying 'No incorporating union'.[33] Together these protest efforts produced remarkable levels of popular engagement in political affairs and brought significant pressure to bear on the government in Edinburgh.

Difficulties arose when national leaders attempted to organise Presbyterian–Jacobite action requiring agreement on more than just the rejection of incorporation. Between November 1706 and January 1707, three successive attempts to disrupt Parliament failed. Focusing on elite politics, historians have blamed this on the duke of Hamilton and his vacillating leadership of the Country Party.[34] It seems clear that Hamilton chose to limit his support for these activities in order to avoid being blamed by the Queen and her ministers for the failure of the treaty.[35] Hamilton's behaviour, however, does not fully explain the collapse of these plans. Discord and distrust also hampered the opposition, from Edinburgh to the localities.

In November 1706, several Jacobite members of parliament supported an attempt to provoke covenanting Presbyterians in the southwest to march in arms to Edinburgh. At the last minute, Hamilton wrote letters calling off the rising, but two key Presbyterian groups had already decided not to cooperate with the Jacobites. With the support of secret government agents, the Hebronites and the Cameronians rejected the venture as too risky for the Revolution and Presbyterian interest. In the end, only a small group of Glaswegians, led by a Jacobite, marched to Hamilton in late November expecting to meet many thousands more. This small band was sent packing home by the staunchly Presbyterian and anti-union duchess of Hamilton who would not countenance an armed march against the Revolution government.[36]

With the collapse of the rising, anti-union leaders called their followers to Edinburgh in hopes of intimidating Parliament with crowds of petitioners and a mass address to the Queen. As hundreds arrived in mid-December, action was stalled by disagreements among the organisers over whether their address should call for the settlement of the succession instead of incorporation. The Jacobites resisted this, having proposed a draft address in generally patriotic terms that avoided the issue of alternatives to union by leaving this up to a new parliament. While the duke of Hamilton demanded that the Hanoverian succession be included, the government dispersed the crowds in Edinburgh by securing an act of parliament against unauthorised gatherings of freeholders. A final attempt to undermine the authority of the nearly-ratified treaty collapsed in early January 1707 as Hamilton refused to lead a planned exodus of anti-unionists from Parliament. In this case, a number of Jacobite members had agreed to join the Country Party walk-out, though a statement to be read out before their departure mentioned the Hanoverian succession. With a mass exit of members likely to weaken the authority of the treaty, the duke of Hamilton chose to opt out of the protest. The other leader of the opposition, the duke of Atholl, failed to step into the breach after objecting to the Hanoverian terms of the protest. Parliament continued undisturbed and completed the ratification of the treaty by mid-January.[37]

If noble leadership, or the lack of it, played a significant role in the disintegration of these protest activities, so did the decisions of ordinary Presbyterians on how far they would go along with the Jacobites to stop the Union. Petitions and parliamentary protests could attract bilateral support in the Country Party and on the ground, but armed activity that might undermine the Revolution government and lead to a Jacobite takeover proved more contentious. Historians have tended to emphasise elite politics in explaining the ratification of the Treaty of Union, but a wider view of public debates and popular resistance indicates the importance of popular opinion in shaping the course of the 1706–7 session. Some Scots rejected the Presbyterian–Episcopalian conflicts of the prior century and saw incorporation as the only way to preserve protestantism in Europe, while also protecting Scottish religious interests and improving Scottish prosperity. Many more people, as covenanting Presbyterians or Jacobite Episcopalians and as petty traders, artisans or simply consumers, saw reasons to question the security of their interests in a closer union with England. Incorporation challenged their deep-seated sense of Scottish national identity, provoking impassioned feelings for the ancient Scottish kingdom and resentment of English hegemony. Yet though ordinary Presbyterians and Jacobites could join in patriotic attacks on the treaty, their unity was compromised by their loyalties to divergent forms of church government and the monarchies that supported these churches. These differences contributed to the making of the Union by preventing the opposition from cooperating to the degree necessary to stop it in 1706–7. Despite deep popular dissatisfaction with the idea and consequences of incorporation, the same dynamics underpinned the continuation of the union as the Jacobites failed to generate national risings to overturn incorporation in 1715 and 1745.

Notes

1 One of the first historians of the Union, the Jacobite George Lockhart of Carnwath, emphasised popular resistance and political management in his memoirs. Daniel Szechi (ed.), *'Scotland's ruine': Lockhart of Carnwath's Memoirs of the Union* (Aberdeen: Association for Scottish Literary Studies, 1995). More recent histories with a similar emphasis include William Ferguson, *Scotland's Relations with England: a Survey to 1707* (Edinburgh: Saltire Society, 1994) and Paul Scott, *Andrew Fletcher and the Treaty of Union* (Edinburgh: Saltire Society, 1994).

2 John Robertson (ed.), *A Union for Empire: Political Thought and the British Union of 1707* (Cambridge: Cambridge University Press, 1995); Christopher A. Whatley with Derek Patrick, *The Scots and the Union* (Edinburgh: Edinburgh University Press, 2006); Jeffrey Stephen, *Scottish Presbyterians and the Act of Union 1707* (Edinburgh: Edinburgh University Press, 2007).

3 [William Seton of Pitmedden], *The Interest of Scotland, in Three Essays* ([Edinburgh], 1700), pp. A3–4.

4 R. A. Houston, *Scottish Literacy and Scottish Identity: Illiteracy and Society in Scotland and Northern England 1600–1800* (Cambridge: Cambridge University Press, 1985).

5 Whately with Patrick, *The Scots and the Union*; Derek J. Patrick and Christopher A. Whatley, 'Persistence, principle and patriotism in the making of the Union of 1707: the Revolution, Scottish parliament and the squadrone volante', *History* (2007) 92:2, pp. 162–86.

6 Colin Kidd, 'Religious realignment between the Restoration and the Union', in John Robertson (ed.), *A Union for Empire*, pp. 145–68.

7 [John Spotiswoode], *The trimmer: or, some necessary cautions, concerning the union of the kingdoms of Scotland and England; with an answer to some of the chief objections against an incorporating union* (Edinburgh, 1706), pp. 4–5.

8 Thomas Thomson (ed.), *Acts of the Parliament of Scotland*, vol. xi ([Edinburgh], 1824), pp. 320–1, 402–3; [Francis Grant], *The patriot resolved, in a letter to an addresser, from his friend; of the same sentiments with himself; concerning the union* ([Edinburgh], 1707), pp. 6, 10.

9 [Seton of Pitmedden], *The interest of Scotland*, pp. 85, 110–11.

10 National Archives of Scotland [NAS], GD 406/1/4976. See also George Mackenzie, Viscount Tarbat, *Parainesis pacifica* (London, 1702).

11 [William Seton of Pitmedden], *Scotland's great advantages by an union with England: showen in a letter from the country, to a Member of Parliament* ([Edinburgh], 1706); William Seton of Pitmedden, *A speech in the parliament of Scotland the second day of November 1706 on the first article of the treaty of union* (London, 1706).

12 NAS, GD 406/1/9747.

13 Colin Kidd, 'Protestantism, constitutionalism and British identity under the later Stuarts', in Brendan Bradshaw and Peter Roberts (eds), *British Consciousness and Identity: the Making of Britain, 1533–1707* (Cambridge: Cambridge University Press, 1998), pp. 321–42.

14 [Seton of Pitmedden], *Scotland's great advantages*, p. 3.

15 Douglas Duncan (trans. and ed.), *History of the Union of Scotland and England by Sir John Clerk of Penicuik* (Edinburgh: Scottish History Society, 1993), p. 174.

16 John Robertson, 'An elusive sovereignty: the course of the union debate in Scotland 1698–1707', in Robertson (ed.), *A Union for Empire*, pp. 198–227.

17 [Seton of Pitmedden], *Scotland's great advantages*, p. 7.

18 NAS, PA 7/28/24–25 (Ayr petitions); Szechi (ed.), 'Scotland's ruine', p. 148; Henry Paton (ed.), *Report on the Manuscripts of the Earl of Mar and Kellie*, vol. I (London, 1904), pp. 312, 316–17, 320, 326, 328, 330–1.

19 T. C. Smout, 'The burgh of Montrose and the Union of 1707 – a document', *Scottish Historical Review*, vol. LXVI, 2:182, October 1987, pp. 183–4.

20 [Spotiswoode], *The trimmer*, p. 3.

21 NAS, CH 1/3/9(60–61); *Manuscripts of the Earl of Mar*, pp. 335–6.

22 See, for example, [Robert Wyllie], *A speech without doors, concerning toleration* ([Edinburgh 1703]); James Hadow, *A survey of the case* (Edinburgh, 1703); *The humble representation of the Commission of the late General Assembly* ([Edinburgh, 1703]).

23 NAS, PA 7/28/22 (petition from south and western shires).

24 NAS, PA 7/28 (petitions from shires, burghs and parishes).

25 Szechi (ed.), '*Scotland's ruine*', p. 149; NAS, PA 7/28/61 (Clackmannan parish petition), 7/28/71 (Hamilton parish petition), 7/28/65 (Culross, Saline, Carnock and Torry[burn] petition).

26 NAS, PA 7/28/65 (Culross, Saline, Carnock and Torry[burn] petition), 7/20/18 (Convention of Royal Burghs petition), 7/28/29 (Cupar petition).

27 NAS, PA 7/28/39 (Lanark town and parish petition).

28 NAS, PA 7/28/56 (Cambuslang parish petition).

29 Murray G. H. Pittock, *Poetry and Jacobite Politics in eighteenth-century Britain and Ireland* (Cambridge, 1994); Roger A. Mason, 'Chivalry and citizenship: aspects of national identity in Renaissance Scotland', in *Kingship and Commonweal: Political Thought in Renaissance and Reformation Scotland* (East Linton: Tuckwell Press, 1998), pp. 165–86; Michael Lynch, 'A nation born again? Scottish identity in the sixteenth and seventeenth centuries', in Dauvit Broun, R. J. Finlay and Michael Lynch (eds), *Image and Identity: the Making and Remaking of Scotland Through the Ages* (Edinburgh: John Donald, 1998), pp. 82–104.

30 [William Forbes of Disblair], *The true Scots genius reviving* ([Edinburgh], 1704), pp. 3–4; [William Forbes of Disblair], *Pill for pork-eaters: or, a Scots lancet for an English swelling* ([Edinburgh], 1705), p. 8.

31 *To the loyal and religious hearts in Parliament, some few effects of the Union, proposed between Scotland and England except God prevent will fall out* ([Edinburgh, 1706]).

32 Szechi (ed.), '*Scotland's ruine*', p. 149. This text tended to be used in the shire petitions, while many burgh and parish petitions employed more Presbyterian language. Karin Bowie, 'Scottish public opinion and the making of the Union of 1707', University of Glasgow Ph.D. thesis, 2004, appendix H.

33 *Manuscripts of the Earl of Mar*, p. 318.

34 Ferguson, *Scotland's Relations with England*, p. 264.

35 National Library of Scotland, Wodrow quarto XL, item 8, letter 3 (2 December 1706); NAS, GD 406/1/7895.

36 Szechi (ed.), '*Scotland's ruine*', pp. 179–84; John Ker of Kersland, *The memoirs of John Ker of Kersland* (London, 1726), pp. 3–11, 30–6; George Harris Healey (ed.), *The Letters of Daniel Defoe* (Oxford: Oxford University Press, 1955), pp. 163–4, 180–1, 183–4; W. R. Owens and P. N. Furbank, 'New light on John Pierce, Defoe's agent in Scotland', *Edinburgh Bibliographical Society Transactions*, vol. VI:4, 1998, pp. 134–43; NAS, GD 406/1/5383.

37 NAS, GD 406/1/7851, 9738; Thomson (ed.), *Acts of the Parliament of Scotland*, pp. 371–2; Szechi (ed.), '*Scotland's ruine*', pp. 184–96.

4

THE TREATY OF UNION: MADE IN ENGLAND

Allan I. Macinnes

The standpoint of England was the most important factor affecting the making of the United Kingdom in 1707. Conventionally, English interest in the Union is associated with political considerations, principally the War of the Spanish Succession, which broke out in 1702 and placed England in direct opposition to France.[1] Scotland appeared to offer a back door to invasion from France under Louis XIV, who favoured the restoration of the exiled house of Stuart. James VII & II had been relieved of the common monarchy at the Revolution of 1688–91 for his professed Roman Catholicism and his authoritarian reliance on the prerogative powers of the crown rather than working with or through parliaments. His son-in-law, William of Orange and his daughter Mary had succeeded him. On his death in 1701, his son James VIII & III was recognised by Louis XIV as the legitimate Jacobite claimant to Scotland, England and Ireland. However, the English Parliament had that same year already determined unilaterally that on the death of William's designated heir, his sister-in-law Anne, the succession should pass to the German house of Hanover as her nearest Protestant heirs. Accordingly, there was a real prospect that the War of the Spanish Succession could turn into the War of the British Succession.

Yet this prospect had been apparent in 1703 when England was content to break off negotiations for union with Scotland and to refuse overtures for union from Ireland one year later. When negotiations for union with Scotland resumed in 1706, France was contemplating suing for peace having been heavily defeated by English forces under the duke of Marlborough at Blenheim and Ramillies. Union itself revived rather than ended the Jacobite threat from Scotland with major risings in 1715 and 1745 and minor ones in 1708 and 1719. Accordingly, we must look at wider considerations of political economy to explain why England became the driving force for the Treaty of Union.

THE SCOTTISH PROBLEM

A key starting point is 1696, when the English Parliament placed oversight of the American colonies and overseas commerce with the Council for Trade and Plantations, more commonly known as the Board of Trade. Its establishment marked a decisive shift in the servicing of England as a fiscal-military state.[2] Under William of Orange, England had been consolidated as a global power by the massive build up of the armed forces to fight the French in the Nine Years War that had commenced in 1688. Military engagements and commercial opportunism on a global scale were fructified by the creation of the National Debt in 1693 that was financed through the Bank of England from 1694. England's war effort was becoming increasingly reliant on indirect taxes on trade and consumption – the customs and excise, respectively – rather than direct taxes on land which required regular parliamentary votes of supply. The largest component of customs was that levied on the colonial trade with the Americas. However, this trade faced significant disruption from Scottish commercial networks that continuously and flagrantly circumvented the Navigation Acts that were contrived to protect English domestic and overseas trade in the later seventeenth century.

English colonial officials from New Hampshire to South Carolina had long noted the clannish cohesion as well as the acquisitiveness of Scottish entrepreneurs who consistently outsold their English competitors by focusing on quantity rather than quality in marketing goods for servants and slaves. Court officials and juries summarily threw out local initiatives by English colonial officials to have the Scots declared foreigners and aliens incapable of wholesale trading or holding public office. Indeed, in the eyes of the officials reporting to the Board of Trade the Scots had become a greater threat to the operation of the Navigation Acts than either the Dutch or even the Caribbean buccaneers. When the Acts were first promulgated in 1660 and 1663, Scots in England and the colonies were accorded the same rights as Englishmen so long as they lived under English jurisdiction. However, Scots based in Scotland and trading to and from the American colonies were treated as foreigners and aliens. These Acts were subsequently modified but never basically altered by further enactments in 1662, 1670, 1671 and 1673. Re-enactment in 1693 instigated a tariff battle with England that endured until the Treaty of Union in 1707. With the establishment of the Board of Trade in 1696, the Acts were again enforced with a particular emphasis on appointing to places of trust in the colonies only natives of England and Ireland, a measure that was particularly interpreted as a licence to treat Scots as aliens and incapable of public employment, be that civil or military.[3] However, the repeated promulgation of these Acts was testimony to the inventive and sophisticated capacity of Scottish networks to circumvent them.

The purpose of the Navigation Acts remained distinctly mercantilist: to advance overseas commerce; increase royal revenue and regulate the colonies, on the one hand; and promote shipping, manufacturing and a favourable balance of trade on the other. No goods or commodities regardless of where they were produced could be imported into or exported out of any English colony except in a ship built in England or in the colonies whose master and three-quarters of its crew were English. Enumerated colonial commodities, such as tobacco, sugar and coffee, should be exclusively traded through English markets. No direct trade was to be permitted between continental Europe and the American colonies. England was the staple for all European goods imported into the colonies and all masters of ships sailing for the colonies were obliged to provide a detailed manifest of their ships and cargos on arrival and lodge a bond for payment of customs in England prior to their departure.[4] Scottish circumvention of these Acts was initially facilitated by Charles II and more significantly by his brother the duke of York, later James VII & II, using the prerogative powers of the crown to grant individual dispensations to merchants wishing to establish sugar works in Glasgow and later in Edinburgh. The development of these 'manufactories' demonstrates the active involvement of Scots in the transatlantic trade to the West Indies, an engagement that also extended to the Chesapeake and Delaware for tobacco.[5]

Significant loopholes and exemptions in the Navigation Acts also facilitated Scottish expertise in circumvention. Scottish entrepreneurs exploited flexible arrangements for the loading and unloading of colonial commodities in the sea lanes rather than just at the ports. Direct shipments to and from the Scottish ports on the Firth of Forth nominally cleared English customs in the Holy Isles rather than at the port of Berwick-upon-Tweed. As long as ships were allowed to land colonial goods in Ireland, the North Channel served the same purpose for ports in the west of Scotland intent on trade with the Americas. There were three areas in particular which were exempt from the Navigation Acts: Newfoundland, where there was a lucrative trade in fish to Spain, Portugal and the Italian states; Guinea, the centre of the African slave trade; and Delaware, the district contested by Maryland, the Dutch and Swedes which remained contested and exempt when incorporated into New York in 1664. In his capacity as colonial proprietor of New York, James, duke of York had encouraged extensive settlement of Scots on the Lower Delaware. Scottish networks engaged in the tobacco trade came to dominate the three southern counties of New Castle, Kent and Sussex, which were eventually assigned to Pennsylvania in 1685. By this juncture, the Scots had established a resident conservator there, Gustavus Hamilton, who oversaw the operation of commercial networks that now stretched from New England to South Carolina.

No less pertinently, there were three key exceptions to the staple provision that all goods had to be exported from England: salt for the fisheries of Newfoundland and New England; servants, horses and provisions from Scotland as well as Ireland; and wines from the Portuguese islands of Madeira and the Azores. These exemptions encouraged tramp trading; that is, the conveying of goods to and from several ports rather than directly across the Atlantic. Tramping, which was the prevailing form of Scottish commerce in the Baltic, was now transferred to the Caribbean and the North Atlantic. It was further encouraged by the concession that ships could trade freely between the colonies in the Americas, a practice which was not checked by the imposition of inter-colonial duties from 1673, since there was only the limited number of colonial officials in place or willing to collect these impositions. The need to provide bonds specifying ships and cargoes to and from the Americas was also circumvented by transferring them from legitimate English to illicit Scottish shipping, through outright forgery, disguised ownership and by smuggling and collusion with colonial officials. These practices became the stock-in-trade of Scottish commercial networks in this period.[6]

Networks headed by London Scots that traded legitimately with the colonies had the added bonus of enrolling their ships in convoys protected by the Royal Navy. However, Scottish entrepreneurs and their colonial associates used Rotterdam, Amsterdam and even Hamburg as commercial hubs. The Atlantic connection certainly contributed to the reinvigoration of Scottish networks in Bordeaux and their presence in Lisbon and Cadiz/Seville by the 1680s. Glasgow, which had developed Port Glasgow further down the Clyde as its Atlantic gateway in 1667, maintained a position of leadership in transatlantic trade which stimulated engagement not only by Ayr but also by lesser ports such as Dumfries in the south and Irvine, Greenock and Dumbarton in the west. Consortia from Edinburgh soon followed through the port of Leith in regular commerce with the Americas, which, in turn, stimulated the engagement of such neighbouring east coast towns as Prestonpans and of Burntisland and Kirkcaldy as well as Bo'ness on the Firth of Forth. Perth soon joined Dundee from Tayside in the Atlantic trade, while Montrose and Peterhead supplemented the endeavours of Aberdeen in the northeast, as did Inverness in the Highlands and even Stromness in the Orkney Isles by the 1680s.

Assiduous commercial networking by Scottish entrepreneurs from Boston to New York and on to Philadelphia was deepened and diversified by steady pressure from the colonies for Scots to serve as servants and in the Chesapeake and Delaware as frontiersmen. In the Caribbean, able-bodied Scots were welcomed to rebuild societies devastated by hurricanes and increasingly fearing internal upheaval from revolts as slavery increased exponentially with the profitability of sugar and rum. Barbados, which was to the fore in providing settlers to consolidate Jamaica – forcibly acquired from Spain in 1655 – was the main promoter of Scottish immigration and open trade through Scottish commercial networks.[7]

English concerns about the autonomy of these networks had been intensified by endeavours to establish Scottish colonies in South Carolina and East New Jersey with the full backing of the duke of York. In 1681, James had established a Committee for Trade which reported that the only effective way for the country to cope with the pressures of mercantilism and growing dependence on English markets was either to seek closer union or develop overseas colonies. Nevertheless, there was little political will either at the court, in the English ministry or in the English Parliament to promote political or commercial collaboration with the Scots at this time. When William and Mary replaced James in all three kingdoms, the interests of England were reaffirmed as paramount. Scotland, like Ireland, was a peripheral consideration to the London elite for the purposes of making peace and war and of conducting trade and commerce. Nevertheless, Scottish commercial networks were still able to exploit the unsettled political situation in North America in the wake of the Revolution. Despite the covert placing of English agents to monitor Scottish shipping, Glasgow merchants expanded their operations into North Carolina. Tobacco was shipped either directly to Scotland or to the stores controlled by Scots on the Lower Delaware. Glasgow also took the lead in forging documentation to pass off its shipping and commodity trading as English. Even on the rare occasions when colonial officials attempted the strict enforcement of the Navigation Acts, Scottish merchants could still charter ships from London and other English ports and travel to the colonies as supercargoes responsible for the actual trading of commodities. In cases of doubt, colonial juries, much to the chagrin of the Board of Trade, still continued to take the Scottish side against crown officials.[8]

In December 1697 and January 1698, the Board completed a review of English trade from 1670 until the recent Peace of Ryswick with the French. It noted that expansion of English trade in the Restoration era had gone into a measurable decline since the Revolution. Serious misgivings were expressed about woollen manufacturing, fishing and the carrying trade, particularly that from the plantations in the Americas. The uncooperative presence of Scottish commercial networks loomed large. Wool was necessary for English manufactures exported out of England, Ireland and Scotland, but Scottish carriers were thought to be dominating the trade from the three kingdoms. In the colonies, the Scots were taking particular advantage of the lack of designated ports for the loading and unloading of overseas vessels.[9]

By the end of the review, the restructuring of colonial governance was proving more impressive on paper than in reality. Scottish commercial networks became particularly adept at using their London contacts to attach their ships to Royal Navy convoys across the Atlantic and then slip away under cover of darkness before the ships entered the English Channel. In addition to using Whitehaven on the western border as an out-station of Glasgow, the Isle of Man became the major centre of smuggling operations in the North Channel. Colonial commodities brought into Whitehaven were re-exported to the Isle of Man, giving the Scots the benefit of a drawback on customs, and then smuggled back via the Firths of Clyde and Solway or into Belfast, Londonderry and Dublin by Irish associates. Newcastle, as well as Berwick-upon-Tweed, was also brought into play on the east coast. For instance, Edinburgh merchant houses engaged in the colonial tramping trade by establishing branches on the Tyne. Bilbao and San Sebastian in northern Spain also became tramping destinations for Scottish ships engaged in the Newfoundland fisheries, where they also encountered New England traders illicitly carrying enumerated commodities for European markets.[10]

From its foundation, the Board of Trade became the main conduit for channelling the antipathies of English diplomatic and colonial officials towards what they conceived to be the rogue behaviour of the Scots. These same officials were the prime movers in encouraging William of Orange to sabotage the Darien venture, a well conceived but poorly executed scheme by the Company of Scotland trading to Africa and the Indies to establish an entrepôt for the East and West Indies at

Darien on the Panama isthmus. Even though William had licensed the Company of Scotland in 1695, there were strong apprehensions voiced through the Board that if the Scots made a success of Darien this would breach the existing British monopoly of the English East India Company and the Lower Delaware might even secede from English control. Its Scottish mercantile community, as practised evaders of the Navigation Acts, was deemed capable of establishing an independent staple for European manufactures. Not only did the Scottish networks already enjoy a competitive edge, but they were also diversifying into textiles and other manufactures prohibited in the colonies. Darien as a free port would be considerably more menacing to English interests in America than that operated by the Dutch on the island of Curaço.[11]

English diplomats and colonial officials lined up to sow doubts at home and abroad about the legality of the Scottish enterprise. However, their concerns for the sovereign rights of Spain over the Isthmus of Panama were far from altruistic and influenced by the lack of current Spanish settlement in the area and by its suitability for an English entrepôt. The region was notably attractive for economic exploitation as the isthmus carried the overland route for the silver mined in Peru prior to its shipping to Spain from Portobello and Cartagena. The ill-fated endeavours of the Scots to settle Darien came to grief in 1700, after successive expeditionary fleets that sailed in 1698 and 1699 failed to establish a permanent colony. Surveying, provisioning and leadership were deficient, notwithstanding additional assistance provided by Scottish mercantile communities in Boston and New York. The defeat of Spanish forces at Tubuganti on 15 February 1700, by a combined force of Scots and Indians offered no more than a brief respite. English polemicists declared open season in ridiculing the audacity of the Scottish enterprise. Duly glossed over was William's instruction to the governors of Jamaica and the other Caribbean colonies in December 1699 to offer no assistance to the Scots. Spanish tenacity on the issue of the Panama isthmus was wholly underestimated by both the English and the Scots.[12]

As Darien turned from a scheme into a fiasco, the call for reparations – for actual losses of no more than £154,000 – contributed to a marked deterioration in Anglo-Scottish relations on the outbreak of the War of the Spanish Succession. For the Scots, the Darien disaster was an expensive demonstration of the need for purposeful British collaboration. Moreover, Darien also hastened a major restructuring of English colonial policy. Imperial consolidation became the over-riding concern among English commercial commentators and colonial officials following the accession of Queen Anne in 1702. Faced with aggressive French competition in the Americas, there was a growing realisation that England did not have the demographic capacity for overseas expansion without draining its domestic manufactures of labour. Indeed, there was no immediate prospect of expanding Empire unless migrants were attracted to England and the colonies or England re-engaged in state formation. Thus, among those shaping English colonial policy, Scottish commercial networks were transformed from being viewed as significant disruptors of trade to a new role as potential pillars of Empire.[13]

COERCIVE PERSUASION

Renewed hostilities with France in 1702, in the shape of the War of the Spanish Succession, altered the English viewpoint on how to service the fiscal-military state. The acquisition of the Spanish crown by Philip of Anjou, a grandson of Louis XIV, not only threatened to create a Bourbon hegemony in Europe, but also made the fate of the Spanish empire a key issue of the war. The English colonies in America were threatened by an arc of menace that stretched from the North Atlantic through to the Gulf of Mexico and into the Caribbean. The West Indies remained particularly vulnerable due to the reluctance of the English ministry to send troops and naval resources from the main European theatres of war.[14] At the same time, the need to harmonise the colonial trade with English manufacturing as soldiers and sailors were being mobilised on an unprecedented scale for war, created a demographic deficit that was likely to threaten English interests in the long and short term.

Although London had grown in the Restoration era to become Europe's largest city, its population, estimated at 530,000 was apparently stagnating, as was that of England as a whole at no more than 5.5 million. These relatively accurate estimates were made by Gregory King in 1696 to demonstrate to the English ministry that England did not have the resources in population and national income to prolong war beyond 1698. King was not arguing that the population was static, rather that its distribution had shifted through intensified, commercial agriculture and diversified manufacturing which had led to gradual urbanisation. However, the natural increase in population, which was seen as the basis of sustainable national prosperity, had been channelled towards emigration to Ireland and the American colonies.[15] The Board of Trade had been relatively sanguine about the prospects for a favourable balance of trade between 1698 and 1701, but, the renewal of war in 1702 led to important shifts in fiscal policy.[16]

In the first place, the balance between direct and indirect taxes to underwrite the costs of the National Debt moved decisively away from the land tax – which had primarily sustained deficit financing during the Nine Years War – towards customs and excise. This reflected not only the dominance of the landed influence in the English Parliament, but also a tilting balance in favour of attaining national prosperity through manufacturing based on landed enterprise rather than overseas trade. In the second place, the size of the army was raised from around 76,000 to 92,000 men. This growth in military manpower masked an increased reliance on foreign auxiliaries: England was becoming more dependent on recruiting continental troops than those raised within the British Isles. During the Nine Years War 26 per cent of the troops raised were foreign auxiliaries, but this proportion rose to between 54 and 67 per cent during the War of the Spanish Succession. As the prevailing strategy in both wars required the offensive commitment of forces by land and sea, costs rose significantly from an annual average of around £2.5 million in the Nine Years War to over £4 million during the War of the Spanish Succession. The Bank of England was overstretched in 1696–7 and again in 1705. The prospect of a renewed war had temporarily stopped the circulation of paper credit in 1701, while the market in government stocks integral to the National Debt remained highly volatile.[17]

These demographic and fiscal pressures led to a renewed debate on the value of colonial commerce. The Board of Trade was especially concerned that the attraction of migrants to the American colonies was not only depriving English manufactures of skilled labour, but also mounting effective competition that undercut English products with respect to price, quality and fashion. Colonial manufactures not only impaired the balance of trade with the Americas, but also diminished the prospect of earning revenue from the re-export of raw materials from the colonies once manufactured in England. These concerns, first raised vociferously in 1702, became a regular feature of Board reports to the English Parliament through to the Union of 1707. Over the same period, English agriculture and manufacturing experienced a war boom with increased demand for grain and textiles in Russia, the Low Countries and Germany. However, this boom also put a premium on retaining population rather than encouraging migration.[18]

If emigration was not to damage the basis for English national prosperity or weaken its military commitments by land and sea, some alternative source of productive and reliable manpower had to be found. French Protestant émigrés fitted both requirements, but in insufficient numbers. Ireland, whose population had reputedly increased in excess of two million, largely through migration within the British Isles, was still predominantly Roman Catholic (at least 80 per cent of the populace) and, therefore, deemed unsuitable. Although its population had in all probability fallen to below a million, Scotland came into the position of favoured nation and was, indeed, identified as such when calls for Scots to be used in the wider service of England won endorsement from the American colonies.[19]

In advance of the War of the Spanish Succession, and no doubt prompted by discreet lobbying on the part of Scottish commercial networks, planters in Barbados and the Leeward Islands had called for free trade with Scotland as a means of securing supplies of servants and militiamen. Colonial governors had also expressed their frustrations from 1703. With English forces stretched to the limits they were disadvantaged by a continuing reluctance to give Scottish officers leading positions of command when confronting the French in the Caribbean. However, as well as complaints from Newfoundland that the Scots as well as the French were encroaching on English fisheries, there were also resurgent fears that clannish Scottish networks in Virginia, east New Jersey and Barbados were subverting English governance. On the one hand, colonial governors were pressing for the services of Scots from Maine and Nova Scotia to Jamaica and the Leeward Islands,[20] while on the other, the English ministry was determined that initiatives to engage Scots in the Americas were only acceptable if firmly under English control. The price of that was political incorporation and, if the Scots would not agree to treat, their commercial networks were to be subject to the same punitive tariffs as foreign traders. In effect, the discrimination applied against Scottish networks in the colonies from 1696 was now to apply in their overland trade to England from 1705 under an Aliens Act. The common monarchy notwithstanding, the Scots were to be treated as aliens unless they accepted the English invitation to negotiate a union. As a further means of coercive persuasion, the English ministry mobilised its troops on the borders and across the North Channel in Ireland.[21]

POLITICAL INEPTITUDE

English desire to control the Scots had become more acute after the accession of, the then childless, Queen Anne in 1702, particularly as

the Scots seemed reluctant to accept the English preference for the
Hanoverian succession. Anne herself played a proactive role in facil-
itating political incorporation. She was outraged by the endeavours
of the Scottish Estates in 1703–4 to impose limitations on the prerogative powers of her eventual successor. If the price of union and
the Hanoverian succession was to be the termination of the Scottish
Parliament, so be it. This royal inclination brought into play a further
consideration favourable to the English ministry. The leading politicians who constituted the Court Party in the Scottish Estates were
intent on preserving the Revolution Settlement without further constitutional limitations on the royal prerogative, on securing the
Presbyterian establishment in the Kirk and on attaining greater career
opportunities through Empire. They promoted union at the expense
of parliamentary sovereignty and achieved additional support from
the New Party or *Squadrone Volante*. This mainly consisted of
Presbyterians who favoured a Hanoverian succession to prevent the
restoration of the exiled house of Stuart and episcopalianism, as
desired by the Jacobite opponents of union. The Jacobites, in turn,
were associated with the opposition Country Party, whose inept leadership ensured that the Scottish commissioners charged to negotiate
union were overwhelmingly drawn from the Court and *Squadrone*.[22]

The Treaty of Union as negotiated and implemented in 1706–7
was not a magnanimous or unprecedented act of altruism in which
England rescued an impoverished Scotland. Undoubtedly, Scottish
commerce had been hit badly by reinforced Navigation Acts after the
Revolution and by the failure to establish a colonial entrepôt at Darien
between 1698 and 1700. Also, as was particularly evident in the aftermath of Darien, Scottish attempts to take retaliatory action against
English mercantilist regulation lacked political clout. Nevertheless, the
tariff battle did facilitate an expansion of Scottish manufacturing. In
turn, the Board of Trade recorded that Scotland enjoyed a favourable
balance of trade of over £29,000 with England, a noted shift from the
purportedly dire position recorded by the Scottish Committee on
Trade in 1681. However, the development of textile manufacturing
and fishing and the reprocessing of imported materials for re-export
primarily rested on the initiatives taken within the mercantile community. At the same time, Scotland was becoming more attractive to
inward investment, notably from displaced Huguenots and from
English consortia usually led by London merchants, which deepened
Scottish interest in textiles, papermaking, leather, mining for minerals
and miscellaneous hardware. Nevertheless, in terms of depth and

diversity, manufacturing had but a limited impact outwith the central belt with only Aberdeen making a distinctive, but subordinate, contribution.[23]

Chronic famine in the later 1690s had proved severely debilitating although not crippling. The crisis can be attributed to a climatic shift, a little ice age which made marginal land unproductive not only in Scotland but also in Nordic areas during the 1690s. Although the shortage of grain was most severe in the aftermath of the successive failed harvests from 1695 to 1698, localised dearth had actually commenced with the harvest of 1694. A mortality crisis, intensified by the spread of typhus and dysentery among the population and compounded by the spread of murrain among cattle, continued in parts of the Highlands and the northeast beyond 1700. From an estimated base of around 1.2 million, the population of Scotland fell by perhaps as much as 15 per cent. This was not only due to increased mortality and decline in births but also to the remarkable increase in emigration to Ulster.[24] Contemporary commentators noted that a third or more of the population had died or fled from some localities. Their testimony was not so much numeric as impressionistic. For the Scots, who had become unused to dearth in the later seventeenth century, were no longer familiar with the coping mechanisms necessary for survival. Yet, by the end of William's reign in 1702, a nationwide recovery was well under way. Landlords no longer felt obliged to rebate rents or accept accumulated arrears in their payment by tenants. Agricultural productivity was restored and demographic stability was returning.[25]

Recovery from the famine demonstrates that the Scottish economy, notwithstanding structural weaknesses and vulnerability to mercantilist policies, was neither primitive nor on an irreversible downward spiral after the Revolution. Official reports, customs records, fiscal returns and deficient military and civil expenditure cannot necessarily be taken as accurate indicators of the Scottish economy, nor do they present an holistic picture of commercial activity, especially of Scottish networks operating from the Baltic to the Caribbean.[26]

Central government in Scotland exercised no meaningful control over exchange rates for trading commodities as these were essentially determined through Amsterdam and London. Scottish coinage conformed to the best international standards in terms of quality but, in the absence of central controls over exchange, tended to trade below its intrinsic value. Although Scotland, since the regal union of 1603, had a fixed exchange rate of £12 Scots to £1 sterling with England, war distorted these rates internationally as Scottish rates of exchange in overseas markets tended to be tied to, rather than assessed separately from English economic performance. Commercial networks operating within Scotland faced a cash flow problem with scarcity of money becoming a frequent complaint, particularly during years of war. In 1696, Scotland endured a financial crisis in the wake of that in England, but in 1704 the situation was reversed with the recently founded Bank of Scotland being obliged to close temporarily that December.[27] However, this crisis was not irreversible or only addressed through union.[28] Private banking funded by merchant houses at home and abroad, which was no less important than the Bank of Scotland to the operation of the Scottish economy, remained resilient. There was undoubtedly a scarcity of money but not a financial crash even in 1705 when the Bank of England ran into difficulties. Commercial networks survived by drawing on family resources, extended credit and ultimately, on the good will of their customers and suppliers.[29]

Considerable caution must also be exercised before accepting claims about impoverishment or even bankruptcy when applied to Scotland as a whole in this period as distinct from its government, central or local.[30] Certainly, when surveyed in 1705 as a preliminary to negotiations for union, the Scottish Estates were presented with a far from healthy balance of trade. Indeed, there appeared to be a chronic deficit of £171,667 that was marginally less than the total value of Scottish exports (£184,333) in relation to imports (£356,000). However, the adverse balance was calculated on trade taxed not on trade actually conducted. These figures, therefore, did not take account of imports processed for re-export or of goods carried to Scotland for re-export to continental or colonial markets, although ten of the top fifteen Scottish imports at this time were capable of some kind of reprocessing. Revenues from manufacturing for domestic consumption taxed as excise were not taken into consideration either, nor were bullion, coin or jewels returned from the profits of the carrying trade. At the same time, money and bullion carried out of the country by politicians and merchants were not factored into the equation. However, the figures presented to the Estates painted an extremely gloomy picture that did little to stiffen the resolve of the Scottish Estates to call the bluff of the Aliens Act which targeted three of the ten principal exports from Scotland and the three in which the landed elite had the prime interest. These statistics, which were also reproduced in committee as the Union was passing through the Scottish Estates in 1706, served as a counter to those who argued for transoceanic trading. Indeed, the critics suggested that the purported global expansion of Scottish trade had not so much stimulated manufacturing as increased imports of luxury and processed commodities.[31]

The political dominance of the landed elite made the Scottish Estates more receptive to specific proposals to secure national prosperity through manufacturing based on landed enterprise rather than through trade. This task was entrusted to a Council of Trade, which especially commended English trade regulations for the promotion of manufactures of assured quality. English and Scottish interests appeared to be coming into line in advance of detailed negotiations for union, with the Scots following the English path in favour of landed enterprise and manufacturing with the establishment of the Board of Trade in 1696. However, the English priority in seeking union in terms of political economy was to secure Scottish labour for English wars, colonies and manufactures, not necessarily to promote manufacturing to retain labour or promote prosperity within Scotland.[32]

Intent on political incorporation, the English ministry were prepared to use the resources of the English Treasury to influence Scottish politics. A sum of £20,000 was eventually advanced to selectively meet arrears of salaries and pensions for Scottish politicians, arrears that were on the whole genuine not fabricated.[33] However, the Scottish politicians who treated for union in 1706 were not a parcel of rogues bought and sold for English gold. They were not corrupt, but they were inept. Their ineptitude was manifested by their negotiating stance on colonial access, reparations and investment in manufactures. All three were secured conditionally. Colonial access, which had been conceded in principle to the Scots during the negotiations of 1702, had been specifically removed from a proposition paper drawn up for the English ministry in 1705. Scots were to be guaranteed only a common market in the United Kingdom. By way of compensation, it was acknowledged that the Scots should receive reparations for Darien, for adjusting to higher rates of taxation and public expenditure and for the standardisation of the currency on the basis of sterling. While equivalents for all but the former purpose had been agreed in 1702, the negotiations then had broken down on reparations for Darien. A composite equivalent now proposed amounted to £600,000 payable in quarterly instalments of £30,000 over twenty years; £230,000 was to be paid as reparation based on a capital sum of £140,000 (£13,000 less than actual losses for Darien) together with interest at 6.5 per cent over eleven years; £110,000 was to be apportioned as compensation to offset incorporation in the English National Debt and the standardisation of the coinage. Higher taxes were to be rebated by an allocation of £260,000 for maintenance of the poor, encouragement of manufactures and other commercial improvements.[34]

Having conceded the Scots free access to the American colonies, the English negotiators did not consent to the recently restructured East India Company being wound up along with the Company of Scotland. The Scottish negotiators concurred that the East Indies remain the preserve of English commercial interests. Reparations for Darien, compensation for augmented public debts and standardised coinage, and encouragement for manufactures were significantly altered from the proposition paper of 1705. Just under £400,000 was offered in a capital or greater equivalent that was to be effected within seven rather than twenty years. Although this represented a higher return in less time than the £340,000 proposed for reparations and compensation in 1705, there was no binding commitment to pay in instalments and the interest rate for the capital lost at Darien dropped from 6.5 to 5 per cent. The money for manufactures was drastically cut back from £260,000 over twenty years to £14,000 over seven years in equal annual instalments. Thus, the promotion of fishing and linen and woollen manufacturing through a rising or lesser equivalent was to receive £2,000 yearly as against £13,000 proposed in 1705. The notion that the Union would serve to boost the Scottish economy was clearly ill served by the Scottish negotiators. Moreover, by agreeing that reparations and investment should be met by the raising of customs, excise and land tax to English levels, the Scots were effectively agreeing to finance their own dividends from Union once it was implemented on 1 May 1707.[35]

However, the Union promptly came under threat before it even came into force. From the beginning of January, Scottish commercial networks at home and abroad sought to profiteer from fiscal circumventions facilitated by the timetable for implementing the Treaty. Great quantities of whalebone from Holland, brandy, claret and salt from France and further salt from Spain, were imported into Scotland with the intent of bringing them into England customs free after the Union. Not only were Scots paying less customs on these commodities before Union, but salt had added value for the curing of fish and whalebone stimulated considerable manufacturing of bodices and stays for colonial as well as domestic markets. News of this activity provoked a backlash in the English Parliament which, in turn, gained momentum from disquiet about the rigorous management of the Union after the Treaty became law. Whereas the Treaty of Union had taken over four months of extensive debate and sophisticated procedural manoeuvring to pass through the Scottish Estates, its ratification in both the Commons and the Lords was achieved within five weeks. The English ministry had attempted to defuse this situation in early April by prescribing that unless the Scots paid full English duties in addition to those already paid in Scotland, the re-export of goods and produce acquired since February would be banned after 1 May. But the ministry were subjected to ferocious lobbying by Scottish politicians and merchants who claimed these prescriptive measures were in direct breach of Union. The Scottish furore and the resultant tension between the Lords and the Commons was only resolved by Queen Anne proroguing Parliament on 30 April before the prescriptions could be enacted. Far from impoverished Scottish commercial networks had invested £300,000 in importing and manufacturing continental commodities in the first four months of 1707. Thus, the true price of a Union made in England was not the £20,000 advanced to cover arrears of salary or even the £232,888 eventually promised as reparations for Darien that took twenty years to deliver, but that of removing the prescriptions at £300,000 in Scotland's favour.[36]

In the final analysis, the making of the United Kingdom in 1707 was the product of power, control and negotiation. England had the military power to coerce and the fiscal power to persuade. The English ministry was intent on controlling through political incorporation what had become a rogue state in terms of commercial exchange. Likewise Queen Anne was intent on terminating what she conceived to be the rogue behaviour of the Scottish Estates in seeking to limit the prerogative powers of the crown. In return for union, Scottish manpower, Scottish enterprise and ultimately Scottish intellectual endeavour were harnessed in service of Empire The Union gave Scotland free access to the largest commercial market then on offer. The unrestricted movement of capital and skilled labour within that market stimulated and fructified native entrepreneurship both domestically and imperially. However, given that England was as much if not more in need of a stable political association, the question remains whether Scottish politicians made best use of their negotiating opportunities. In uniting with England, the Scots prioritised the attainment of sustainable prosperity through manufacturing stimulated by landed enterprise rather than by overseas trade. The former option was also reinforced from 1707 by territorial acquisitiveness through Empire that opened up opportunities for Scots, if not necessarily Scotland, through colonies, manufactures and war. Political incorporation, however, was not an end in itself. The fortunes of the Union have been umbilically linked to the Empire. As the British Empire has declined in the twentieth century, Union has moved from a constitutional fixture to a constitutional option.

Notes

1 A. I. Macinnes, *Union and Empire: The Making of the United Kingdom in 1707* (Cambridge: Cambridge University Press, 2007), pp. 12–50.

2 C. M. Andrews, *The Colonial Period of American History: England's Commercial and Colonial Policy* (New Haven: Yale University Press, 1943), pp. 157–68, 272–317; H. A. Curson, *Companion of the Laws and Government Ecclesiastical, Civil and Military of England, Scotland and Ireland, and Dominions, Plantations and Territories thereunto belonging* (London, 1699), pp. 497–9, 510–12, 527–32.

3 M. J. Braddick, *The Nerves of State: Taxation and the Financing of the English State, 1558–1714* (Manchester: Manchester University Press, 1996), pp. 27–45; T. C. Smout, *Scottish Trade on the Eve of Union, 1660–1707* (Edinburgh and London: Oliver & Boyd, 1963), pp. 205, 244–51; C. A. Whatley, *Scottish Society, 1707–1830* (Manchester: Manchester University Press, 2000), pp. 31–9.

4 Andrews, *The Colonial Period of American History*, pp. 50–177; J. M. Soisin, *English America and the Restoration Monarchy of Charles II: Transatlantic Politics, Commerce and Kinship* (Lincoln: University of Nebraska Press, 1980), pp. 39–73.

5 Smout, *Scottish Trade on the Eve of Union*, pp. 175–8, 242; T. Barclay and E. J. Graham, *The Early Transatlantic Trade of Ayr, 1640–1730* (Ayr: Ayrshire Archaeological and Natural History Society, 2005), pp. 21–38.

6 Macinnes, *Union and Empire: The Making of the United Kingdom in 1707*, pp. 155–62; N. C. Landsman, 'Nation, migration, and the province in the first British Empire: Scotland and the Americas, 1600–1800', *American Historical Review*, (1999), 104, pp. 463–75.

7 S. Murdoch, *Network North: Scottish Kin, Commercial and Covert Associations in Northern Europe, 1603–1746* (Leiden and Boston: Brill, 2006), pp. 13–83; C. Dalhede, *Handelsfamiljer på Stormakstidens Europamarknad*, 2 vols (Stockholm: Warne Förlag, 2001), I, pp. 13–46.

8 Macinnes, *Union and Empire*, pp. 162–71, 181–4; Sir John Clerk of Penicuik, *History of the Union of Scotland and England*, D. Duncan (ed.) (Edinburgh: Scottish History Society, 1993), pp. 81–3. Scottish networks in the Americas were usually dominated by literate laymen not averse to litigation and willing to represent each other in a diversity of jurisdictions covering commerce by land and sea. These networks were also able to take advantage of differing traditions of jurisprudence and legal practice in the colonies. In the middle colonies of New York, New Jersey, Pennsylvania and, to a lesser extent, Maryland, the normal prac-

tice of conforming to English statute and common law had to take account of Dutch and Scottish affinities for and grounding in civil law. Moreover, in all colonies from New England to the Carolinas, juries became notorious in the eyes of English officials for their disregard of the alleged facts in returning, even with repeated redirection, not guilty verdicts against practised evaders of the Navigation Acts.

9 British Library [BL], Papers relating to Trade etc., Sloane MS 2902, ff. 115–16, 137–8, 171–80, 218, 244; Charles Davenant, *Discourses on the Publick Revenues, and on the Trade of England* (London, 1698). The Board of Trade had become particularly apprehensive about the purported dominance of Scottish commercial networks in Ireland since the Revolution. Not only did Scottish merchants in the trading towns and the Scottish gentry in plantation districts actively collude, but they 'are generally Frugall, Industrious, very nationall, and very helpful to each other agst any Third [party]'. Associated claims that an additional 50,000 Scots emigrated to Ireland in the 1690s should be viewed as guesstimates rather than estimates. Nevertheless, Scottish dominance of the Irish carrying trade was recognised in reports from America. Dublin no less than Belfast and Londonderry was locked into Scottish commercial networks during that decade (John Cary, *A Discourse concerning the Trade of Ireland and Scotland as they stand in Competition with the Trade of England* (Bristol, 1695 and London, 1696); National Aarchives of Scotland [NAS], Journal of William Fraser, London, 1699–1711, CS 96/524, pp. 18–73).

10 Macinnes, *Union and Empire*, pp. 184–9; W. R. Brock, *Scotus Americanus: A Survey of the Sources for Links between Scotland and America in the Eighteenth Century* (Edinburgh: Edinburgh University Press,1982), pp. 11–12; J. M. Soisin, *English America and Imperial Inconstancy: The Rise of Provincial Autonomy 1696–1715* (Lincoln: University of Nebraska Press, 1985), pp. 23–36.

11 Macinnes, *Union and Empire*, pp. 173–81; D. Watt, *The Price of Scotland: Darien, Union and the Wealth of Nations* (Edinburgh: Luath Press, 2007), pp. 145–57.

12 Edward Ward, *A journey to Scotland giving a character of that country, the people and their manners* (London, 1699); Anon., *Caledonia; or, the Pedlar turn'd Merchant. A Tragi-Comedy, as it was acted by His Majesty's Subjects of Scotland in the King of Spain's Provinces of Darien* (London, 1700); C. Storrs, 'Disaster at Darien (1698–1700)? The persistence of Spanish imperial power on the eve of the demise of the Spanish Habsburgs', *European History Quarterly*, (1999), 29, pp. 5–38.

13 A. I. Macinnes, 'Union for Ireland failed (1703), Union for Scotland accomplished (1706–7)', in D. Keogh and K. Whelan (eds), *Acts of Union: The Causes, Contexts, and Consequences of the Act of Union of 1801* (Dublin: Four Courts Press, 2001), pp. 67–94; Huntington Library, San Marino, California [HL], Blathwayt Papers, BP 33–4, 416

and Bridgewater & Ellesmere MSS, EL 9611; BL, Papers Relating to English Colonies in America and the West Indies, 1627–1694, EG. 2395, ff. 574–8.

14 B. Lenman, *Britain's Colonial Wars 1688–1783* (Harlow: Longman, 2001), pp. 13–46; HL, Blathwayt Papers, BL 14, 26–7, 361, 415 and Huntington Manuscripts, Manuscript Newsletters from London to Tamworth (1690–1704), HM 30,659/87.

15 *Two Tracts by Gregory King*, G. E. Barnett (ed.) (Baltimore, 1936); E. A. Wrigley and R. S. Schofield, *The Population History of England, 1541–1871: a Reconstruction* (Cambridge: Cambridge University Press, 1981), pp. 174–9; 207–15; J. Hoppit, *A Land of Liberty? England 1689–1727* (Oxford: Oxford University Press, 2000), pp. 52–5.

16 Charles Davenant, *Discourses on the Publick Revenues, and on the Trade of England: Part I – Of the Use of Political Arithmetick, in all Considerations about the Revenues and Trade* (London, 1698); John Pollexfen [JP], *Of Trade* (London, 1700); Macinnes, *Union and Empire*, pp. 189–94.

17 D. W. Jones, *War and Economy in the Age of William III and Marlborough* (Oxford: Blackwell, 1988), pp. 1–65, 131–68; Hoppit, *A Land of Liberty?*, pp. 123–31; HL, Stowe Papers: Brydges Family Papers, ST 8/vol. 1, 'The Account of James Brydges, Esq., Paymaster General of her Majesties Forces acting in Conjunction with those of her Allies' and vol. 2, 'Three Year Accounts of ye Payments made to the Forces in Flanders by the Rt. Hon. James, Earl of Carnarvon from 1706 to 1709'.

18 Macinnes, *Union and Empire*, pp. 194–7; Jones, *War and Economy*, pp. 169–210. The Great Northern War had dislocated grain supplies from the Baltic and textile production in Saxony and Silesia, while the discovery of gold in Brazil fuelled increased sales of goods to Portugal.

19 HL, Huntington Manuscripts, HM 1264, '(Nehemiah) Grew, The Meanes of a most Ample Encrease of the Wealth and Strength of England in a few years humbly presented to Her Majesty in the 5th Year of Her Reign'; M. Flinn, *Scottish Population History from the 17th century to the 1930s* (Cambridge: Cambridge University Press, 1977), pp. 7–8, 187–200.

20 HL, Huntington Manuscripts: Sunderland Collection, HM 9916 and 22,281; Lenman, *Britain's Colonial Wars 1688–1783*, pp. 35–8.

21 Clerk of Penicuik, *History of the Union of Scotland and England*, pp. 81–5; P. W. J. Riley, 'The Union of 1707 as an episode in English Politics', *English Historical Review*, (1979), LXXXIV, pp. 498–527.

22 C. A. Whatley, *The Scots and the Union* (Edinburgh: Edinburgh University Press, 2007), pp. 202–42; Macinnes, *Union and Empire*, pp. 243–76.

23 G. Marshall, *Presbyteries and Profits: Calvinism and the Development of Capitalism in Scotland, 1560–1707* (Oxford: Clarendon Press, 1980), pp. 284–319; W. R. Scott, *The Constitution and Finance of English,*

Scottish and Irish Joint-Stock Companies to 1720, 3 vols (Cambridge, 1911–12), II, pp. 123–98; Aberdeen University Library [AUL], Duff House (Montcoffer Papers), MS 3175/A/801; Glasgow City Archives [GCL], Records of the Maxwells of Pollock, T-PM 113/439, 575, 613 and TD 1022/11, Research Papers and Notes compiled by R. F. Dell, Register of Deeds, B.10.15/2143–4, 2397, 2490.

24 Flinn, *Scottish Population History from the 17th century to the 1930s*, pp. 164–86; T. C. Smout, *A History of the Scottish People, 1560–1830* (Glasgow: Collins, 1979), pp. 143–5, 225.

25 Anon., *A Call to Scotland for threatening famine* (Edinburgh, 1698); Sir Robert Sibbald, *Provision for the Poor in Time of Dearth and Scarcity* (Edinburgh, 1699); Patrick Walker, *Six Saints of the Covenant*, D. H. Fleming (ed.), 2 vols (London, 1901), II, pp. 28–33; James Donaldson, *Husbandry anatomized* (Edinburgh, 1697); Andrew Fletcher of Saltoun, *Selected Political Writings and Speeches*, D. Daiches (ed.) (Edinburgh: Scottish Academic Press, 1979), pp. 27–66, 106–37; NAS, Letter and Account Book, John Watson yr, merchant Edinburgh, 1695–1713, CS 96/3309.

26 Smout, *Scottish Trade on the Eve of Union*, pp. 205, 244–56; Whatley, *Scottish Society*, pp. 31–9.

27 Aberdeen City Archives, Aberdeen Council Letters (1682–1699), 7/224; AUL, Leith-Ross MSS, MS 3346/12/11 and Duff House (Montcoffer Papers) MS 3175/A/2380; HL, Huntington Manuscripts, Manuscript Newsletters from London to Tamworth (1690–1704), HM 30,659/51–2; GCA, Records of the Maxwells of Pollock, T-PM 113/30 and TD 1022/11, Research Papers and Notes compiled by R. F. Dell, Register of Deeds, B.10.15/2136, 2180; Scott, *The Constitutions and Finance of English, Scottish and Irish Joint-Stock Companies to 1720*, I, pp. 356, 372–4; S. Checkland, *Scottish Banking: A History, 1695–1973* (Glasgow and London: Collins, 1975), pp. 31–9, 46. Scottish transactions in London that were based on bills or other paper transactions were not necessarily accorded the fixed exchange of 12:1 and rates were frequently pushed up by financial traders demanding discounts. While this was a customary practice in English as in continental markets, Scottish dealers effectively faced a double indemnity of added discounts when converting Scots currency into its sterling equivalent. Accordingly, from its inception in 1695, the Bank of Scotland preferred to issue its notes in sterling.

28 R. Mitchison, *Lordship to Patronage: Scotland 1603–1745* (London: Edward Arnold, 1983), p. 131; Smout, *Scottish Trade on the Eve of Union*, p. 262; Whatley, *The Scots and the Union*, pp. 184–202; Watt, *The Price of Scotland*, pp. 219–42.

29 Checkland, *Scottish Banking*, pp. 68–9; NAS, Letter and Account Book, John Watson, yr, merchant Edinburgh, 1695–1713, CS 96/3309; AUL, Leith-Ross MSS, MS 3346/12/8.

30 R. Mitchison, *A History of Scotland* (London: Methuen, 1977), pp. 215–16; A. L. Murray, 'Administration and law', in T. I. Rae (ed.), *The Union of 1707: Its Impact on Scotland* (Glasgow: Blackie, 1974), pp. 30–57.

31 Macinnes, *Union and Empire*, pp. 229–31; AUL, Duff House (Montcoffer Papers) MS 3175/A/2380. The principal Scottish exports cited were, in descending order, linen, herring, wool and wool skins, black cattle, stockings, plaiding and serges, coal, lead and lead ore, salmon and salt. The principal imports were, again in descending order, muslin and fine cloths, leather, household furnishings, tobacco, iron and copper, flax and hemp, wines, brandy and spirits, timber and tar, woollen manufactures from England, Spanish wool and camel hair, dye stuffs, ships and ships furniture and sugars and candy.

32 AUL, Crathes Papers (Burnet of Leys), MS 3661/2/81/5 and Duff House (Montcoffer Papers) MS 3175/A/236/20; NAS, Mar and Kellie Collection, GD 124/10/438, 445 and Hamilton Papers, GD 406/1/5435; BL, Sydney, 1st Earl of Godolphin: Official Correspondence, Home 1701–1710, Add. MSS 28,055, ff. 300–02; Checkland, *Scottish Banking*, pp. 39–44.

33 Macinnes, *Union and Empire*, pp. 293–5; Whatley, *The Scots and the Union*, pp. 266–9.

34 BL, Hanover State Papers, vol. I (1692–1706), Stowe 222, ff. 343–4; Dumfries House, Ayrshire, Loudoun Papers, A240/2.

35 Rigsarkivet Copenhagen, T. K. U. A. England, *Akter og Dokumenter nedr Sofart og Handel: Order med Bilag*, 1705–6, A.III/ 214, 216; Macinnes, *Union and Empire*, pp. 278–83.

36 HL, Stowe Papers: Brydges Family Papers, ST 57/vol. 1, pp. 81–2, 93, 94–6, 110–11, 126 and ST 58/vol. 1, pp. 115–16, 144–5, 149–52, 175–7; NAS, Mar and Kellie Collection, GD 124/15/491/2 and Journal of William Fraser, London, 1699–1711, CS 96/524 and Letter and Account Book, John Watson yr, merchant Edinburgh, 1695–1713, CS 96/3309; BL, Blenheim Papers, vol. DXXI, fo. 19; W. A. Speck, *The Birth of Britain: A New Nation 1700–1710* (Oxford: Blackwell, 1994), pp. 117–18. Scottish commercial networks were also involved in the exploitation of drawbacks on customs granted in England on colonial products like tobacco that were subsequently exported. Accordingly, they imported tobacco wholesale from England prior to 1 May with a view to earning a further drawback after the Union when the tobacco was exported to continental markets. The English ministry also attempted to proscribe these double drawbacks claimed by Scots on colonial goods.

PART TWO
HISTORY

5

THE LEGACY OF UNIONISM IN EIGHTEENTH-CENTURY SCOTLAND

Alexander Murdoch

The tercentenary of British parliamentary union has led to more interest in the legacy of that union in Scotland than England, but should this surprise us? There was no English interest in union with Scotland after the arrival of a Scottish king to take the throne of Scotland in 1603, and the incorporation of Scotland into the Cromwellian protectorate after 1652 was based on military conquest. As Maurice Lee wrote about the English rejection of James VI & I's plans for British union after 1603: 'The union would mean more Scots, quarrelsome, beggarly, covetous, and proud, in England's green and pleasant land. The English wanted none of it'.[1] In 1604 Sir Edwin Sandys 'argued that an English parliament could not make decisions about "Great Britain" alone, and spoke of English precedency "believing that Scotland should yield and take the famous name of England" '.[2] Bruce Galloway wrote that English assumptions of superiority to Scotland 'went beyond the stereotypes of English riches and Scots poverty. Material fortunes merely confirmed the feudal and indeed moral supremacy of the southern kingdom', although he did note that there were those in both nations in 1603, as there would be 1707, who hoped that ancient animosities might be overcome.[3] During debates over naturalisation of Scots in the English House of Commons in 1607 Sir Christopher Piggot, MP for Buckinghamshire, ended his speech against the proposal by concluding with 'a bye-Matter of invective against the Scots and Scottish nation; using many words of obloquy' including the assertion that the Scots 'have not suffered above two kings to die in their beds, these two hundred years'.[4] In short, opposition in the English House of Commons in 1607 made it impossible for King James of England to argue that the English would willingly consent to union with his original kingdom.

James's son Charles I had not sought political union between Scotland and England but instead projected religious uniformity, which cost him his kingdoms and his life, and cast England along with Scotland and Ireland into the vortex of civil war and sectarian violence. In turn, Scottish and English hopes of Presbyterian unity offered no resolution to conflict. Only military conquest and Cromwell's protectorate, with its formidable garrisons in Scotland at Leith, Perth, Inverness and Inverlochy achieved that. Arguably this achievement (or aggression) offered a modern precedent for English claims of ancient authority over Scotland under feudalism, and overturned the powerful myths of Scottish ability to protect their sovereignty by military means that went back to the Scottish medieval wars of independence and the legends of Wallace and the Bruce. Even those Scots who argued that Scotland had never been conquered and was never subservient to England in ancient times had to concede that this had not been the case between 1651 and 1660.[5] Much of the ethereal quality of Restoration culture and politics originated in this, along with English recognition that each of the restored Stuart monarchs saw Scotland and Ireland as independent kingdoms whose resources could be used against political opposition in England. Although Conrad Russell quipped that Charles I might be seen as unfortunate to lose one kingdom, by losing three he demonstrated how careless he really was, Charles II forgot the importance of being earnest and to a large extent forfeited the credibility of his dynasty as a result.[6] His younger brother, vacuous but well intentioned, could not overcome this handicap.

There were many Scots politicians who would have welcomed political union with England in the aftermath of the collapse of the Stuart regime in 1688, but it was English opposition to foreign conquest and belief in an exceptional destiny that made it impossible for a Glorious Revolution engineered by the Dutch to acknowledge connections with events in Scotland and Ireland to the bloodless regime change in London. Christopher Whatley and Derek Patrick are right to argue that for Scotland, union with England started in 1688 (if it had not already begun in 1651, or 1603, or 1560) but that was not the case for England.[7] For most Englishmen, the idea of union with Scotland was something they could not have foreseen before 1702 or even 1705, when negotiations began in earnest. It is true that Queen Anne, the last genuinely Stuart monarch, played a key role in enabling the Scots to negotiate a union that recognised their ancient sovereignty despite the depth of English assumptions of constitutional superiority over Scotland.[8] There was an unshakeable English conviction that liberty was unique to their constitution and that it was an unknown concept in Scotland. In that sense the English really did believe that the union of 1707 extended the benefits of Englishness to a less fortunate people.[9]

In 1707 a significant number of English Tory MPs in the House of Commons argued that this would be a mistake. P. W. J. Riley began to explore this in his research on the Union, and Professor David Hayton has added to our knowledge in his introduction to the History of Parliament volumes on the House of Commons from 1690–1715.[10] More research is needed on the subject to complement and contextualise the great strides that have been made with the publication of new research on the situation in Scotland that has coincided with the tercentenary. English politicians knew that union with Scotland would increase the power of the court in parliamentary politics. Francis Annesley wrote to Archbishop King of the proposed Scottish representation in the House of Commons and House of Lords after the Union as 'so many dead votes one way will be a great stroke in the legislature . . .'.[11] As Riley has pointed out, English court policy in the negotiations accepted the idea put forward by Whig Junto supporters to satisfy as many Scottish demands as possible and still win English parliamentary approval for the resulting treaty. Scottish negotiators enjoyed a great deal of success in achieving generous terms for Scotland as part of the Union settlement. That makes those Scots responsible for the Union more patriotic than they were often portrayed by Robert Burns and others who wrote off all unionist Scots politicians as scoundrels and even traitors. For many English observers, however, it meant that the Union was a bad job that gave foreigners preferential access to English court influence and the riches of both the English Treasury and the English Empire.[12] They were not pleased. They portrayed Scots as corrupt politicians who would corrupt parliamentary politics.[13] English politicians had supported union as a means of winning favour at court with the Queen, but once a treaty had actually been approved in Scotland, they began to contemplate the upsetting element Scottish MPs and peers would have on English politics.

High Church Episcopalian Tories led the charge. Charles Caesar raised 'scruples against the union' in opening the debate on the Treaty of Union in the House of Commons that observers did not specify in their reports but which related clearly to fears about Scottish Presbyterians in Parliament expanding the religious dissenting interest in England and weakening the Church of England.[14] Later there would be a Tory motion to add a clause to the Treaty of Union to prevent any 'oath, text or subscription' being imposed by any post-Union government that would undermine the 'government, worship and disciplines' of the Church of England.[15]

The real star of the English parliamentary opposition to union was Sir John Pakington (or Packington). His contribution to the debate in the House of Commons began by stating that:

> People [in England] without Door had been, for a long time, tongue-tied by a special Order of council, which not reaching them within [Parliament], he would very freely impart his Thoughts about it. That, for his part, he was absolutely against this incorporating Union, which he said, was like the marrying a Woman against her Consent: An Union that was carried on by Corruption and Bribery within Doors, and by Force and Violence without.[16]

He went on to accuse Scottish unionists of betraying their own country and:

> in thus basely giving up their independent Constitution, had actually betray'd the Trust reposed in them, and therefore he would leave it to the Judgement of the House to consider, whether or no Men of such Principles were fit to be admitted to sit amongst them?[17]

The core of Pakington's case, like that of most opponents of the Union in the English Parliament, was that the Church of England was in danger. What was to become of the Church of England if Presbyterian Scots were to be allowed a voice in English affairs? For dissenting English Protestants such as Daniel Defoe, the answer was that the Scots were welcome as reinforcements to the idea that the 'Protestant Interest' in England should never be defined narrowly as the Church of England.[18] In the House of Commons during March 1706/7, however, 'little was said in Answer' to Pakington. Once a great majority rejected the motion to postpone consideration of the first article of the Treaty, which established the United Kingdom of Great Britain, many members of the opposition withdrew from the House.[19]

In the Lords the ministerial majority was established, but the earl of Nottingham led the opposition in emphasising that English liberty and the Church of England were both in danger. In a speech which was published later as a pamphlet, Lord Haversham pointed out to the House just how strong popular opposition to the Union was in Scotland, and asserted that 'I think an incorporating union one of the most dangerous experiments to both nations, in which, if we happen to be mistaken, however we may think of curing things hereafter, the error is irretrievable'.[20] The bishop of Bath and Wells recorded that:

> he was altogether against the Union which he could wish with all his Heart had been completed an hundred Years ago; because, said he, all the

Ferment and Discord which were likely to ensue upon it, would by this time have had their Course: That he could no better compare it, than to the mixing together strong Liquors, of a contrary Nature, in one and the same Vessel, which would go nigh to be burst asunder by their furious Fermentation.

He called for Scots peers who would sit in the House of Lords in the future to be barred from voting on legislation affecting the Church of England.[21]

Nottingham returned to the attack to claim that the end of the laws and constitution of England was at hand and that he prayed that God would 'avert the dire effects which might probably ensue from such an incorporating union', and that he rued the day that 'he had out-lived all the Laws and the very Constitution of *England*'.[22] Numerous statements of dissent were recorded by the minority after they had been defeated on most votes by majorities of 90:20, including the following by the Lords Beaufort, Buckingham, Stawell, Guilford and Granville:

> Because the constitution of this Kingdom has been so very excellent, and therefore justly applauded by all our Neighbours for so many Ages, that we cannot conceive it prudent now to change it, and to venture at all those Alterations made by this Bill, . . . that, as the Inconvenience and Danger of them (in our humble Opinion) is already but too obvious, some think it more proper and decent to avoid entering further into the particular Apprehension we have from the passing of this Law.[23]

Few speeches were made in favour of the treaty in the Lords due to the government's anxiety to secure parliamentary approval as soon as possible. The Queen was delighted, and in her message to Parliament, in addition to reminding its members that they had still to approve the 'Equivalent' of financial incentives promised to the Scots by the treaty, expressed the hope that all her subjects would 'act with all possible respect and Kindness to one another, that so it may appear to all the World, they have Hearts disposed to become one People'.[24]

Of course, they didn't. It took a century, and four or five major wars (depending on how you count them), to make British union a reality. Ironically, Britain as a state only succeeded once it began to expand beyond the island itself. Although the British union did not expand its parliamentary representation until the union with Ireland in 1801, it was the heavy British involvement in what Americans came to call 'the French and Indian' war from its undeclared skirmishing in 1754 to its formal conclusion with the Peace of Paris in 1763 that formalised Scottish involvement in British overseas empire. The Scots had penetrated English colonies before the union of course, but it was the acute need for fighting men (and reluctance to impress them in England) that led to Scottish regiments contributing such a disproportionate element to the British war effort from 1756 to 1763. In the face of increasing English prejudice against the raised profile of Scots in politics and at court some Scots even claimed that it was the Scots who had conquered North America for a British state which by 1763 manifestly had become an empire.[25]

However, the domestic Scottish experience of union from 1707 to 1763 and beyond was anything but positive. Even Hanoverians and unionists in Scotland (and they were not always the same people), found that the fruits of union were not always sweet. Christopher Whatley and Derek Patrick document widespread economic depression and disillusion with union in their recent book, particularly along the eastern coast of Scotland.[26] Scottish textile production was opened to increased competition in domestic markets and yet lacked the technical expertise to raise the quality of its goods to make them competitive elsewhere. Even Scots success in the west in engaging in colonial trade was limited to a small number of merchants who increasingly became concentrated in Glasgow and remained largely detached from the rest of Scottish society and the Scottish economy. There were two major Jacobite rebellions, as is well known, and a further minor outbreak in 1719, as well as an attempted descent by the French army and navy in 1708. The end of war with France in 1713 brought Scottish calls to end the union, attempts by the government to extend the English tax on malt to Scotland (as they were entitled to do under the terms of the Treaty of Union) and widespread unrest in Scotland.[27] After the arrival of the Elector George of Hanover from the Holy Roman Empire in 1714 to take the throne in succession to Queen Anne this led to open rebellion the following year headed by the formerly pro-Union earl of Mar. Of course, the Jacobite rebellions all failed, because there was little support for Jacobite restoration in London and the 'Home' counties, but they accentuated the growing disparity between the metropolitan centre of Britain and the rest of the country, including the English regions. Jacobite rebellion, however, gave credence to the impression that all Jacobites were Scots, and Scottish Jacobite incursions into England in 1715 and 1745 led many Englishmen to conclude that the British military intervention that followed in Scotland in 1716 and 1746 meant that the Union was a sham. Had not Oliver Cromwell, as the English

Commander of the Forces in Scotland in 1747 commented, demonstrated that the most effective means of dealing with Scotland was through English conquest and the extension of English laws and culture into that barbarous country?[28] There were Scots who agreed with him, although Anglophilia does not quite explain satisfactorily the phenomenon that we now think of as the Scottish Enlightenment.[29]

Nor did the Union experience serious problems only from Jacobite rebellion and subsequent British military intervention. During the long period of peace from post-1716 to 1739 presided over by Sir Robert Walpole as first minister to both George I and George II at Westminster, governing Scotland became increasingly more, rather than less, problematic. It has been suggested that this was due at least in part to Walpole's inclination to trust to the duke of Argyll to preserve order in Scotland through the enormous extent of his property, power and consequent influence there. He embarked on this policy after major Scottish resistance to tax collection reached something like open rebellion in 1725 with the so-called Shawfield riots in Glasgow and related disturbances in Edinburgh.[30] This ended up over time increasing divisions among the Scottish Whigs, some of whom saw 'completing the union' on an incorporating basis as a means of liberating the country from dominance by a single member of the nobility and his kin group. Others backed the 'Argathelians' as the only means of preserving national interest in a political union in which the economic interests of the dominant member would always take precedence. Still others continued to perceive the house of Argyll, despite evidence to the contrary, as guardians of the Presbyterian cause in Scottish society.

In 1741 Argyll went over to the opposition and the government lost a parliamentary election in Scotland for the only time in the eighteenth century. The death of the second duke of Argyll in 1742 following direct approaches to him by the Old Pretender for political support, and the rebellion in Scotland three years later, set in motion a period of transition in which Argyll's brother and successor as third duke cultivated the role of senior statesman in Scotland and became, as a series of Allan Ramsay portraits demonstrate, a talisman of economic and cultural 'improvement', as a national movement to complete the Union by achieving parity, or something like it, with England economically and culturally.[31] Argyll looked back to the days of his brother and Walpole, but in semi-retirement worked at reforming the country's church and universities. In essence he secularised both to a degree that led to successful integration by the time of the American Revolution, and a generation later the identification of Scotland as a major centre of conservative support for king and country politically and through military recruitment in a renewed war with France.[32] New research, however, is demonstrating that the conservative breakthrough in economic and cultural development in Scotland from c. 1750 to c. 1790 associated with a 'Scottish Enlightenment' committed to British unionism also spawned popular political opposition which identified, paradoxically, the political conservatism of the country's landowning elite as a legacy of Scottish feudalism, and associated the limited integration of the parliamentary union of 1707 as intended to safeguard the feudal privileges of those who dominated the former kingdom in the form of the nobility and their creatures.[33]

After the initial impact of events in France on Scotland, in which popular unrest was directed at Scottish targets such as the Scottish politician Henry Dundas, discontent with the narrow basis of the existing political constitution was directed at political institutions in Scotland that had been preserved under the terms of the Treaty of Union. The extension of political liberty to the majority of the population in Scotland was not seen in terms of national self-determination, which was beginning to find expression in parts of Europe, but re-negotiation of the Union to ensure that Scots had access to English political liberties. There were claims to the legitimacy of a Scottish political tradition of liberty most obviously made by a revival of the cult of William Wallace, but the 'Unionist Nationalism' Graeme Morton has identified incorporated renewed commitment to British union while emphasising, not the independence of Scots law and institutions, but the moral and cultural integrity of a country with an important contribution to make to an expanding United Kingdom and Empire.[34]

What was the influence of the Scottish example of parliamentary union with England on implementation of unionist ideology in British North America? Was it a model used in the project to incorporate the former kingdom of Ireland from 1801 in an expanded United Kingdom that survived until 1922, and in turn ensured that part of Ireland remains within the modern British state? The legacy of Anglo-Scottish union did not attract favourable attention in British North America including the West Indies in the early eighteenth century, although it did increase interest in recruiting Scots as indentured servants in the West Indies (often compared favourably on ethnic or sectarian grounds by plantation overseers and colonial authorities), and as settlers in colonies struggling to attract English immigrants by the early eighteenth century.[35] In 1710 the French territory of Arcadia was renamed Nova Scotia by New England commercial and colonial interests keen to extend their influence there, informed by Scottish contacts of long abandoned seventeenth-century Scottish efforts to settle the territory under royal charter which provided a convenient 'British' claim that could be used eighty years later.[36] The first dynamic move for British North American union was led by Benjamin Franklin in forwarding the 'Albany' plan for mutual defence against the French and their Indian allies in 1754. Ned Landsman has pointed out that many of Franklin's closest associates in this project were Scots. The 'very idea of a united America was originally a British invention', Landsman has pointed out, citing a pioneering essay by the American historian John Murrin.[37]

In other words, Scots in North America at the time of the challenge to colonial expansion by France drew on the Scottish experience of union to 1754 as a model for defence of interests that were essentially imperial rather than national, and identified in terms of a modernising commercial 'improvement' associated with Protestant societies such as Lowland Scotland repelling French-supported incursions against its development by a Highland population that was beginning to be portrayed in Scotland as aboriginal. Landsman identifies Scots such as James Abercromby, James Alexander, Cadwallader Colden, Archibald Kennedy and William Livingston as associates of Franklin.[38] Most of these men had left Scotland in the problematic period (for unionists) before 1745, but research is needed as to how far they were influenced by the increase in favourable comment on the benefits of union for Scotland over the longer term, such as Adam Smith's reflections on the Union:

> The Union was a means from which infinite Good has been derived to this country. The Prospect of that good, however, must then have appeared very remote and very uncertain. The immediate effect of it was to hurt the interest of every single order of men in the country . . . The views of Posterity are now very different; but those views could be seen by but few of our forefathers, by those few in but a confused and imperfect manner.[39]

In North America, this scenario did not unfold, as is made clear in Franklin's response to correspondence from the Scottish judge and intellectual luminary Henry Home, Lord Kames of the Scottish Court of Justice. We can deduce that Kames's letters to Franklin, now lost, argued that American grievances were best pursued within an expanded parliamentary union between Britain and the North American colonies. Franklin was having none of it. He was already inventing an American identity that turned its back on the feudalism of Europe in order to realise to the full the possibilities of the American continent. Scotland and Ireland would forever be condemned to the status of a Celtic periphery in a British union dominated by London. America, on the other hand, if united, would sooner than many realised become more powerful than perhaps Britain itself. 'I have lived so great a part of my life in Britain, and have formed so many Friendships in it, that I love it and wish its Prosperity, and therefore wish to see that Union on which alone I think it can be secur'd and establish'd,' wrote Franklin. America was different, however:

> As to America, the Advantages of such an Union to her are not so apparent. . . Scotland and Ireland are differently circumstanc'd. Confin'd by the Sea, they can scarcely increase in Numbers, Wealth and Strength so as to overbalance England. But America, an immense Territory . . . will in a less time than is generally concern'd be able to shake off any Shackles that may be imposed on her, and perhaps place them on the Imposers.[40]

In another letter, this time to the American Joshua Babcock, Franklin expressed his scepticism of the advantages of British unionism after a tour of Ireland and Scotland:

> Had I never been in the American Colonies, but was to form my Judgement of civil Society by what I have lately seen, I should never advise a Nation of Savages to admit of Civilisation: For I assure you, that in the Possession and Enjoyment of the various Comforts of Life, compar'd to these People [the people of Ireland and Scotland] every Indian is a Gentleman: And the Effect of this kind of Civil Society seems only to be, the depressing Multitudes below the Savage State that a few may be rais'd above it.[41]

In Scotland, after victory in the war with France in 1763, there were some striking statements of belief in the dynamic of an expanding British polity that included accepting that in time the epicentre of British union would move from Britain itself to the Britain overseas that came into existence after 1763. Archibald Grant of Monymusk was an improving landowner in Aberdeenshire who had links to relations involved in colonial trade. His aspirations to extend his 'estate' overseas echo ambitions of other Scottish landowners just before and after the Treaty of Union, but they also looked forward to the grandiose schemes of the earl of Selkirk to use capital raised from the sale of his estates in Kirkcudbrightshire to realise what he envisaged as virtually a private kingdom after 1815 in the Red River Valley in what is now Manitoba.[42]

Ned Landsman has developed an analysis of Scottish experience of union in the eighteenth century that drew on the now dated but still stimulating essay by Bernard Bailyn and John Clive published more than half a century ago that sought to compare that part of British North America that became the United States with Scotland as 'cultural provinces' of eighteenth-century Britain. Provincial culture over the course of the eighteenth century began to gain in confidence to define itself as more virtuous and more industrious than an increasingly decadent British metropolis, but the sting in the tail was that provincial America declared political independence, whereas provincial Scotland remained just that, despite the cultural and scientific glories of the Scottish Enlightenment.[43]

When certain Scots argued that the problematic nature of the relationship of the kingdom of Ireland with Great Britain after 1782 could be best solved by application of the model of the Scottish union of 1707 to Ireland, increasing numbers of Irishmen looked (and many emigrated) to a very different model polity that subordinated unionism to nationalism. Scottish unionism became stronger as Britain expanded and, by implication, the imbalance caused by the dominance of England over the other British nations was diluted by an imperial dynamic that many Scots, influenced by entrenched Presbyterian concepts of a dynamic moral commonwealth that would change the world.[44] A former member of the faculty at Edinburgh University taught his students that the power of what Adam Smith presented as his central message was that it was possible to be both rich and good. It was a dream that defined unionism in Scotland.[45]

Notes

1 Maurice Lee, Jr, *Government by Pen: Scotland Under James VI and I* (London: University of Illinois Press, 1980), p. 37.

2 Quoted in Bruce Galloway and Brian Levack (eds), *The Jacobean Union* (Edinburgh: The Scottish History Society, 1985), p. xx.

3 Bruce Galloway, *The Union of England and Scotland 1603–1608* (Edinburgh: John Donald, 1986), p. 11.

4 Galloway, *The Union of England and Scotland 1603–1608*, p. 104.

5 Allan Macinnes, *British Revolution, 1629–1660* (Basingstoke: Palgrave Macmillan, 2005); F. D. Dow, *Cromwellian Scotland 1651–1660* (Edinburgh, John Donald, 1979).

6 Alexander Murdoch, *British History 1660–1832* (Basingstoke: Macmillan, 1998), p. 17, citing Conrad Russell, 'The British problem and the English Civil War', *History*, 72, 1983, p. 397.

7 Christopher A. Whatley with Derek J. Patrick, *The Scots and the Union* (Edinburgh: Edinburgh University Press, 2006), ch. 3.

8 Whatley, *The Scots and Union*, pp. 4, 6, 53, 215–16, 262.

9 Alexander Murdoch, 'The creation of the United Kingdom of Great Britain in 1707', *The Historian*, 94, Summer 2007, p. 16.

10 P. W. J. Riley, *The Union of England and Scotland* (Manchester: Manchester University Press, 1978); D. W. Hayton, *The History of Parliament: The House of Commons 1690–1715* (Cambridge: Cambridge University Press, 2002), vol. I.

11 Riley, *Union*, p. 164, citing *Reports of the Historical Manuscripts Commission Archbishop King MSS*, 244, 1706.

12 Riley, *Union*, p. 170.

13 Riley, *Union*, p. 300.

14 Riley, *Union*, p. 302. Also see Mark Knights, 'Charles Caesar', *History of Parliament*, III, p. 438, which records Caesar repeating 'some scruples against the union' in a Commons debate on 7 December 1707.

15 R. [Chandler], *The History and Proceedings of the House of Commons* (London, 1741–44), IV, p. 60.

16 [Chandler], *History*, p. 54. See Stuart Handley, 'Sir John Pakington', in *History Parliament*, III, pp. 68–9.

17 [Chandler], *History*, IV, p. 54.

18 Whatley with Patrick, *Scots*, pp. 54, 72. Also see the entry on Defoe in the *Oxford Dictionary of National Biography* (Oxford: Oxford University Press, 2004).

19 [Chandler], *History*, IV, p. 55. See J. Bruce, *Report on the Events and Circumstances which Produced the Union of England and Scotland* (London: 1799), I, 372–3.

20 E. [Timberlake], *The History and Proceedings of the House of Lords* (London: 1742–3), II, pp. 174–5. See the *Oxford DNB* entry for Thompson, John, first Barone Haversham (1648–1710). Defoe compared Haversham's rhetoric with 'a dog baying at the moon'.

21 [Timberlake], *History*, II, p. 175. See the *Oxford DNB* entry for Hooper, George (1640–1727), bishop of Bath and Wells.

22 [Timberlake], *History*, II, p. 176.

23 [Timberlake], *History*, pp. 178–9.

24 [Chandler], *History*, IV, p. 59.

25 Ned C. Landsman, 'The provinces and the Empire: Scotland, the American Colonies and the development of British provincial identity', in Lawrence Stone, (ed.), *An Imperial State at War* (London: Routledge, 1994), p. 267.

26 Whatley with Patrick, *Scots*, ch. 9.

27 [Timberlake], *History*, II, pp. 393–8.

28 Alexander Murdoch, *The People Above: Politics and Administration in Mid-Eighteenth Century Scotland* (Edinburgh, John Donald, 1980), p. 43.

29 Colin Kidd, *Subverting Scotland's Past* (Cambridge: Cambridge University Press, 1993), ch. 9.

30 John M. Simpson, 'Who steered the gravy train, 1707–1766', in N. T. Phillipson and Rosalind Mitchison (eds), *Scotland in the Age of Improvement* (Edinburgh: Edinburgh University Press, 1970, reissued 1996), pp. 53–4.

31 See the entries by this author in the *Oxford DNB* for the second and third dukes of Argyll. For the Ramsay portraits of the third duke see Alastair Smart, *Allan Ramsay: A Complete Catalogue of his Paintings*, John Ingamells (ed.) (London: Yale University Press, 1999).

32 Atle L. Wold, 'Scottish attitudes to military mobilisation and war in the 1790s', in Bob Harris (ed.), *Scotland in the Age of the French Revolution* (Edinburgh: John Donald, 2005); Atle L. Wold, 'The Scottish government and the French threat 1792–1802', University of Edinburgh Ph.D., 2003.

33 Gordon Pentland, 'Patriotism, universalism and the Scottish conventions, 1792–1794', *History*, 89, 2004, pp. 340–60; Gordon Pentland, 'Scotland and the creation of a national reform movement, 1830–1832', *The Historical Journal*, 48, 2005, pp. 999–1023; Bob Harris, *The Scottish People and the French Revolution* (London: Pickering and Chatto, forthcoming 2008).

34 Graeme Morton, *Unionist Nationalism* (East Linton: Tuckwell Press, 1999); Graeme Morton and R. J. Morris, 'Civil society, governance and nation, 1832–1914', in R. A. Houston and W. W. J. Knox (eds), *The New Penguin History of Scotland* (London: Penguin, 2001), pp. 355–416.

35 T. M. Devine, *Scotland's Empire 1600–1815* (London: Penguin, 2003), p. 227; Hilary McD. Beckles, *White Servitude and Black Slavery in Barbados* (London: University of Tennessee Press, 1989).

36 Whatley with Patrick, *Scots*, p. 361; John G. Reid et al., *The 'Conquest' of Acadia, 1710: Imperial, Colonial and Aboriginal Constructions* (London: University of Toronto Press, 2004).

37 Landsman, 'The provinces and the Empire', p. 267; John Murrin, 'A roof without walls: the dilemma of American national identity', in Richard Beeman et al. (eds), *Beyond Confederation: Origins of the Constitution and American National Identity* (London: University of North Carolina Press, 1987), pp. 333–48.

38 Landsman, 'The provinces and the Empire', p. 267.

39 To William Strahan, 4 April 1760, in Ernest Campbell Mossner and Ian Simpson Ross (eds), *The Correspondence of Adam Smith* (Oxford: Clarendon Press, 1977), p. 68.

40 25 February/11 April 1767, in William Willcox (ed.), *The Papers of Benjamin Franklin*, vol. 14 (London: Yale University Press, 1970), pp. 69–70.

41 13 January 1772, in William Willcox (ed.), *The Papers of Benjamin Franklin*, vol. 19, pp. 6–7.

42 Landsman, 'The provinces and the Empire', p. 266; Bernard Bailyn, *Voyagers to the West* (London: I. B. Tauris, 1986), pp. 436–7, 462–4; J. M. Bumsted, *The People's Clearance 1770–1815* (Edinburgh: Edinburgh University Press, 1982), ch. 8.

43 Landsman, 'The provinces and the Empire'; Landsman, 'Introduction', in Ned C. Landsman (ed.), *Nation and Province in the First British Empire: Scotland and the Americas, 1600–1800* (London: Associated University Presses, 2001), pp. 15–35.

44 This has yet to be fully explored, but see Morton and Morris, 'Governance and nation 1832–1914' and works such as R. D. Anderson, *Education and Opportunity in Victorian Scotland* (Oxford: Oxford University Press, 1983, reissued Edinburgh University Press, 1989); George Davie, *The Democratic Intellect: Scotland and her Universities in the Nineteenth Century* (Edinburgh: Edinburgh University Press, 1961) and J. David Hoeveler, Jr, *James McCosh and the Scottish Intellectual Tradition* (London: Princeton University Press, 1981).

45 Paul Edwards in conversation with David Dabydeen, Open University A206 course, *The Enlightenment* programme for television broadcast, 'Equiano and the Noble Savage', *c.* 1993.

6

THE SPOILS OF EMPIRE

T. M. Devine

By the middle decades of the eighteenth century Scotland was at a crossroads between the old world and the new. In the 1760s and 1770s the social and economic structure of the nation began a process of transformation unparalleled among European societies in its speed, scale and intensity. Indeed, no other area of the Continent achieved a similarly fast revolution in its economy until the state-initiated and planned industrialisation of Soviet Russia in the 1920s. The great Scottish leap forward towards an urban and industrial society was without precedent. England was, of course, in the vanguard of modernity but it took around 200 years to achieve what its northern neighbour managed in a couple of generations. Scottish industrialisation was explosive; that of England, cumulative, protracted and, for the most part during the seventeenth and eighteenth centuries, evolutionary in character.

Consider, for instance, the rates of urban expansion, a crucial confirmation of the emergence of a new society. Between 1750 and 1850 the growth of towns and cities in Scotland was the fastest in Britain or on the Continent. In 1750 the country lay seventh in a league table of 'urbanised societies', fourth by 1800 and second only to England and Wales in 1850, by which time over a third of Scots were urban dwellers. Critically, however, this was a revolution which had a transformational effect on the whole of Scotland. The effects of the new order were apparent even in the most remote corners of the land. They embraced the islands of the Hebrides and Orkney and Shetland in the far west and north of the country, the innumerable farms and small villages of the rural Lowlands as well as the booming urban areas. The voracious demands of industry and the towns for food, drink, raw materials and labour radically altered economic and social relationships throughout Scotland. The buoyant markets for kelp, fish, whisky, slate, cattle, timber and sheep to c. 1815 helped to transform Gaelic society, dissolved the traditional townships, encouraged land division into single crofts and subordinated the ancient responsibilities of the landed classes to the new imperatives of profit. In parallel, customary relationships between clan elites and followers swiftly disintegrated as the entire fabric of society was recast in response to the new rigour of landlord demand, ideological fashion and, above all, the overwhelming force of market pressures emanating from the south. Over less than two generations Scottish Gaeldom had moved from tribalism to capitalism.

The scale and speed of the revolution was no less remarkable in the rural Lowlands. There, too, the steep rise in grain and meat prices after c. 1780 as a result of urbanisation was the basic dynamic in rapid commercialisation. In the two or three decades after c. 1760 a recognisably modern landscape of enclosed fields, trim farms, individual holdings and new roads started to take shape in the countryside. The single farm under one master became the norm as the old holdings were brought together between 1760 and 1815. By 1830, most of those who toiled in Lowland agriculture were landless men and women servants. Their lives were often as much subject to the unrelenting pressures of labour discipline as those employed in the new industrial workshops and factories. The market forces unleashed by industrialisation and urbanisation spanned the length and breadth of the land. There had been a decisive break with the past and the country was set firmly on the path towards an industrial society.

Historians are able to show that a range of factors helped to make this new order. These included such influences as growing markets, the natural advantages of water, coal and iron ore resources, cheap labour and fertile sources of enterprise among other causes. Most existing accounts, however, fail to address convincingly or sometimes even fail to mention a major puzzle at the core of Scotland's rapid progress to modernity. In earlier centuries, the country had been recognised as one of the poorest in Europe with high levels of emigration and low standards of living. In the 1690s the population had endured several years of famine and a serious economic crisis triggered by the failure of the Darien expeditions and severe difficulties in overseas trade. As late as 1738–41 Scotland experienced one of the worst depressions of the eighteenth century. Two consecutive harvest failures led to acute price inflation, a fall in agricultural output and a marked decline in average incomes. Yet the transformational process, especially in its early stages from the 1760s before productive gains came through, required investment and a lot of it. From where did the new resources come?

Again, a contrast with England is worth making. Historians there spend little time pondering over the sources of capital for eighteenth-century trade, agriculture and industry. This is hardly surprising because England far exceeded Scotland in national income. It was a country with the wealth not only to make war on a global scale but also to provide the resources needed to sustain its existing economic expansion, primarily through the reploughing of profit into new investment. Scotland differed in three key respects is that it was a much poorer country, the economic revolution took place rapidly over a few decades and unprecedented levels of investment were needed simultaneously not only in industry, town and the transport infrastructure of roads, harbours and canals but also crucially in agriculture. Significant injections of capital were required not only in niche development or in some sectors but across the whole range of the economic system.

The evidence from the revolution in agriculture is compelling in this respect: in its first phase at least, the process of innovation was led and managed by the lairds and their agents. Only by the 1790s were there clear signs that the tenantry had become the prime driving force. This top-down approach involved lavish expenditure either on loans to tenants or in outright payments on liming, roads, enclosures, ditching, timber plantations, wells, dykes, drains and village development. Three examples from many illustrate the magnitude of the required investment. Over a five-year period from 1771 to 1776, the earl of Strathmore laid out £22,223 in a large-scale programme of improvement on his Angus lands, while over six months in 1803 Richard Oswald's expenditure on Auchencruive in Ayrshire was of the order of £2,600.[1] On the Crawford estate in South Lanarkshire in 1772, the annual spend was over £4,700.[2] In addition, it is reckoned that from 1780 to 1815 between £2.5 million and £3 million was paid out by the new turnpike trusts on the construction of roads and bridges in Scotland, a scale of investment which revolutionised the country's formerly inland primitive system of communications.[3] It must be remembered, too, that much of the nation's industries of textiles, mining, printing and quarrying were rural-based in this period and were capitalised by collective partnerships of landowners and entrepreneurs.

All of this improvement does not take into account the astonishing rise in the levels of conspicuous consumption among the Scottish aristocracy and gentry classes which were occurring in parallel. The costs of landownership spiralled in the eighteenth century. These were the

decades of competitive display when social standing became defined
by material status designed to impress. Magnificent country houses,
opulent furnishings and the adornment of estate policies were not
only fashionable but essential in order to maintain and demonstrate high position in the social hierarchy. It is noteworthy how many
of the great houses of Scotland were either built or much reno-
vated during this period: Inverary, Culzean, Hopetoun House and
Mellerstain were only the most famous examples. This was the era
when the remarkable Adam family of architects did their best work,
much of which involved the comprehensive remodelling of the old
castellated houses and fortified dwellings of an earlier and more tur-
bulent age. In the later eighteenth century the number of aristocratic
and laird houses built from scratch also multiplied. Nearly twice as
many were constructed in the 1790s (over sixty) as between 1700 and
1720. Most of Robert Adam's commissions were for the laird class,
although his best known work was for the nobility.[4] Also driving up
costs was the revolution in interior design. At the time of the Union
the domestic furnishings of a typical laird's house were simple in the
extreme. Less than fifty years later the aristocracy was aspiring to
standards of unprecedented splendour with gilded ornamentation,
framed paintings, lavish fabrics and elaborate ceiling mouldings.
Mahogany furnishings based on the designs of Chippendale, Sheraton
and Hepplewhite enjoyed remarkable popularity. Over time the
resources for elite spending on the grand scale would come through
from the fatter rent rolls generated by improved methods and booming
markets. Yet this explanation still leaves out of account the problem
of the crucial pioneering decades of the 1760s and 1770s when
modern agrarian capitalism first became established in Scotland.
The argument here is that one prime source of the new wealth was the
profits of Empire gained through trade with the Americas, the
Caribbean and India, together with the impact of 'sojourners' returning with fortunes made in merchanting, plantation ownership, the
professions and colonial administration, some of which found its way
into large-scale productive investment.

AN EMPIRE OF TRADE

An empire of transoceanic Scottish trade would not have existed on
such a scale but for the Union of 1707, that resulted in Scottish inclu-
sion within the English system of tariff protection, the protection of
the Royal Navy and the long series of wars fought successfully

against France in the West Indies and the Caribbean for territorial and commercial hegemony. In the final analysis, the British markets in the Americas and India rested on the deployment of force backed by the massive financial resources of the state. One recent argument has it that there was a definable difference between the 'Scottish' and 'English' Empires.[5] The latter, it is suggested, was driven by the urge to conquer, while the former was more benign and concerned with making money and settling emigrants. This supposed distinction is illusory. Even if the Scots were dedicated to profit rather than conquest (itself a highly questionable proposition), the colonies where they traded only remained British, and hence open markets for them, because of the muskets of the army and the firepower of the navy. The governing assumption among all eighteenth-century European states was that global wealth was finite. Any increase in the share of one nation could only take place at the expense of another. Aggression, predatory behaviour and an obsession with protection of national interests by commercial regulation and armed force were inevitably built into these mercantilist beliefs. The Scottish trading communities were usually enthusiastic for colonial conflicts if they resulted in real commercial gains, hence the open letter of gratitude sent to the dying George II in 1760 by the Scottish Convention of Royal Burghs. Praise was heaped on the monarch for the military successes in the West Indies and Canada culminating in the glorious capture of Quebec. Scottish interests were quick to spot the opportunities that opened up as a consequence of these victorious campaigns. As early as October 1759, Edinburgh publishers were already selling maps of Guadeloupe, Louisburg, Quebec and Montreal, all areas soon to attract Scottish adventurers when the Seven Years' War came to an end. They would have agreed with the famous aphorism that: 'Trade is the source of finance and finance is the vital nerve of war'.[6]

Equally, the only effective guarantor of Scottish colonial commerce in such a hostile environment was the Royal Navy. That protection in turn depended on the Treaty of Union of 1707. A year before it was signed, the pro-unionist, William Seton of Pitmedden, calling to mind the bitter lesson of the Darien disaster, recognised the harsh realities of an international world riven by mercantilist jealousies and mighty rivalries. The 'Course of Commerce' could only be exploited 'where there's force to protect it'. That force could not come from Scotland. The country was too poor and possessed tiny naval forces. Therefore, only 'the Protection of some powerful Neighbour Nation' could provide the support necessary in a world of expansionist maritime powers.[7] These arguments soon became reality in the years after the Union. Scottish Atlantic traders then enjoyed the protection of a navy expanded on the fiscal-military resources of the English state against the foraging wolf packs of enemy predators. Coastal shipping was also better protected by the twelve cruisers despatched to 'North Britain' under the Cruiser and Convoy Act 1708. However, it was only during the Seven Years War (1756–63) that the naval presence in home waters really became vital as, before then, enemy privateers tended mainly to infest the English Channel and the Southern Approaches where there were richer pickings. In 1759 and early 1760, the formidable French Commodore Thurot sailed north into Scottish waters with three heavily armed frigates, two corvettes and 1,300 troops. Such, a force could have created mayhem. However, thanks to the arrival of a substantial Royal Navy squadron, Thurot's expedition ended in disaster. The whole affair was a striking demonstration of British naval power. It was this protection which enabled the Scottish merchant marine to expand dramatically from a tonnage of 47,751 in 1759 to 91,330 on the eve of the American War in 1775.[8]

This was the context for success in the colonial trades. Scottish overseas commerce became dominated by Atlantic trade for most of the century after *c.* 1730. By 1762 just under half of Scottish imports and 52 per cent of exports were of colonial tobacco. Even when that lucrative trade declined after the American War imperial markets remained fundamental. The sugar and cotton trades from the West Indies became the new money-spinners. As late as 1814, nearly half of all the vessels leaving the Clyde ports sailed for the Caribbean, Jamaica, Grenada, Barbados and the remaining British North American territories took double the Glasgow exports destined for the USA in that year. The West Indian connection was also a key element in the development of Scottish cotton manufacture in the early decades of its expansion. Until near the end of the eighteenth century, the Caribbean was the great source of cheap and abundant 'sea-island' cotton for the industry. Imports rose from 2,700,000 lb to 8,400,000 lb between 1790 and 1805 to supply the needs of the numerous spinning mules springing up across the western Lowlands.

Fortunes made from tobacco, sugar and cotton had a direct impact on the agricultural revolution especially in the counties around Glasgow. Money poured from the Atlantic trades into land as wealthy merchants bought up properties. At least 44 per cent of the Glaswegian merchant aristocracy owned at least one landed estate and the really rich managed to acquire a number of them spread across several counties. Huge sums were often involved. Partners of the giant West India house of Alexander Houston and Company had bought up several properties to the value of £287,000 by 1800. Alexander Spiers, the so-called 'mercantile god of Glasgow', who headed one of the three great syndicates in the tobacco trade, had by his death in 1783 secured estates in Renfrewshire and Stirlingshire worth over £174,000. James Dunlop, another famous Virginia tycoon, held £130,000 of property in land in 1793.[9]

It may have been that some of this opulent breed of merchant gentry were content to live out their lives at leisure, engaging in hunting, building mansions, entertaining and beautifying the grounds of their estates. Many, however, were gripped by the contemporary mania for 'improvement' and were keen to see their properties as assets to be exploited for profit as effectively as their shares in cotton mills or in trading ventures. As observed by Adam Smith in *The Wealth of Nations*, merchants were 'generally the best of all improvers'. He noted that they were 'not afraid to lay out at once a large capital upon the improvement of lands' when there was 'a profitable prospect of raising the value of it in proportion to the expense'.[10] Sir John Sinclair, the most knowledgeable commentator on matters agricultural in Scotland, was equally impressed: 'employing part of their capital in the purchase of land and improvement of the soil [merchants], became most spirited cultivators'.[11] Sustained developments took place in some areas. The Monklands parishes in Lanarkshire were said to be 'in a huge degree of cultivation' in the 1790s because 'when a merchant has been successful, he purchases a piece of land, builds an elegant villa and improves his property at the dearest rates'.[12] Other enthusiastic comments came from Renfrewshire where the McDowall and Speirs families were very active. In Ayrshire and Kirkcudbright the very wealthy Richard Oswald, who had made an immense fortune in arms contracting as well as slave-trading in Africa and merchanting in the Caribbean and Europe, poured many thousands of pounds into his estates of Auchencruive and Cavens. But he was only the most prominent of a number of rich traders who were doing the same thing throughout the county. The record also shows that few merchants gave up their commercial activities when estates were purchased. The profits from the colonial trades continued to be pumped into schemes of landed improvement as well as the coal-mining ventures and factory villages which were also often established on country properties.

Nevertheless, one should take care not to be too Clydecentric when the eighteenth-century imperial economy is considered. Linen rather than cotton was far and away Scotland's greatest manufacture of the period, and by 1813–17 the industry was producing 27,000,000 yards annually. A few decades earlier, it was reckoned that full and part-employment in linen occupied almost a quarter of a million men, women and children. In 1790, John Naismith thought it 'the most universal source of wealth and happiness introduced into Scotland'.[13] Most Scots producers concentrated on the cheaper and coarser lines with Fife, Angus and Perthshire the dominant centres where the cloth was primarily destined for overseas markets. The home population in Scotland grew only slowly in the later eighteenth century, at a rate under 1 per cent per annum and well below the increases for Ireland and England. The total of 1.25 million in 1755 had only reached 1.6 million by 1801. Compare this with the massive increases across the Atlantic of 2.3 million in 1770 in the North American colonies from 265,000 in 1707 and 877,000 in 1815 in the British Caribbean in contrast to 145,000 at the start of the century. Of that 1815 total, 85 per cent of the population in the West Indies were slaves.

Scottish linen producers eagerly fed these booming markets. From 1745 linen bounties were extended to low-priced cloth which generated a dramatic increase in linen exports to the plantations across the Atlantic in the years that followed. Throughout the eighteenth century 80 to 90 per cent of these exports were supported by the bounty. The colonial markets were critical to growth. European consumption was marginal and Ireland was of minor significance. Nine-tenths of all Scottish linen exported from Scotland went to North America and the West Indies. Thus, after the American War, the Caribbean became even more fundamental. In the last quarter of the eighteenth century, the standards of living of numerous working-class families in the eastern Lowlands of Scotland came to depend on the huge markets for cheap linen clothing among the teeming slave populations of Jamaica and the Leeward Islands.[14]

THE FISCAL-MILITARY STATE

In 1707 the Scots joined in parliamentary union with a bellicose nation, which in the later seventeenth century was already building the fiscal, political and military foundations for imperial expansion.

This 'fiscal-military state' has been convincingly described as 'the most important transformation in English government between the domestic reforms of the Tudors and the major administrative changes in the first half of the nineteenth century'.[15] Like most European governments of the time, the English state spent most of its resources either on waging war or in preparation for future conflict. It is estimated that over most of the eighteenth century between 75 per cent and 80 per cent of annual government expenditure went on current military needs or in servicing debt accruing from previous wars. For Britain, by far the biggest outlay was on the navy, the 'senior service', vital for the home defence of an island people and for the prosecution of a 'blue water' policy around the globe, safeguarding trade routes and establishing secure overseas bases for the protection of colonies. Sir Walter Raleigh's dictum of over a century before still rang true: 'Whosoever commands the sea, commands the trade of the world; whosoever commands the riches of the world, and consequently the world itself'.[16] The problem was, however, that navies were fearsomely expensive. Wooden ships rotted fast, maintenance costs were enormous and the huge dockyards and shipyards required for repair and construction were inevitably a major drain on the public purse. Abundant finance rather than military force *per se* was reckoned to be the crucial sinew of war.

The English state had been pursuing a policy of aggressively extending its economic and military resources since *c.* 1650 and the process was virtually complete by the time of the Anglo-Scottish Union in 1707. It amounted to a financial revolution which made available to both the army and navy vast sums for the prosecution of war. The key components included a huge extension of the National Debt, sharp increases in taxation, a government bank (the Bank of England) and the flotation of long-term loans on the London capital market which also attracted funds from the Continent. No other state in Europe (apart perhaps from the Netherlands, which did not link its mercantile prowess so effectively to war strategy as England) was quite as successful in this financial transformation.[17] The costs of the revolution were borne mainly by taxes, especially customs and excise on imported and home-produced goods. Undeniably, as a result, Scotland was faced with an increased tax burden after 1707.

Scottish taxes did rise on consumer items, most notoriously in 1711 with the salt and linen taxes and 1725 with the malt tax. Yet, one estimate suggests that, in the half century after the Union, up to 80 per cent of the revenue take was absorbed in Scotland itself to cover the routine costs of the civil administration rather than being transferred to London.[18] Moreover, before the 1740s, the Westminster government tended to tread carefully in Scotland, conscious of the extent of Jacobite disaffection there and of the popular fury the malt tax increases had provoked in 1725. Revenue burdens on a per capita basis were, therefore, much lighter in both Scotland and Wales than in the richer counties of southern England. In addition, the Scots customs service was much less effective in collecting revenue in the first few decades after the Union than its counterpart in the south. Underpayment and smuggling were endemic. A black economy ran through Scottish society from top to bottom. To the anger of their rivals in the English outports, the Clyde tobacco merchants were estimated to have paid duty on only half their imports in the first two decades after 1707. The Records of the Scottish Board of Customs also teem with cases of widespread intimidation, violent assaults on officers and gang attacks on the warehouses of the Revenue.[19]

Tax evasion on this massive scale could not disguise the fact that the Union with England presented the Scottish elites with a golden opportunity. The benefit of naval protection for merchants engaged in the American trade was obvious. Even more fundamental, however, were the possibilities now opening up for the landed classes, the real masters of Scotland in this period. An historic anxiety for the aristocracy and the lairds was the challenge of achieving gainful employment for younger sons which would not only provide income but an acceptably genteel position in society. Landed estates in Scotland, whether great or small, descended by primogeniture on the eldest male child. His siblings had to make their own way in the world, either by the family acquiring some landed property for their remaining progeny or by younger sons achieving army and naval commissions, entering the law, the church or being apprenticed to a merchant house. This was the basic social dynamic which for centuries had impelled the offspring of the Scottish gentry to seek careers and fortunes in Europe. But the European connection was fading fast in the later seventeenth century and there is some evidence that the decline of career opportunities there was beginning to stoke up anxieties among the laird classes. Something of this came through in the plans for the Scottish colony in East New Jersey in the 1680s. The project was dominated by landowners from the eastern counties of Scotland, especially the northeast region, formerly a major supplier of Scots army officers and merchants to Scandinavia. The projectors envisaged a colony of landed estates and among those who eventually emigrated to the New World were a very high proportion of younger sons of the northeast gentry. Thus, three members of the Gordons of Straloch purchased proprietary shares, but only the two younger bothers actually travelled to the colony. Several other emigrants can be identified as sons of minor, cadet branches of landed families. Robert Gordon of Cluny probably spoke for many of his fellow proprietors when he stated that his own reason for being attracted to the project of colonisation was to provide land for his younger son, 'since I had not estate whereby to make him a Scotch laird'.[20]

However, perhaps even more intense pressures were building up by the early eighteenth century. Scottish landed families simply had more surviving adult children as infant mortality levels started to fall rapidly at that time. Although no exact figures exist to prove the point conclusively from a specifically Scottish perspective, research on the demography of British ducal families for the period can provide a useful surrogate source of information on changing patterns of population growth among the nation's governing classes. Family size among this elite was relatively stable until the later seventeenth century, but then, a few decades later, rapid growth started among the aristocracy at a rate which was considerably higher than in the general population increase in the country as a whole. The percentage of children of the nobility dying under the age of sixteen was 31.1 per cent between 1480 and 1679; from 1680 to 1779, the figure fell to 25.9 per cent and declined further to 21.1 per cent between 1780 and 1829. There were now many more sons surviving into adulthood. If this pattern was replicated across the Scottish landed classes, the concerns for placing younger sons in employment which was both gainful and socially acceptable must have become even more acute.

Yet this was not all. Changes in the composition of the Scottish landed structure added to the challenge. In 1700 there were around 9,500 landowners in Scotland, only about half of whom had the right to inherit or sell the land they possessed. The structure was dominated by the great aristocratic landlords and their associated kinship groups. This elite was expanding its territorial control at the expense of the lesser lairds between the later seventeenth century and the 1770s. Thus, the number of proprietors in Aberdeenshire fell by a third between *c.* 1670 and *c.* 1770 (621 to 250) and the steepest decline occurred among the smallest group of landowners. The trend was repeated all over Scotland. The total of 9,500 landowners at the beginning of the eighteenth century had dropped to 8,500 by the

1750s and fell further to around 8,000 at the start of the nineteenth century. Manifestly, the minor lairds were under considerable economic pressure before the 1750s. Rental income was relatively stagnant and increases in farm productivity did not really encompass most of Scottish agriculture until the 1760s. At the same time, as the number of estates possessed by this class was squeezed, one traditional option exercised to solve the problem of young sons, namely purchasing additional properties in their name, became much more difficult. In a sense, then, imperial employment after 1707 in the armed forces, colonial administration, trade and the professions came both as a crucial lifeline and a golden opportunity. In the decades after the Union, streams of eager Caledonians from genteel but impoverished backgrounds poured into the British Empire at every point from the Arctic wastes of Canada to the teeming cities of Bengal. The bureaucratic growth of the fiscal-military state ensured that career openings were now much more abundant than before and the Scots were very keen to exploit them. It was a form of resource transfer from the metropolis to Scotland, a kind of eighteenth-century variant on the twentieth-century Barnett Formula, with the prime beneficiaries being the landed classes of the nation.

THE OPPORTUNITIES OF EMPIRE

What one writer has described as the 'luscious opportunities' of Empire became even more enticing in the second half of the eighteenth century.[21] Especially after the Seven Years War (1756–63), there were enormous British territorial gains as a result of conquest, annexation and victory over the French. By c. 1770 the population of the North American colonies had grown to around 2.3 million. Georgia, East and West Florida, Quebec and Nova Scotia had all been won from France and Spain. Then came the American Revolution in 1776 and the emergence of an independent United States, born out of the thirteen British colonies. Their departure left only a rump of underpopulated territories in the north of the American mainland. Known as British North America they would in due course become the Dominion of Canada. Elsewhere, however, the momentum of territorial expansion seemed unstoppable. In the West Indies the Ceded Islands and Trinidad were acquired in 1763, while the most spectacular gains were achieved in India where the whole of the eastern subcontinent and a large part of the Ganges valley were under the administration of the English East India Company by 1815. At that date, it is calculated that 40 million Indians were living under British rule which was also fast extending into Ceylon and Mauritius. The Company at the same time was raising some £18 million in taxation within its territories, a sum amounting to around one-third of peacetime revenue in Britain itself. Exploration was also being pursued in the vastness of the Pacific Ocean by the voyages of such famous navigators as Captain James Cook. A permanent British colony was established for the first time in Australia when the First Fleet arrived in New South Wales in 1788. By 1815 Britain ruled over a global population in America, the Caribbean, Asia and the Antipodes of about 41.4 million people. By 1820, British dominion encompassed a fifth of the world's population. Contemporaries, such as Sir George Macartney in 1773, revelled in the scale of this vast empire 'on which the sun never sets and whose bounds nature has not yet ascertained'.[22] Patrick Colquhoun's *Treatise on the Wealth, Power and Resources of the British Empire* of 1814 had the revealing subtitle 'in every Quarter of the Globe'.

All this hugely increased demand for soldiers, arms and store contractors and the colonial bureaucracies ranging from governors of huge territories at the top to humble clerks at the bottom of the administrative hierarchies. The number of men under arms rose from around 113,000 during the War of the Austrian Succession of 1739 to 1748 to 190,000 in the American War, while the cost of war, standing at £8.75 million per annum in the 1740s spiralled to over £20 million in the 1770s. The fiscal-military state had never held out more alluring prospects for ambitious officers and colonial administrators.[23]

Moreover, in India the victories at Plassey (1757) and Buxar (1763) became the military foundations for a veritable bonanza of pillage. The years *c.* 1757 to *c.* 1770 were those when the subcontinent became notorious as the place where easy riches could be made quickly. Mortality rates among servants of the East India Company were horrendous, but there were compensations. As one historian has noted: 'these years were the only time during the eighteenth century when survival in Bengal virtually guaranteed that a man would return home with a fortune'.[24] It was not company salaries which fuelled the rapacity but rather returns from private trade, prize money and tax revenues extracted from the newly conquered Indian territories. Edmund Burke summed it up as 'the annual plunder of Bengal'.[25]

The Scots *par excellence* were to the fore in the exploitation of this new imperial bounty. They were outnumbered as a nation by the

Table 6.1 Scottish ratios in the eighteenth-century imperial elite

Period	Territory	
1680–1780	American colonies	One-third of university-educated men from Europe trained in Scotland
1707–75	Antigua	60 per cent of planter elite
1707–1800	North America	Thirty Scottish-born governors and lieutenant governors
1740	India	One in three of colonel rank in EIC army
c. 1750	Antigua	60 per cent of doctors
c. 1760	North America	One in four of British army officer corps
1763	Ceded Islands (West Indies)	Three governors appointed, all Scots
1771–5	Jamaica	45 per cent of inventories at death above £1,000
1774–85	Bengal	47 per cent of writers: 50 per cent of surgeon recruits (EIC)
c. 1775	Bengal	One in three of the EIC army's officer corps
1776–85	Bengal, Calcutta, Madras	60 per cent of 'free' merchants
1799	British North America (Hudson Bay Company)	78 per cent of staff from Orkney
1800	British North America (North West Company)	62 per cent of staff from counties of Inverness, Banff and Aberdeen
1813	Calcutta	37 per cent of private merchant houses

Source: T. M. Devine, Scotland's Empire, 1600–1815 (London: Allen Lane, 2003), passim.

English in the ratio 5:1 but, as the figures in Tables 6.1 and 6.2 confirm, the Scots achieved a much greater share of the imperial spoils than their population size within the United Kingdom justified.

The reasons for what one writer has termed these 'absurdly high proportions' of imperial Scots have been explored by the present author elsewhere and the interested reader is directed to the relevant sources listed in the Notes to this chapter.[26] Here the focus is primarily on the impact which the spoils of Empire had on Scotland,

Table 6.2 Scottish ratios in Indian service, 1720–1813

Territory	Period	Occupation	Scottish ratio (%)
Bengal	1774–85	Writer	47
Bengal	1750	Writer	38
Calcutta	1813	Private merchant houses	37
EIC provinces	1754–84	Officer class, EIC service	62
Madras	1720–57	Principal medical officer	100
Madras	1800	Physician and surgeon	40
East India	1740–60	Sea captains	39

Source: T. M. Devine, *Scotland's Empire, 1600–1815* (London: Allen Lane, 2003), *passim*.

especially in helping to provide much of the capital for the great transformation of the country which accelerated from the 1760s.

BRINGING HOME THE IMPERIAL SPOILS

Repatriation of the profits of Empire from the Caribbean and India was likely since most Scots who went there to make their fortunes were transients, 'sojourners in the sun', who had no intention of settlement and were committed to return as soon as their ambitions were achieved. They were temporary exiles whose roots remained in the mother country. Return, of course, did not always mean to Scotland because several came back to London, Bristol and elsewhere in England. Moreover, both the West Indies and Bengal, for all their economic allure, had the reputation of being the graveyards of the white man. One East India Company officer in 1780 had not yet made enough to come back home but he still intended to leave rather than die 'in this vile country' while another admitted: 'I'd almost as soon live in Hell as in India'. Over the period 1707 to 1775, 57 per cent of the Company's servants succumbed to fatal diseases.[27]

As seen earlier in this chapter, some of the tobacco and sugar princes of Glasgow's transatlantic trading empire made great fortunes, but even these could not compare to the colossal riches repatriated, some to relatives after the death, of the Indian 'nabobs'. Thus, John Johnstone of Westerhall returned to Scotland in 1765 with an estimated fortune of £300,000 which helped him to acquire three landed estates and a parliamentary interest. It was said of him that he pursued wealth with an enterprise and a dedicated ruthlessness second only to the victor of Plassey, the famous Robert Clive himself. Equally celebrated was William Hamilton, arguably the most famous doctor to serve in India during the whole three centuries of the Empire. A cadet of the family of Hamilton of Dalziell in Lanarkshire he first went to the East as a naval surgeon in 1711. His major claim to fame was his successful treatment of the Mogul Emperor for venereal disease. Hamilton was showered with gifts including an elephant, 5,000 rifles, two diamond rings, a set of gold buttons and a presentation set of all his own surgical instruments fashioned in gold. He also brought untold benefits to the East India Company when its rights to free trade in Bengal, Bihar and Orissa were confirmed in consequence of Hamilton's cure of the royal patient. John Farquhar, however, outdid both Johnstone and Hamilton in rapacity. At his death in 1826 he was worth £1.5 million, making him one of the richest Britons of the nineteenth century. Farquhar's commercial ruthlessness was matched only by his eccentricity. On his return from India he was said to have offered to endow one of the Scottish universities with the immense sum of £100,000 to establish a Chair of Atheism, only to be disappointed when his generosity was summarily rejected. Only one year in India for General Hector Munro, the victor of Buxar, yielded around £20,000, a sum reckoned to be equal in value to the thirty-eight years of income from his estate in northern Scotland.[28]

The recent pioneering research of George McGilvaray of Edinburgh University has provided new insights into the scale of these capital flows.[29] He estimates that between 1720 and 1780 at least 1,668 Scots were in East India Company service as naval and military officers, surgeons and civil servants. Of these and other groups, 124 are reckoned to have returned affluent, thirty-seven with 'large' fortunes (£40,000+), sixty-five medium (£20,000 to £40,000) and twenty-one small to middling (£10,000 to £20,000). McGilvaray argues that this known figure is probably a relatively small proportion of the real total of inflows over the period and hence estimates that something of the order of £500,000 may have been repatriated annually to Scotland from India in the 1750s, 1760s and 1770s, the decades of transformation in the country's rural economy.

Success in the Empire became the solid political foundation of the Union by the later eighteenth century, but it was also a crucial source of capital, one factor enabling Scotland to achieve an unprecedented rate of economic growth in a remarkably short period of time.

Notes

1 National Register of Archives (Scotland) 885, Earl of Strathmore Papers, vol. 22a, Ledger of P. Proctor's Accounts as Clerk to the Works, 1771–6; National Archives of Scotland, SC6/72/1, Sheriff Court Records (Ayr), Register of Improvements on Entailed Estates (1803).

2 Hamilton Public Library, 631/1, John Burrell's Journals, June 1772.

3 Sir John Sinclair, *General Report of the Agricultural State and Political Circumstances of Scotland* (Edinburgh: Constable, 1814), III, p. 339.

4 T. M. Devine, *The Scottish Nation, 1700–2007* (London: Penguin, 2006 edn).

5 Michael Fry, *The Scottish Empire* (Edinburgh: Birlinn, 2001).

6 Quoted in T. M. Devine, *Scotland's Empire, 1600–1815* (London: Allen Lane, 2003), p. 329.

7 There is an abbreviated version of Seton's speech in C. A. Whatley, *'Bought and Sold for English Gold?': Explaining the Union of 1707* (Dundee: Economic and Social History Society of Scotland, 1994), pp. 48–50.

8 Eric J. Graham, *A Maritime History of Scotland, 1650–1790* (East Linton: Tuckwell Press, 2002), pp. 101–16.

9 T. M. Devine, *Clearance and Improvement: Land, Power and People in Scotland, 1700–1900* (Edinburgh: John Donald, 2006), pp. 54–92.

10 J. R. McCulloch (ed.), Adam Smith, *An Inquiry into the Nature and Causes of the Wealth of Nations* (Edinburgh, 1861), Book III, p. 181.

11 Sinclair, *General Report*, VII, pp. 377–9.

12 Sir John Sinclair, *The Old Statistical Account of Scotland* (Edinburgh, 1791–8), VII, p. 377.

13 John Naismith, *Thoughts on Various Objects of Industry pursued in Scotland* (Edinburgh, 1790), p. 93.

14 Alastair J. Durie, *The Scottish Linen Industry in the Eighteenth Century* (Edinburgh: John Donald, 1979), pp. 151–2.

15 John Brewer, *The Sinews of Power: War, Money and the English State, 1688–1783* (Cambridge, MA: Harvard University Press, 1990), p. xvii.

16 Quoted in Devine, *Scotland's Empire*, p. 65.

17 The pioneering work on this is Brewer, *Sinews of Power, passim*.

18 T. M. Devine, *Exploring the Scottish Past: Themes in the History of Scottish Society* (East Lothian: Tuckwell Press, 1995), pp. 42–3.

19 P. K. O'Brien'Inseparable connections: trade, economy, fiscal state and the expansion of "Empire"', in P. J. Marshall (ed.), *The Oxford History of the British Empire, Vol. 2, The Eighteenth Century* (Oxford: Oxford University Press, 1998), p. 63–70; P. K. O'Brien, 'The political economy of British taxation, 1660–1815', *Economic History Review*, (1988), 2nd series, xli, pp. 1–32.

20 This and the following two paragraphs summarise the arguments in T. M. Devine, 'Scottish elites and the Indian Empire, 1700–1815', in

T. C. Smout (ed.), *Anglo-Scottish Relations from 1603 to 1900* (Oxford: Oxford University Press, 2005), pp. 213–31.

21 Neal Ascherson, *Stone Voices. The Search for Scotland* (London: Granta Books, 2002), p. 237.

22 Sir G. Macartney, *An Account of Ireland in 1773 by a late Secretary of that Kingdom* (London, 1773) cited in Thomas Bartlett, ' "This famous island, set in a Virginian sea": Ireland in the British Empire, 1690–1801', in P. J. Marshall (ed.), *Oxford History*, p. 262.

23 P. J. Marshall, *The Making and Un-making of Empires* (Oxford: Oxford University Press, 2005), pp. 58–9.

24 P. J. Marshall, *East India Fortunes* (Oxford: Oxford University Press, 1976), p. 234.

25 Quoted in Devine, *Scotland's Empire*, p. 259.

26 Ascherson, *Stone Voices*, p. 237.

27 Quoted in G. J. Bryant, 'Scots in India in the eighteenth century', *Scottish Historical Review*, (1985), LXIV, p. 27.

28 Devine, *Scotland's Empire*, p. 253.

29 George McGilvaray, *East India Patronage and the British State: the Scottish Élite and Politics in the Eighteenth Century* (London: I. B. Tauris, 2008), pp. 161, 176, 182–203.

7

IMPERIAL SCOTLAND

T. M. Devine

So intense was the Scottish engagement with Empire that almost every nook and cranny of national life from economy to identity, religion to politics and consumerism to demography were affected by this powerful force.[1] The great industries of the nation in the nineteenth and early twentieth centuries were believed to depend for their success on imperial markets. Typical were those of Dundee which became 'Juteopolis', its major industry founded on the importation of raw jute from India. Gordon Stewart, later an historian who went on to write an important study of that manufacture, recalled the imperial connections of his native city in the 1950s:

> I grew up in Dundee and I thought that the Scottish city was the centre of the world jute trade. This impression was dinned into me by my geography lessons at school and by a host of childhood encounters with jute. When I felt depressed by the drabness of life amidst the row of identical, rain-stained buildings on the housing scheme where I lived, I would pedal my bike down to the docks and watch hundreds of bales of jute being unloaded from the holds of great cargo steamers which had sailed half-way round the world from Chittagong and Calcutta. On the way home from school I would sit on city buses crowded with women workers coming off their shifts with wisps of jute sticking to their hair and clothes and their hands roughened red by the handling of jute in the factories . . . Because of the names on the sterns of the cargo ships and the faces of the crewmen, I understood there was an Indian dimension to jute. I also learned of this connection by listening to family stories about relatives and friends of my parents who had spent time in India.[2]

In Glasgow, the economic connections were seen as equally deep. It arrogated to itself the description 'Second City of the Empire' (a term first used as early as 1824), while the broader west of Scotland region was later celebrated as 'The Workshop of the British Empire'. Scottish society more generally had the strongest of ties to Empire. As one author has put it, the Scots professional and middle classes claimed 'not merely a reasonable but a quite indecent share of the [imperial] spoils'.[3] As seen in Chapter 5, throughout the eighteenth and for much of the nineteenth centuries, Scottish educators, physicians, soldiers, administrators, missionaries, engineers, scientists and merchants relentlessly penetrated every corner of the Empire and beyond so that when the statistical record for virtually any area of professional employment is examined the Scots were over-represented.

This elite emigration was but one element in a greater mass diaspora from Scotland. Between 1825 and 1938 over 2.3 million Scots left their homeland for overseas destinations. This placed the country with Ireland and Norway in the top three European countries with the highest levels of net emigration per capita throughout that period.[4] The emigrants had three main destinations: USA (after 1783); British North America (which became the Dominion of Canada in 1867); and Australia. After c. 1840 the USA was the choice of most who left but Canada predominated in the early twentieth century. Also in the 1850s Australia, for a period, was taking more Scots than each of the two North American countries considered individually. These huge levels of emigration generated a vast network of family and individual connections with the colonies and dominions which were consolidated by return migration (in one estimate averaging more than 40 per cent of the total exodus in the 1890s), chain migration, letter correspondence and widespread coverage of the emigrant experience in Scottish popular press and periodical literature.

The British Empire also had a potent influence on Scottish national consciousness and identity. For the Scots elite in the years before 1914 nationalism was not in conflict with the Union but rather was closely integrated with it. The Empire was the means by which the Scots asserted their equal partnership with England after 1707.[5] In the Victorian era it was commonplace to assert that substantial imperial expansion only occurred *after* the Union and hence was a joint endeavour between the partners in which the Scots had played a full part. This was no empty boast. Scottish publicists through such works as John Hill Burton's *The Scots Abroad* (2 vols, 1864) and W. J. Rattray's monumental four-volume magnum opus, *The Scot in British North America* (1880), were easily able to demonstrate the deep mark that Scottish education (especially at college and university level), presbyterianism, medicine, trading networks and philosophical enquiry had had on the colonies. Pride in the Scottish achievement was taken even further by those who saw the Scottish people as a race of natural empire-builders. Thus, Andrew Dewar Gibb argued in 1930:

> the position of Scotland as a Mother nation of the Empire is at all costs to be preserved to her. England and Scotland occupy a unique position as the begetters and defenders of the Empire. They alone of all the Aryan peoples in it have never been otherwise sovereign and independent. Ireland and Wales, mere satrapes of England, can claim no comparable place. Scotsmen today are occupying places both eminent and humble through-out the Empire, and Scottish interests are bound up with every colony in it.[6]

Exposure to the imperial experience started early in Scotland. In 1907 the Scottish Education Department in its memorandum on the teaching of history in schools directed that the curriculum should develop from the study of Scotland to British and then international themes but always throughout stressing the nation's role in the Empire. Text books embodying this approach were soon available in schools. The most popular was *Cormack's Caledonia Readers* which placed very considerable emphasis on the imperial project. The British Empire had a key part to play in late nineteenth-century history teaching because it provided the kind of blend of British and Scottish history which reflected Scotland's position in the Union state.[7] The 1900s also saw the widespread celebration of Empire Day when flags were exchanged between Scottish schools and those elsewhere in the empire. The stories of such imperial heroes as General Gordon, Sir Colin Campbell (of Indian Mutiny fame), the missionary Mary Slessor and, above all, David Livingstone, would all have been very well known to Scottish schoolchildren. Biographies of Livingstone, the 'Protestant Saint' and the most famous and venerated Scotsman of the nineteenth century, were widely read and also awarded as prizes in schools and Sunday Schools, a practice which continued unabated through to the 1960s. Of course, it was not simply children who were taught to respond to these imperial heroes. They were also celebrated by the trades union movement, working men's clubs and Labour politicians, such as Keir Hardie, as models of Scottish virtue and exemplars for the nation. Knowledge of and loyalty to empire was also communicated by such organisations as the Junior Empire League with around 20,000 members and the Boys' Brigade, which not only promoted Christian values but also inculcated fidelity to the imperial ideal within its membership. The 'BBs' were enormously popular among ordinary young Protestant Scots boys well into the twentieth century.

Among the mass of the population, however, perhaps the main symbols of Empire were the Scottish regiments. Recognised as the spearheads of imperial expansion, and widely celebrated in music, story, painting and public monuments as the tartan-clad icons of the Scottish nation, they enjoyed the supreme status as symbols of Scotland's identity. Ironically, however, despite the fame of the Highland soldier, the kilted battalions were mainly recruited during the Victorian age from the working class of the Scottish cities. Nonetheless, their exploits were widely reported not simply in the popular press but in such famous portrayals of their heroic actions as *The Thin Red Line*. The regiments made a remarkable impact on Scottish consciousness. Seen as the heirs of a martial national tradition which went back for centuries, they also acted as important catalysts for the wide diffusion of the military ethic throughout the country. One major spin-off was the Volunteer movement, the ancestor of the Territorial Army, which developed into a permanent reserve force for the forces and attracted many thousands of young Scotsmen. The Volunteers were a focus for local pride but they also strongly identified with the British Empire. Both the Volunteers and the Boys' Brigade adopted army ranks and nomenclature, undertook military drill and were regularly inspected by army officers. The important influence of both organisations goes a long way to explaining the exceptional scale of voluntary recruitment into the army in Scotland when war broke out in 1914.[8] More generally, the fame and significance of the Scottish military tradition lives on in the present as is graphically illustrated by the extraordinary and continuing success of the Edinburgh Military Tattoo and the political controversies during the 2005 General Election over the proposed reorganisation of the historic Scottish regiments.

Despite this long-term and profound engagement with Empire, however, the Scots seem to have responded to the loss of the colonial territories in the 1950s and 1960s with remarkable equanimity. Perhaps inevitably, the Highland regiments were to the fore once again as the imperial retreat gathered pace. This time, however, they were the pallbearers rather than the spearhead of empire. 'Auld Lang Syne' was played in 1947 as the British Army in India signalled the independence of the sub-continent, while the pipers of the Black Watch marked the handover of Hong Kong to Chinese rule in July 1997 as the Union Jack was lowered for the last time. At home, however, the disintegration of Empire from the 1940s to the 1960s seems to have occurred with little fuss. Indeed, as scholars have noted, the British as a whole accepted decolonisation with an extraordinary sang-froid, bordering on indifference.[9] Most reported activity in Scotland in the 1950s favoured the acceleration of decolonisation. Thus, the Church of Scotland's General Assembly, still a formidable force in shaping public opinion in that period, strongly supported the cause of black nationalism in Africa: 'Africa for the Africans' became its catchphrase.[10] Only the strongly imperial *Daily Express* and some voices from the right-wing of the Conservative and Unionist Party dissented from the majority.

Thereafter, the Scots seem quickly to have developed an acute case of imperial amnesia. Between the publication of Andrew Dewar Gibb's polemic, *Scottish Empire*, in 1937 and 2001 no major study of the nation's central role in the imperial project appeared. Only in the 1990s did some pioneering articles by the imperial historian of Scottish birth, John Mackenzie, demonstrate how fruitful a field for scholarly investigation this area could be. The 1970s and 1980s were decades of remarkable growth in Scottish historical studies with many monographs published, an unprecedented expansion in the number of research students and a major extension in the range of topics studied. Yet the theme of Scotland and Empire, arguably to be counted among a small number of really major influences which have shaped the modern nation, remained of only marginal interest.[11] Only in the early years of the new millennium has it become an active area of Scottish historical scholarship. Before then, the imperial aspects of the nation's modern history were woefully neglected. Instead, 'victim history' took centre stage in the 1960s, more especially at the popular level with the huge sales achieved by the Canadian writer, John Prebble, on subjects such as the Highland Clearances, the Massacre of Glencoe, Culloden and other Scottish tragedies. These were published as the politics of grievance within the Union, associated with the rise of the SNP, became a popular factor in Scotland. The notion that the Scots could have been eager and exploitative collaborators with England in the global project of Empire did not at all conform with the national mood at the time. Needless to say Scottish history in schools failed to rectify this imbalance, not only because the nation's history was not a core part of the history curriculum but because it did not feature among those topics which were the most popular in the classroom. In 2007 the ten most widely taught Scottish themes in the five-to-fourteen curriculum included the Romans in Scotland, Mary, Queen of Scots, Jacobites and the Clearances. Empire and Scotland was nowhere to be seen on the list.[12]

It is easy to argue that this marginalisation of the imperial past can be explained in terms of Scotland's developing modern identity. A nation which has consistently voted overwhelmingly for left of centre parties, whether Labour or SNP since the 1980s, is hardly likely to be comfortable with the story of the Scots as pre-eminent and dominant builders of Empire. But the key argument of this chapter is that the roots of indifference to decolonisation go back much further in time to the decades when the territorial expansion of the British Empire was still underway. A good starting point is the end of the First World War. On the face of it, of course, imperial sentiment still flourished after 1918. The massive war losses suffered by Scotland, formally counted at 74,000 but unofficially reckoned to be over 110,000, were commemorated in stone in the impressive Scottish National War Memorial, completed in Edinburgh Castle in 1927. It was not simply a remarkable tribute to the nation's fallen but also to the sons and grandsons of Scotland from the Empire. The Roll of Honour included all those who had served in Scottish regiments and in those of the dominions overseas, an eloquent affirmation of the continuing impor-tance of the imperial bond.[13] The link between Empire and the national Church also seemed robust. The cult of David Livingstone reached its apotheosis in the 1920s when many small donations by ordinary Scots financed the creation of the Livingstone Memorial Centre in Blantyre, Lanarkshire in the cotton mill complex where the legendary explorer and missionary had worked as a boy. The Centre remained a very popular place of pilgrimage for schools and Sunday Schools well into the 1950s.[14] In addition, the public face of imperial Scotland seemed to have changed little. A great Empire Exhibition was held in Glasgow in 1938, the fourth in a series which since the 1890s had attracted millions of visitors.[15] As late as 1951 a colonial week was held in the same city. Empire was also still very much on the political agenda. In the inter-war years factional arguments raged in the nascent Scottish nationalist movement over the nature of the relationship which a self-governing Scotland would have with the Empire.[16] Even the Labour Party temporarily diluted earlier hostility and some of its leading intellectuals in Scotland, including John Wheatley, argued that through the Empire could come not only eco-nomic regeneration but also the hope of protecting a socialist Britain from the menace of international capitalism.

In some ways, however, all this was a mirage, a false image of continuity after the trauma of the First World War. The colonies of white settlement – Canada, South Africa, Australia and New

Zealand – with which the Scots mainly identified were given self-governing dominion status in the Statute of Westminster, while retaining links to the mother country through the crown and the Commonwealth. This change was of deep relevance to Scotland since these were the very countries where the nation's ties of kindred, friendship and association were especially close, due to the mass Scottish emigrations of the nineteenth and early twentieth centuries. Arguably, this major constitutional change of the 1930s, granting autonomy to the 'white' Commonwealth, was of greater significance to Scots than the independence of India and the African states with which personal connections were considerably more limited by comparison. Dewar Gibb in 1937 recognised the transformation. With the granting of dominion status to the colonies of white settlement, he observed 'the hegemony of Britain in the Empire is steadily becoming more formal and more ornamental'.[17] Popular imperialism also waned. The Glasgow Empire Exhibition of 1938 is now regarded not so much as a catalyst for regenerating imperial enthusiasms as an event of primarily nostalgic significance.[18] In the 1945 election both Scottish Tory and Labour candidates referred even less frequently in their manifestos to imperial themes than their English counterparts. This was a symbolic prelude to the results of that election, when the Unionists, *par excellence* the party of Empire, were roundly defeated by Labour which had a quite different set of political and social priorities for the future governance of Scotland.[19]

The traditional career route of middle-class Scots into some areas of imperial administration was also crumbling. In this respect the Indian Civil Service (ICS) had long enjoyed pre-eminence in the rank order of colonial administrations. By 1939, Scots still accounted for 13 per cent of the Europeans on the ICS books. This was marginally greater than the Scottish proportion of the UK population. Nonetheless, it was a significantly lower ratio than in the eighteenth and for much of the nineteenth centuries. Indeed, demoralisation was rampant in the ICS after 1918 because of a decline in career prospects as Indian self-government became an ever closer and inevitable prospect. Though recruitment to the service did not dry up entirely, the ICS was confronted with a critical shortage of satisfactory recruits from Britain which became especially acute from the 1920s.[20]

Yet Scottish elite families were still exporting their male progeny overseas. The key point was that they were no longer constrained to the same extent by opportunities within the formal Empire. The great Scottish business syndicates of Jardine, Matheson and Co., the

Hongkong and Shanghai Bank, Burmah Oil Company, Guthries and Company and many others had by the twentieth century become global rather than simply imperial corporations. The USA, Latin America, China and Japan, in addition to British colonies, now all provided rich pickings for ambitious and educated Scots. They no longer felt, if they ever had done after 1707, inhibited by imperial frontiers. Above all, career goals were still more easily satisfied in London than in faraway places. Historians have been more interested in the exotic and have, therefore, tended to concentrate on Scottish transoceanic activities. In truth, the London financial and business world had always been crucial. The 'Scottish Raj' in the UK Cabinet and the high-profile Scottish presence in the British media and the financial services of the capital in 2007 were simply the latest variant in a trend which goes back a very long way.[21]

No single cause conspired to weaken the emotional attachment of the Scots to Empire but the profound crisis which overwhelmed the nation between the world wars was arguably of primary significance. To understand this fully, however, we need to back much further. This perspective suggests that the disastrous inter-war experience, which will be described later, was the culmination of structural weaknesses reaching much further back in time. Admittedly, the close connections with imperial markets helped boost productive capacity enormously in Victorian Scotland. One significant consequence was a marked increase in Scottish population as the economy created more employment opportunities for the new generation. In 1701, Scotland had a population of around 1.1 million. By 1831 the figure stood at 2.3 million, and in 1911 reached 4.7 million. Further confirmation of the dynamic nature of the economic system was the large increase in immigration in the Victorian era, most notably from Ireland, but also including significant numbers of Italians, Jews and Lithuanians. This level of immigration over such a short period was something quite new in Scottish history, and eloquent testimony to the economy's new vitality.

Again, trading with the Empire made some Scots very rich indeed. A handful of families amassed colossal fortunes. Sir Charles Tenant of the chemical empire; William Baird, ironmaster, Sir James and Peter Coats of the thread-making dynasty; and William Weir, colliery owner and iron manufacturer, were among the forty individuals in Britain reckoned to be worth £2 million or more in the nineteenth century. The super-rich were as well represented in Scotland as in any other part of the United Kingdom.[22] In addition to these tycoons, there were the solid ranks of the prosperous middle classes, who ranged in occupational status from highly paid professionals, such as lawyers, to small businessmen and senior clerks. In his analysis of national income, published in 1867, the Victorian economist R. Dudley Baxter estimated that the 267,300 people who were in this group in Scotland had an annual income of between £100 and £1,000 and represented nearly one-fifth of the total number of what he termed 'productive persons' in the country.[23] The impact of the spending of this middle class could be seen in the elegant suburbs that blossomed around the major cities in the nineteenth century: Broughty Ferry, near Dundee; the graceful terraces of the West End of Glasgow; and the substantial villas of Newington and Corstorphine in Edinburgh.

The increases in the outflow of capital from Scotland after 1870 was also reflected in the new affluence of the Scottish middle classes. Most of this came through Scottish solicitors and chartered accountants, who raised funds on behalf of overseas clients from professional and business families at home. It was said that Edinburgh in the 1880s was 'honeycombed' with agents of these companies, who were the main channel for this substantial mobilisation of middle-class capital. This level of overseas investment was one of the most telling manifestations of the new wealth. It grew from an estimated £60 million in 1870 to £500 million by 1914. Not all of this went to the imperial territories – land, mining and railway developments in the United States were also major beneficiaries – but much did. In the 1880s it was reckoned that three-quarters of all British companies established for overseas investment were of Scottish origin. Nearly half of all Australian borrowing in the late nineteenth century came from Scotland. Tea planting in Ceylon, jute production in India and railways in the Canadian west also benefited. One estimate for 1914 suggested that the value of overseas investment was equivalent to £110 for every Scot, compared with the per capita average of £90 for the United Kingdom as a whole. Here was unambiguous confirmation that Scotland's imperial economy had indeed generated huge increases in capital. The social elites and many in the business and professional classes had done rather well out of Empire.[24]

The picture is, however, somewhat gloomier for the rest of the population. Scotland was a grossly unequal society in the heyday of its imperial success. R. D. Baxter's contemporary calculations for 1867 suggest that around 70 per cent of 'productive persons' in Scotland, almost a million people, belonged to his two bottom categories of 'lower skilled' and 'unskilled', which consisted of male workers who earned on average less than £50 per annum.[25] For many at this level, short-term unemployment was always a threat. In 1908, unemployment among Clydeside shipyard workers rose to almost 25 per cent. In the four major cities there were large pools of seasonal and casual labour, reckoned in the early 1900s to number around 25 per cent of the workforce, engaged in jobs such as portering, catering and street selling in which earnings were both paltry and volatile. For most of the period between 1830 and 1914, Scottish industrial wage rates were lower than the English average. Living costs, on the other hand, were higher. Glaswegians paid on average over 5 per cent more for their food and rent (which accounted for four-fifths of the weekly working-class budget) than did the population of Manchester, Leeds, Salford or Nottingham – and this against a background of low wages and fluctuating levels of employment on Clydeside.[26] That Victorian industry founded on Empire was not a source of general prosperity is confirmed by the examples of Scottish migration and housing in this period. Precisely when manufacturing was achieving remarkable success in overseas markets, the Scots, as noted above, were leaving their native land in large numbers for the United States, Canada and Australasia. Over 2 million people emigrated from Scotland overseas between 1815 and 1939, a rate of outward movement that, per capita, was around one and a half times that for England and Wales. This figure did not include another 600,000 who moved south of the Border. Scotland was, therefore, almost alone among European countries in having experienced both large-scale industrialisation and a great outward movement of population. Most other societies prone to high levels of emigration suffered from poor rural economies. It seemed that many Scots were voting with their feet in the search for better prospects than those easily available at home.[27]

The condition of working-class housing confirmed that mass poverty was a marked feature of Scotland's age of Empire. One scholar has concluded that 'by the eve of the First World War Scotland stood on the brink of a housing catastrophe'.[28] In 1911 nearly 50 per cent of the Scottish population lived in one- or two-room dwellings, compared with just over 7 per cent in England. Rents were significantly higher north of the Border – 10 per cent greater than in Northumberland and Durham, and almost 25 per cent higher than the other English midland and northern counties. In 1914 more than 2 million Scots, nearly half the population, lived more than two persons to a room, the contemporary definition of 'overcrowding'. The housing problem reflected the reality of low and fluctuating incomes. For families on limited earnings, it made economic sense to take small tenement flats at a rental sufficiently affordable to allow them to avoid arrears or eviction. The problem was not so much the availability of reasonable housing as the inability of very many to pay for it. In 1914, for instance, in Glasgow alone there were over 20,000 unoccupied houses, or about a tenth of the city's total stock – the most striking manifestation of the depth of Glasgow's poverty in the very decade when it proclaimed itself 'Second City of the Empire'.[29]

The conclusion has to be that, despite high levels of emigration, Scotland suffered from a chronic oversupply of labour in the heyday of Empire. Low pay, underemployment, casual work and broken time are all consistent with that pattern. Some Scots had grown wealthy, but the majority, despite modest gains in the later nineteenth century, remained mired in poverty and endured a hard daily struggle to make ends meet. The imperial economy was also building up potential problems for the future. The dependency on low wages and semi-skilled or unskilled labour placed the nation at a strategic disadvantage in the twentieth century, when home demand was the force which propelled the new consumer economy with its focus on household goods, motor vehicles, bicycles, furniture and electrical products. Scotland missed out on most of this 'Second Industrial Revolution'. Even before 1914 the economic structure seemed precarious. The heavy industries were all interconnected, geared to overseas markets, especially in the Empire, and at risk from such potentially mighty competitors as the United States and Germany. The threat was especially real because the Scots excelled at making simple capital goods such as iron, steel, locomotives, bridges and the like, which could be easily and rapidly imitated by emerging competitors. Imperial markets had, therefore, left a flawed legacy with serious consequences for Scotland by 1914 when international trade collapsed during several years between the world wars.

Unemployment soared to unprecedented levels in the early 1930s. In the industrial heartland of the western lowlands, the famed 'Workshop of the British Empire', over a quarter of the entire labour force, nearly 200,000, were out of work in 1932. New industries failed to develop and poor housing and slum conditions remained as bad as ever with overcrowding six times greater in 1935 than south of the Border. Fears were expressed in the business community of long-term economic decline and the erosion of indigenous Scottish control as several failing firms were bought up by financial interests from England. The unprecedented scale of emigration in the 1920s intensified these anxieties. So great was the exodus that the Scottish population actually fell by nearly 40,000 in that decade, the only period since records began in which absolute decline between censuses occurred. As several observers noted, many of those who left were skilled and semi-skilled workers, the economic lifeblood of an industrial nation.

Now, rather than being seen, as it had been in Victorian times, as evidence of the virility of an imperial race, emigration was viewed as absolute confirmation of terminal national crisis. The novelist and poet, Edwin Muir, saw it as a 'silent clearance' in which 'the surroundings of industrialisation remain, but industry itself is vanishing like a dream'.[30] The most arresting illustration of the economic irrelevance of Empire to Scottish prosperity was the experience between the wars of the Dundee jute industry. Already, by the 1890s, Bengal had overtaken its Scottish parent to become the world's dominant centre for the jute sacks and hessian cloth which carried the world's foodstuffs and raw materials. Not surprisingly, in the depressed market conditions of the 1930s, Dundee jute interests pleaded on numerous occasions for tariffs to be imposed on the cheap imports from Calcutta. But their pleas were in vain. Now it was Dundee which looked more like the colony, and Bengal the metropole: 'jute presents an unusual example of a powerful industry emerging in a colonial setting which almost destroyed the rival industry back in Britain while the empire was still flourishing'.[31]

All this shattered faith in Scotland as the powerhouse of Empire. Long before decolonisation took place, the old imperial markets were no longer seen to be of vital benefit. Though the economy recovered during the Second World War and the immediate post-war period, the fully enfranchised masses now had other and more pressing social priorities which could be delivered through the ballot box. It was, therefore, hardly surprising that the majority of the Scottish people reacted to the end of Empire with equanimity, despite Scotland's historic role before 1914 in imperial expansion. After 1945, as imperial decline set in, government intervention in industry, political commitment to full employment and, above all, the beginning of the welfare state, slowly delivered unprecedented security and material improvement to the mass of Scots. These were the issues which now had widespread popular appeal, especially in the light of Scotland's history of chronic working-class poverty over the previous century. The age of Empire may have passed, but, ironically, the Union in the 1940s and 1950s was now even more important than before. As one of the poorer parts of the United Kingdom, Scotland was likely to gain more than most other regions from the introduction of an interventionist social and economic policy guaranteeing decent standards of life introduced in the very decade when India, the jewel in the imperial crown, won independence. It was now state support from cradle to grave rather than the old connections of Empire which became the sheet anchor of the Union state.

Notes

1 John M. Mackenzie, 'Essay and reflection: On Scotland and Empire', *International History Review*, (1993), 15, pp. 714–39.

2 Gordon Stewart, *Jute and Empire* (Manchester: Manchester University Press, 1998), p. ix.

3 David Allan, *Scotland in the Eighteenth Century: Union and Enlightenment* (Harlow: Longman, 2001), p. 185.

4 Dudley Baines, *Migration in a Mature Economy* (Cambridge: Cambridge University Press, 1985), p. 10.

5 John M. Mackenzie, 'Empire and national identities. The case of Scotland', *Transactions of the Royal Historical Society*, (1998), 6th series, 8, pp. 215–32.

6 A. D. Gibb, *Scotland in Eclipse* (London: Humphrey Toulmin, 1930), p. 187.

7 R. D. Anderson, *Education and the Scottish People, 1750–1918* (Oxford: Oxford University Press, 1995), pp. 212–13, 218–19.

8 Heather Streets, *Martial Races. The Military, Race and Masculinity in British Imperial Culture, 1857–1914* (Manchester: Manchester University Press, 2004).

9 See, for example, John Darwin, *The End of the British Empire. The Historical Debate* (Oxford: Oxford University Press, 1991).

10 M. Fry, *The Scottish Empire* (Edinburgh: Birlinn, 2001), pp. 412–24.

11 See the papers in 'Whither Scottish History' and 'Writing Scotland's History', *Scottish Historical Review*, (1994), lxxiii, pp. 1–116 and (1997), lxxvi, pp. 1–114.

12 Peter Hillis, 'Scottish history in the school curriculum', forthcoming in *Journal of Scottish Historical Studies*. I am most grateful to Professor Hillis for sending me a draft of his valuable survey.

13 Catriona M. M. Macdonald and E. W. McFarland (eds), *Scotland and the Great War* (East Linton: Tuckwell Press, 1999), pp. 1–2.

14 John M. Mackenzie, 'David Livingstone: the construction of the myth', in G. Walker and T. Gallagher (eds), *Sermons and Battle Hymns* (Edinburgh: Edinburgh University Press, 1990), pp. 24–42.

15 P. Kinchin and J. Kinchin, *Glasgow's Great Exhibitions* (Bicester: White Cockade Publishing, 1985).

16 R. J. Finlay, ' "For or Against?" Scottish nationalists and the British Empire, 1919–39', *Scottish Historical Review*, (1992), 71, pp. 184–206.

17 Gibb, *Scotland in Eclipse*, p. 187.

18 R. Crampsey, *The Empire Exhibition of 1938: The Last Durbar* (Edinburgh: Mainstream, 1988).

19 I. F. C. Hutchison, *Scottish Politics in the Twentieth Century* (Basingstoke: Macmillan, 2001), pp. 121–2.

20 A. Kirk-Greene, *Britain's Imperial Administration, 1858–1966* (Basingstoke: Macmillan, 2000), pp. 17, 88. Scottish recruitment was falling away from the 1850s in comparison with eighteenth-century levels. See Scott B. Cook, 'The Irish Raj: social origins and careers of Irishmen in the Indian Civil Service, 1855–1899', *Journal of Social History*, (1987), 20, Spring, pp. 507–29.

21 Fry, *Scotland's Empire*, pp. 477–89.

22 W. D. Rubinstein, 'The Victorian middle classes: wealth, occupation and geography', *Economic History Review*, (1977), 2nd series, 30, pp. 609–11.

23 T. C. Smout, *A Century of the Scottish People, 1830–1950* (London: Fontana, 1997), pp. 109–10.

24 C. H. Lee, 'Economic progress: wealth and poverty', in T. M. Devine, C. H. Lee and G. C. Peden (eds), *The Transformation of Scotland: The Economy since 1700* (Edinburgh: Edinburgh University Press, 2005), pp. 138–41.

25 Smout, *A Century of the Scottish People*, pp. 109–11.

26 T. M. Devine, 'Scotland', in Roderick Floud and Paul Johnson (eds), *The Cambridge Economic History of Modern Britain, Vol. 1: Industrialisation, 1700–1860* (Cambridge: Cambridge University Press, 2004).

27 T. M. Devine (ed.), *Scottish Emigration and Scottish Society* (Edinburgh: John Donald, 1992), pp. 1–15.

28 C. H. Lee, *Scotland and the United Kingdom* (Manchester: Manchester University Press, 1995), p. 46.

29 Lee, *Scotland and the United Kingdom*, p. 46.

30 Edwin Muir, *Scottish Journey* (Edinburgh, 1935), p. 110.

31 Stewart, *Jute and Empire*, pp. 2–4.

8

THE POLITICS OF THE UNION IN AN AGE OF UNIONISM

Ewen A. Cameron

Three events in the early 1920s shaped the history of the Union down to the 1960s: the partition of Ireland, the Church of Scotland Act, and the general election of 1922. The first two disposed of complications, the third altered the party political structure. The election of 1922 was the occasion of the 'breakthrough' of the Labour Party in Scotland. For all its precocity of development in Scotland and the prominence of Macdonald and Hardie, Labour had struggled in Scotland and 1922 marked a new beginning in which it would be an area of strength for the party, its vote never sinking below the 32.3 per cent achieved then. The partition of Ireland produced a view – exposed in the long term as horribly complacent – that the 'Irish question' had been solved. This was important in Scotland as the debate on Scottish home rule had, since 1886, been firmly attached to that on Ireland. This had fewer implications for Scottish nationalism than for Unionism. After 1922 it was not entirely clear which Union exercised the Unionists. The defence of the 1801 Union had brought the label before the electorate in 1886 and was currently controversial at the time of the incorporation of the Liberal Unionists by the Conservatives in 1912.[1] The continuation of the Union with Ulster was important, but it would be the late twentieth century until the Anglo-Scottish union came more clearly into focus.[2] This does not mean, however, that the Unionists were advocates of Anglo-Scottish uniformity. After all, since 1912 the Conservative cause north of the Border was advanced by the Scottish Unionist Party. Unionists acknowledged that recognition of the diversity of its component parts was central to the durability of the Union.[3] Indeed, it might well be argued that the Unionists were more aware of the Scottish dimension of politics and identity in the United Kingdom than was the Labour Party.

The third significant event was the reform of the Church of Scotland. In 1707 the presbyterian settlement of 1689–90 seemed to have been guaranteed in the Treaty of Union. This helped to sell the

Union project and prevented the controversies over religion which emerged in Ireland and Wales in the nineteenth century. This aspect of the Union was not uncontroversial, however. Reforms of 1712 reintroduced patronage in the Church of Scotland; this, along with neglect of Scottish church matters by both Whig and Tory governments in the 1830s and early 1840s, provoked the Disruption of 1843. By the 1920s the task of restoring the unity of Scottish presbyterianism was well under way. The United Free Church had been created in 1900 after a union between most of the Free Church and the voluntaries of the United Presbyterian Church, and the next step was a further union with the Church of Scotland, which was ultimately achieved in 1929.[4] In order to appease the voluntary tradition in the United Free Church the status of the Church of Scotland had to be altered, its spiritual independence confirmed without eroding its established status. This was tricky. After lengthy negotiations, however, a new constitution for a united church was thrashed out and recognised by the Church of Scotland Act 1921. This provided that the Kirk be 'subject to no civil authority . . . in all matters of doctrine, worship, government and discipline'. This seemed to contradict the guarantees of the nature of the Church of Scotland as enshrined in the Union settlement. This was not merely a narrowly legal question, nor was it a purely theological one concerning the status of the Westminster Confession of Faith. The 1921 Act has the potential to test the nature of the Union: is it a fundamental law of the United Kingdom or, in the Diceyian view, subordinate to the sovereignty of Parliament.[5] Nevertheless, the issue has not arisen in this context and the ecclesiastical legislation of the 1920s bolstered the Union through neutralisation of the church–state issue, the complexities of which had dogged the Union since 1712.

A brief review of electoral patterns in Scotland demonstrates the existence of an apparent unionist consensus.

The inter-war period saw a profound realignment in Scottish politics. The Liberal Party, which had dominated Scottish politics since the reforms of 1832, was no longer a significant force. It was now largely confined to the geographical peripheries of Scotland and, by the 1930s, found electoral competition harsh even there. At the general election of 1945 the party lost all its Scottish seats. Although other aspects of the Liberal tradition, notably free trade and the principle of international cooperation, were kept alive by the Labour Party, advocacy of home rule declined with the Liberal Party. Although it is possible to find a strand of thinking in the Labour Party,

Table 8.1 General elections in Scotland, 1910–35

Election	Cons		LU/CL/NL		Lib		Lab		ILP		Comm	
	Seats	Vote (%)	Seats	Vote (%)	Seats	Vote (%)	Seats	Vote (%)	Seats	Vote (%)	Seats	Vote(%)
1910 (Jan)	7	39.6	2		59	54.2	2	5.1				
1910 (Dec)	6	42.6	3		58	53.6	3	3.6				
1918	28	32.8	25	19.1	4	15.0	7	22.9				
1922	13	25.1	12	17.7	15	21.5	29	32.3			1	1.4
1923	14	31.6			22	28.4	34	35.9			0	2.4
1924	36	40.8			8	16.5	26	41.1			0	0.7
1929	20	35.9			13	18.1	36	42.3			0	1.1
1931	48	49.5	8	4.8	7	8.6	7	32.6			0	1.4
1935	35	42.0	7	6.7	0	6.7	20	36.8	4	5.0	1	0.6

Table 8.2 General elections in Scotland, 1945–70

Election	Lab		Cons		Lib		SNP		ILP		Comm		Ind	
	Seats	Vote (%)	Seats	Vote (%)	Seats	Vote (%)	Seats	Vote (%)	Seats	Vote (%)	Seats	Vote (%)	Seats	Vote (%)
1945	37	47.6	27	41.1	0	5.0	0	1.2	3	1.8	1	1.4	3	1.9
1950	37	46.2	32	44.8	2	6.6	0	0.4					1	1.0
1951	35	47.9	35	48.6	1	2.7	0	0.3						
1955	34	46.7	36	50.1	1	1.9	0	0.5						
1959	38	46.7	31	47.2	1	4.1	0	0.5					1	0.7
1964	43	48.7	24	40.6	4	7.6	0	2.4						
1966	46	49.9	20	37.7	5	6.8	0	5.0						
1970	44	44.5	23	38.0	3	5.5	1	11.4						

especially in the Independent Labour Party (ILP), which believed in home rule, the mainstream of the Labour movement became central-ist in the 1930s.[6] The challenges of politics in that traumatic decade of economic depression and social dislocation seemed to leave little room for the niceties of constitutional debate.[7] Although Ramsay MacDonald had been secretary of the London branch of the Scottish Home Rule Association in the late 1880s, as Labour leader and Prime Minister he did little or nothing to advance the cause.[8] Home Rule may also have been a casualty of the perception, fostered by the rise of fascism in Europe, that nationalism was an unhealthy right-wing phenomenon. Indeed, nationalism in Scotland in this period was not devoid of regressive aspects. The National Party of Scotland had been founded in 1928 and it contained some evidence of the radical traditions from which some of its originators had emerged. By the time of the formation of the Scottish National Party (SNP) in 1934, after a merger between a cleansed National Party and the right-wing Scottish Party, an imperialist version of Scottish nationalism was dominant. Electoral impotence was another important characteristic. Sir Alexander MacEwen had performed creditably in the Western Isles in 1935, but other candidacies resulted in many embarrassments and lost deposits. Indeed, nationalist politics provided more material for comic novelists such as Eric Linklater – whose *Magnus Merriman* (1934) drew on his disastrous involvement in the East Fife by-election of 1933 – than it did for serious political commentators.[9]

What about the Conservatives, or more properly the Unionists? Until his death in 1923 they had been led by the tough and ascetic Glasgow businessman, Andrew Bonar Law. Law had antecedents in Ulster and in 1912 had placed his party squarely behind an uncom-promising Ulster Unionism. Other Scots, such as Sir John Gilmour and Walter Elliot, held senior cabinet positions in the inter-war period. Unlike the Labour Party, however, their Scottish electoral per-formance, although quite strong, lagged behind that achieved in England. Nevertheless, if there was a Liberal culture in Scotland in the nineteenth century, a Unionist equivalent emerged in the 1920s. Both the *Glasgow Herald* and *The Scotsman* were Unionist and many local newspapers had also abandoned liberalism. Key issues for the Liberal agenda, such as land reform, temperance and Ireland, had been rele-gated in the 1920s. The church unification of 1929 also favoured Unionism in that an important series of issues which had ener-gised liberalism were no longer prominent. More important was the unambiguously rightward shift of the leadership of the Presbyterian churches in the 1920s.[10] The social conscience evident in the late nineteenth century was abandoned, perhaps to curry favour with right-wing governments in order to secure concessions required for unification. This is not to say that the reunited Church of Scotland was merely the Unionist Party at prayer. In some of their campaigns, most notably that against the Irish in Scotland, they went far beyond what the party could tolerate.[11] Political conditions also favoured the Unionists. As we have seen, the Liberal Party was divided, and ultimately decimated and Labour had been weakened by the financial crisis which engulfed its second minority government in 1931. This led to the division of the party over the issue of the formation of the Conservative-dominated National Government of that year. In the following year the radical and intellectually stimulating ILP disaffiliated from the Labour Party.

During the 1930s the Unionists pushed forward important changes in the government of Scotland. The Scottish Office had been established in 1885 and the status of its senior minister raised to a full Secretary of State in 1926, but there were still weaknesses. Most of the autonomous functional boards which looked after various elements of Scottish administration – health, agriculture, prisons, lunatic asylums, the crofting system – had been consolidated into a structure of departments in the 1920s. Nevertheless, the Scottish Departments of Education, Health, Home and Agriculture did not come under the full control of the Scottish Office until 1939. Further, the Scottish Office had little Scottish infrastructure and a limited staff in Edinburgh. These matters were investigated by a committee under the chairmanship of Sir John Gilmour, whose recommendations were partly implemented in 1939. This momentous year also saw the opening of St Andrew's House on the site of the old Calton Jail in Edinburgh. These events gave the Scottish Office greater authority and a tangible presence in Scotland's capital, where previously it had occupied a townhouse in Drumsheugh Gardens in the west end of the city. Scotland was now subject to a considerable degree of 'administrative devolution'. Legal and institutional distinctiveness had been recognised with improved machinery of government. In the long term, the creation of a powerful territorial ministry may have made the absence of a parliament even more glaring, but this did not seem evident in the late 1930s when such a body was not widely advocated.[12]

The economic travails of the 1930s were also directly relevant to the history of the Union. There may have been a rough consensus between the major political parties on the efficacy of centralised economic planning, but there were suspicions that the Scottish dimension of the problem was not receiving sufficient attention. Unemployment was very high in the industrial areas and, aside from the antiquated nature of the Scottish economy built around declining heavy industries, there were the seemingly perennial problems of the Highlands. To some extent these issues were addressed by the Special Areas legislation of the mid-1930s, but this did little to alleviate high unemployment and did nothing for the Highlands. There was a widespread feeling in Scotland in the 1930s that Whitehall government was remote from, and uncomprehending of, the economic and social problems of Scotland. These problems, compounding the effects of massive emigration from Scotland in the 1920s as well as erosion of a Scottish business sector with the takeover of banks and railway companies, led to a feeling that Scottish identity was in crisis. This was articulated by nationalists and was also evident in the work of the Scottish Economic Committee, a business-orientated organisation which analysed a series of key problems in the Scottish economy in the late 1930s. In 1937 the Unionist Secretary of State, Walter Elliot, wondered aloud to his cabinet colleagues about the corrosive effects of these difficulties and he was in no doubt that administrative reforms were an insufficient response.[13] These processes might have challenged many aspects of the Union settlement had they not been overtaken by rearmament and the outbreak of the Second World War.

Much attention has been paid to Scotland's rebelliousness during the First World War. The Second World War, by contrast, has not received the same scrutiny. An exception is the attention which has been lavished on the relative autonomy of the Scottish Office under Thomas Johnston. Johnston regarded himself as Scotland's man in the cabinet rather than *vice versa*. Since Scottish politics and administration were something of a sideshow for the government during the war, Churchill could afford to grant licence to his Scottish Secretary. Johnston claimed that he had been granted permission to undertake 'large-scale reforms' leading to 'Scotia resurgent'.[14] He did suggest some innovations when he accepted office in February 1941: first, that Scottish MPs should meet in Edinburgh and have access to Scottish Office civil servants; secondly, that Scottish legislation should merely be rubber-stamped by Westminster if it had been approved in Edinburgh; and thirdly, the formation of a 'Council of State' composed of former Scottish Secretaries, 'acting as a sort of

Scottish equivalent to the coalition cabinet' or even 'a sort of informal home rule' according to one historian.[15] Since the British system does not allow for alternative sources of sovereign power, especially not on an informal basis, these innovations were less important than Johnston claimed. The Council of State, however, made suggestions in areas such as housing and industrial policy, but it was one voice among many in the debate over the shape of post-war society and it is not clear that it was influential.[16] Walter Elliot, who used the Council to maintain his profile after his political marginalisation, argued that more ought to be done to attract war industry to Scotland. The subsequent creation of the Scottish Council on Industry in February 1943 helped to maintain the pressure on this issue and may have contributed to subsequent improvements in the position of Scottish industry. Far from being an innovation, however, the Council of State gave expression to a pre-existing consensus in Scottish politics. One of the most important characteristics of the Union is its inherent flexibility. It has proved possible to accommodate Scottish distinctiveness throughout its history and the Second World War was no exception.

Johnston's hints that all was not well in Scotland were not entirely baseless. There were serious industrial disputes, especially over the position of female workers at the vast Hillington aircraft factory outside Glasgow.[17] There was also resentment at the way in which 'Scotland' was expected to contribute to the war effort. Some of this was at a decidedly low level, such as irritation about the interruption to work caused by frequent soundings of air raid sirens in false alarms.[18] There was resentment at the movement of female labour, mostly younger women without families, to work in the English midlands. The war effort was more important than Scottish feeling in this regard and the transfer of labour continued, although women under the age of twenty were not taken and absolute compulsion was recognised as counterproductive.[19] At one level this was something which exercised those who saw England as a 'foreign' land, but there was a more serious dimension. The controversy was linked to the nature of the Scottish economy and the fact that war production facilities were located in the English midlands rather than in the central belt of Scotland.[20] That large proportions of Scottish factory space was used for storage rather than production was another facet and Johnston made a point of appearing to fight hard for more war contracts – some 7,000 or 13.5 per cent of the total by the end of the war – to be awarded to Scotland.[21] This was not a partisan position, most

Scottish MPs were Unionists and did not dissent from Johnston's portrayal of his role as a defender of Scottish national interests. In this 'campaign' he was certainly not above attempting to scare his cabinet colleagues with the spectre of Scottish nationalism. Once again, this was not entirely without foundation as Scottish wartime party politics demonstrates.

In contrast to the First World War the experience of Scottish by-elections indicates a certain querulousness. There were eleven contested by-elections out of thirteen vacancies, a much higher proportion than in England. The principal reason for this was the fact that the SNP was not privy to the truce between the main parties. Neither was the ILP, and there was one intervention, at North Midlothian in February 1943, by Common Wealth, the main body for left-wing opposition to the coalition government. Government candidates criticised their opponents for stimulating frivolous and unnecessary contests during a dire national emergency.[22] For example, the Conservative in Argyll in April 1940 was none too subtle in his suggestion that William Power, his SNP opponent, was unpatriotic. He suggested that 'soldiers would feel that they had been stabbed in the back' were the county not to elect him to Parliament. Power, emphatically not an anti-war candidate, was careful to argue that the conditions in the Highlands, rather than the war (or, indeed, home rule), were the main issue.[23] In other by-elections, notably at Kirkcaldy in February 1944, the SNP took a slightly different line. On this occasion their candidate was Douglas Young, a divisive figure in the party, who had opposed conscription on the grounds that it was a breach of the Treaty of Union and was imprisoned as a result. At Kirkcaldy he polled 41 per cent and an explicitly anti-war candidate, who took 7 per cent of the vote, allowed him to argue that there was a bare majority for the government. The main issue, he argued, was the 'shift south of industries and workers' rather than the 'war effort'.[24] The high watermark of the SNP's wartime performance, however, was Dr Robert MacIntyre's victory over Labour at Motherwell in April 1945. Although he did his best in the House of Commons, causing a fuss over some of its conventions as well as making substantial interventions on social and economic issues, Labour regained the seat at the general election in August. The history of nationalist politics provides some qualified evidence that there was a general air of dissatisfaction abroad, but the SNP could not capitalise on it. Contested Scottish wartime politics indicates a distinct political tradition, although but for fringe parties like the SNP and the ILP this would have been less obvious. That the Second World War represented a blip in the trajectory of Scottish political development is suggested by what came afterwards. The 1940s and 1950s, when Labour and the Unionists dominated Scottish politics, suggests that wartime grievances were not translated into a general dissatisfaction with Scotland's position in the United Kingdom. The SNP and the Liberals were condemned to the margins of a bi-polar political system until the 1960s.

As can be seen from the tables of election results the post-war political landscape appears to be fairly flat. The two main parties had virtually exclusive occupation of the ground, neither the Liberals nor the SNP were very active and put up few candidates. The ILP did not long survive the death of James Maxton and the sole Communist MP, Willie Gallacher, was ousted in West Fife in 1950. The political agenda of this period had a strong 'British' feel to it. Post-war reconstruction, nationalisation, the establishment of the National Health Service and the extension of the social welfare system seemed to provide British solutions to generic problems. Nevertheless, the history of the Union was not entirely relegated to the sidelines as political life was dominated by the advance of the state. There was, it is true, administrative distinctiveness to the structures of the welfare state in Scotland, but the potential of an analysis of the period between 1945 and 1960 does not stop there.[25] The Labour Party carried over the centralism of the 1930s and wartime into the peace. Johnston's successor, Arthur Woodburn, appeared even to distance himself from the patriotic tactics of his illustrious predecessor:

> I knew it was possible to build a reputation at the Scottish Office by pretending to be . . . a Scottish St George fighting the English dragon in the shape of my colleagues in Cabinet but I made clear in my first speech to the Scottish Council of the Labour party that I felt this attitude was to demean the importance of the Secretary of State being a member of the Cabinet. He was not there only to keep his colleagues informed on Scotland, its progress, problems and needs but to accept equal responsibility with his other colleagues for running the whole country. Scotland did not need to beg for favours so long as she had rights.[26]

Unfortunately this approach did not stand Woodburn in good stead; he was sacked in 1949 because he was not deemed to be sufficiently subtle to counter manifestations of Scottish nationalism. The late 1940s and early 1950s were an odd period in the history of the national question. As we have seen, the SNP was a marginal force at the polls, hardly able to register a presence due to a lack of candidates. The wartime divisions in the SNP had released John MacCormick to take forward his conception that the national question would be more effectively advanced with a non-party campaign. This he did through his Convention, collecting signatures for a mass petition which, with historical overtones, he called a 'Covenant'. Over two million Scots indicated their support for the following rather general statement:

> We the people of Scotland who subscribe to this Engagement, declare our belief that reform in the constitution of our country is necessary to secure good government in accordance with out Scottish traditions and to promote the spiritual and economic welfare of our nation.[27]

There were also a series of 'National Assemblies' in the late 1940s and early 1950s in a further attempt to demonstrate a consensus for constitutional change. The difficulty which these movements faced was that in order to achieve widespread cooperation the stance taken up was so general as to be largely meaningless. Chief among nationalist stunts of this period was the removal by a group of Glasgow students of the Stone of Destiny from Westminster Abbey on Christmas Day 1950. Although it was returned to London in April 1951, its brief liberation gave publicity to the nationalists and exposed the reverence with which such symbols were regarded by establishment figures in London, as well as by high-spirited Scottish nationalists. Also outside the formal organisation of the SNP were the Scottish Patriots, led by Wendy Wood; they took exception to public buildings flying the Union flag and after 1952 to pillar boxes marked 'E II R'. This was a revival of a periodic complaint, last heard at the accession of Edward VII in 1901, that the royal numeral took no account of the Union of the Crowns and the creation of a new kingdom in 1707. In 1952–3 it was pointed out, correctly, that the first Elizabeth preceded the Union of the Crowns and that the new royal numeral was not only wrong but insensitive. This matter was tested in the Court of Session in the famous case of *MacCormick* v. *The Lord Advocate* in 1953. As with the Church of Scotland Act 1921, this touched on the issue of the nature of the Union of 1707, the argument being that since Article One of the Treaty of Union expressly created a new kingdom the offending royal numeral was a breach of that Treaty. Lord Cooper, a former Unionist Lord Advocate, in an incidental comment during the case suggested that 'parliamentary sovereignty' was an exclusively English doctrine and had no place in Scots law. This statement is frequently appealed to by nationalists and forms one base of the argument that in Scotland a doctrine of 'popular sovereignty' can be identified. This was especially prominent in the 1980s when it was held that the Conservative governments lacked a 'mandate' to govern Scotland. The notion also figured prominently in the *Claim of Right* of 1988, the founding document of the Scottish Constitutional Convention. *MacCormick v. The Lord Advocate* failed as it was found that MacCormick and his co-pursuers had no title in a matter of public right and that the royal numeral was a matter for the monarch under the royal prerogative.[28] Thus, once again, the fundamental question of the nature of the Union was not decisively resolved. In subsequent cases arguments based on alleged breaches of the Treaty of Union have cut little ice with the civil courts in Scotland, challenges to the tolls on the Skye bridge and the Community Charge/'Poll Tax' being good examples.

Away from the rarefied atmosphere of the Court of Session these matters had political consequences, but did not challenge prevailing unionist political consensus. As we have seen, Labour tried to up their game by replacing as Secretary of State for Scotland the lumbering Woodburn with the high-flying Hector McNeil. Attlee was hostile to the Covenant movement, refusing in 1950 to meet one of its delegations and his instincts in this regard were given greater substance by the Unionists' attempts to use it play the Scottish card. This was most tangibly represented by John MacCormick's 'National' candidacy at the Paisley by-election of 1948. On this occasion both the Unionists and the Liberals stood down in order to give MacCormick a straight run against Labour. This tactic was in vain, the nature of MacCormick's claim to the label 'National' being unclear, as was the meaning of that label. In addition, the sophisticated voters of Paisley did not care to have their party loyalties trifled with in this way.[29]

Unionist rhetoric of this period is interesting and indicates again that in this era of great success for the party they were not afraid to use the Scottish card and to go beyond a unitary understanding of the nature of the British state. This went right to the top of the party, Churchill told a meeting at the Usher Hall in Edinburgh in 1950:

> I do not . . . wonder that the question of Scottish home rule and this movement of Scottish nationalism has gained in strength with the growth of Socialist authority and ambitions in England.[30]

This was also evident in Unionist attempts to turn the policy of nationalisation against Labour in Scotland. It was argued that nationalisation equalled centralisation and that Socialist policies were a threat to the autonomy of Scotland because so much political and economic decision making was being concentrated in London. At the Aberdeen South by-election of 1946, the Unionist candidate, Lady Tweedsmuir, pointed out:

> Scotland's position under the various nationalisation schemes of the government has been the subject of acute anxiety by Scottish MPs. Under socialist administration the tendency has grown to concentrate power in Whitehall, remote from Scotland and inevitably leading to a neglect of the special conditions ruling in that country.[31]

Unionists used this argument to try to explain the rise in demands for Scottish home rule. They were opposed to this, but argued that the Scottish Office administration should be strengthened:

> the whole attitude of the Socialists is one of complete indifference to the special circumstances and distinctive needs and conditions of Scotland both in legislation and administration. Unionists believe that the revolutionary change in the conduct of Scottish affairs being brought about by the Socialists will result not only in unnecessary delays and inefficiency, but in a disastrous loss of Scottish prestige. Complaint is sometimes made that through the congestion of business at Westminster Scottish affairs are neglected.[32]

It is worth remembering that this was a period of success for the Unionists, not only in their achievement of a popular majority in the election of 1955, but by the fact that in the four general elections from 1945 to 1955 their Scottish vote was closer to their English vote than at any point in their history. This was very much in the tradition of Scottish Unionists of the inter-war period, who were not only progressive in their social outlook but also subtle in their understanding of the nature of the Union. It was also handy that this was a convenient stick with which the beat the centralist Labour Party. The 1950s saw Scottish home rule formally disappear from Labour's Scottish appeal. The Unionists could also point to solid achievements in the 1950s, although as we shall see, this was less convincing by the end of the decade. Their vote began to decline in 1959 and continued to do so until 1979. Further changes were made to the Scottish Office, adding a Minister of State, Lord Home, who mostly worked in Scotland. They developed an increasingly sophisticated mechanism for regional policy, although it is fair to point out that Labour advocated similar measures to attract industry. They also invested heavily in major infrastructure projects, especially the Forth and Tay bridges. Finally, in an initiative which seemed like a good idea at the time, they persuaded a reluctant Colvilles to accept government assistance for a strip mill at Ravenscraig in Lanarkshire.[33] Above all the Unionists were successful in housing policy. This was the key Scottish issue of the day and the fact that the Unionists had established the Scottish Special Housing Association in 1938 serves as a reminder that they had a track record in this area. Investigations during the Second World War had confirmed what everyone knew: Scottish housing was a national disgrace and was a priority in post-war reconstruction. The Labour government struggled with uncooperative local authorities in the major urban areas, a lack of materials and labour, and completion rates did not match the extremely high expectations. In the 1950s the Unionists made more progress but this slowed down later in the decade as subsidies were cut and cheaper forms of building, especially high-rise flats, began to be used.

By the end of our period the long dominance of Scottish politics by the Unionists seemed to be coming to an end. Why was this? One local association was fairly clear in its diagnosis of the problem:

> There appeared to be some doubt as to whether ministers were sufficiently aware officially that the lack of expanding industries in Scotland was likely to lose the Government some seats. The popular 'you've never had it so good' slogan was a mistake in the west of Scotland where the incidence of unemployment was so high.[34]

This suggests a number of concluding points. First, while the Unionists were not plumbing the depths of unpopularity and insensitivity that would mark the 1980s, they did seem to be losing touch with Scottish opinion. The social and institutional background to their electoral success was becoming less secure. The press, for example, was becoming more diverse and populist organs like the *Scottish Daily Express* were less dependable allies than the traditional broadsheets. In any case, *The Scotsman* under Alistair Dunnett moved away from Unionism. The Church was not only much more left-wing in the 1950s than it had been in the 1930s, but in the later part of the decade its strength and influence began to decline. Earlier successes in housing policy were, as we have seen, not sustained and despite regional policy and other investment the economy had scarcely been transformed. Nevertheless, if Unionism was less popular than it had been, a unionist consensus seemed firm as the 1960s began. The Labour Party was the principal beneficiary of Unionist unpopularity; the SNP and the Liberals, who showed more interest in home rule, remained on the margins of Scottish politics, although there were incremental accretions of strength and confidence. When Labour returned to power in

1964 they remained true to their unionist colours. The Secretary of State for Scotland, Willie Ross, was as unionist as they came and the empowerment of the state in economic planning was a prominent theme for the new government. Scottish politics was becoming less subtle and sophisticated by the late 1950s. There were not many high-ranking Scots in either party: other than the Secretary of State for Scotland there were few Scots in the Cabinets of the 1950s and early 1960s. Walter Elliot had been marginalised after Munich, Thomas Johnston had eschewed party politics and the brightest Scottish Labour politician, Hector McNeil, showed signs of frustration with the limitations of the Scottish scene prior to his untimely death in 1955. When the main parties attempted to play the Scottish card again, in the aftermath of Hamilton and following the SNP surge in 1974, their efforts appeared clumsy compared with the initiatives of the 1930s or early 1950s. That said, conditions had changed: the SNP provided a new kind of threat to the traditional parties and the social, economic and educational changes of the 1960s had produced a new and younger electorate sceptical of Unionism's rather tired appeal. From the early 1920s to the late 1950s there was a bipartisan consensus on the continuing relevance of the Union. It was bolstered by the outlook and continuing influence of important national institutions and it was defended by politicians who understood the need to recognise Scottish distinctiveness within its framework. By such methods was it steered through the depression, total war and reconstruction. What came after was very different, but the forty years after 1920 serve as a warning against whiggish interpretations of Scottish political history. The twentieth century was not a straightforward 'road to home rule'.

Notes

1 C. Burness, *'Strange Associations': The Irish Question and the Making of Scottish Unionism, 1886–1918* (East Linton: Tuckwell Press, 2003).
2 J. Mitchell, 'Contemporary unionism', in C. M. M. Macdonald (ed.), *Unionist Scotland, 1800–1997* (Edinburgh: John Donald, 1998), pp. 117–39.
3 P. Ward, *Unionism in the United Kingdom, 1918–1974* (Basingstoke: Palgrave, 2005).
4 See the essays in J. Kirk (ed.), *The Scottish Churches and the Union Parliament, 1707–1999* (Edinburgh: T. and T. Clark, 2001).
5 F. Lyall, *Of Presbyters and Kings: Church and State in the Law of Scotland* (Aberdeen: Aberdeen University Press, 1980), pp. 66–84.

6 W. W. Knox and A, MacKinlay, 'The re-making of the Scottish Labour in the 1930s', *Twentieth Century British History*, (1995), 6, pp. 174–93.

7 Although I. S. Wood, 'The ILP and the Scottish national question', in D. James, T. Jowitt and K. Laybourn (eds), *The Centennial History of the Independent Labour Party* (Halifax: Ryburn, 1992), pp. 63–74, argues valiantly for a sustained interest in home rule.

8 C. M. M. Macdonald, 'Following the procession: Scottish Labour, 1918–45', in M. Worley (ed.), *Labour's Grass Roots: Essays on the Activities of Local Labour Parties and Members, 1918–45* (Aldershot: Ashgate, 2005), pp. 33–53.

9 R. J. Finlay, *Independent and Free: Scottish Politics and the Origins of the Scottish National Party, 1918–1945* (Edinburgh: John Donald, 1994).

10 I. G. C. Hutchison, 'Scottish Unionism between the two world wars', in Macdonald (ed.), *Unionist Scotland*, pp. 73–99.

11 S. J. Brown, ' "Outside the covenant": the Scottish Presbyterian churches and Irish immigration', *Innes Review*, (1991), 42, pp. 19–45.

12 J. Mitchell, *Governing Scotland: The Invention of Administrative Devolution* (Basingstoke: Palgrave, 2003); J. Mitchell, 'The Gilmour report on Scottish central administration', *Juridical Review*, (1989), 34, pp. 17–88.

13 R. H. Campbell, 'The Scottish Office and the special areas in the 1930', *Historical Journal*, (1979), 22, pp. 16–83; R. J. Finlay, 'National identity in crisis: politicians, intellectuals and the "end of Scotland", 1920–1939', *History*, (1994), 79, pp. 24–59.

14 T. Johnston, *Memories* (Glasgow, 1952), p. 147; G. Walker, *Thomas Johnston* (Manchester: Manchester University Press, 1988).

15 C. Harvie, 'Labour and Scottish government: the age of Tom Johnston', *Bulletin of Scottish Politics*, (1981), 2, pp. 1–20.

16 R. H. Campbell, 'The committee of ex-Secretaries of State and Industrial policy', *Scottish Industrial History*, (1979), 2, pp. 1–10.

17 H. L. Smith, 'The problem of "equal pay for equal work" in Great Britain during World War II', *Journal of Modern History*, (1981), 53, pp. 663–5; H. L. Smith, 'The womanpower problem in Britain during the Second World War', *Historical Journal* (1984), 27, pp. 625–45.

18 *The Scotsman*, 31 October 1939.

19 A. Calder, *The People's War: Britain, 1939–1945* (London: Jonathan Cape, 1969), p. 333.

20 S. O. Rose, *Which People's War? National Identity and Citizenship in Britain, 1939–45* (Oxford: Oxford University Press, 2003), pp. 225–8.

21 C. Harvie, *No Gods and Precious Few Heroes: Scotland Since 1914*, new edn (Edinburgh: Edinburgh University Press, 1993), p. 53.

22 P. Addison, 'By-elections of the Second World War', in C. Cook and J. Ramsden (eds), *By-elections in British Politics* (London: Macmillan

1997), pp. 130–50; S. Fielding, 'The Second World War and popular radicalism: the significance of the "movement away from party"', *History*, (1995), 80, pp. 48–52.

23 *The Scotsman*, 5 April 1940.

24 *The Scotsman*, 19 February 1944, p. 4; 22 February 1944, p. 4; Finlay, *Independent and Free*, pp. 224–32; Harvie, 'Labour and Scottish government', pp. 8–10.

25 M. McCrae, *The National Health Service in Scotland: Origins and Ideals, 1900–1950* (East Linton: Tuckwell Press, 2003).

26 National Library of Scotland (NLS), Woodburn MSS, Acc. 7656/4/1/145.

27 J. M. MacCormick, *The Flag in the Wind: The Story of the National Movement in Scotland* (London: Gollancz, 1955), p. 128.

28 N. MacCormick, 'Does the United Kingdom have a constitution? Reflections on MacCormick versus the Lord Advocate', *Northern Ireland Legal Quarterly* (1978), 29, pp. 1–20.

29 M. Dyer, ' "A nationalist in the Churchillian sense": John MacCormick, the Paisley by-election of 18 February 1948, home rule and the crisis in Scottish Liberalism', *Parliamentary History*, (2003), 22, pp. 285–307.

30 *Glasgow Herald*, 15 February 1950.

31 NLS, Tweedsmuir MSS, Acc. 11884/1/3/56.

32 NLS, Tweedsmuir MSS, Acc. 11884/1/4/29.

33 A. Seldon, *Churchill's Indian summer: the Conservative government, 1951–55* (London: Macmillan, 1981), pp. 130–40; G. McCrone, *Regional Policy in Britain* (London: Allen & Unwin, 1969), pp. 106–26; P. L. Payne, *Colvilles and the Scottish Steel Industry* (Oxford: Oxford University Press, 1979), pp. 368–405.

34 NLS, Central Ayrshire Conservative and Unionist Association, Acc. 9079/3, Executive Committee minutes, 29 October 1959.

PART THREE
CHALLENGES

9

THE CHALLENGE OF NATIONALISM

T. M. Devine

The most sensational by-election result in Scotland since 1945 came in Hamilton, Lanarkshire in November 1967 with the victory of the young Glasgow solicitor, Winifred Ewing, over Labour.[1] The SNP won with 46 per cent of the vote and this in one of the safest Labour seats in the party's political heartland of the west of Scotland. Mrs Ewing travelled to London in triumph by train, accompanied by large numbers of enthusiastic SNP supporters, before being driven to Westminster in a scarlet Hillman Imp built at the Linwood car plant. The victory truly put the SNP on the British political map and attracted huge press and television interest, while at the same time sending shock waves through the other political parties. Hamilton was no freak result. At the local elections in May 1968, the SNP had won a remarkable 34 per cent of the votes cast, had performed strongly in the Labour fiefdom of Glasgow, which was afterwards ruled by an SNP–Conservative coalition, and made 101 net gains as against overall Labour losses of eighty-four. The Labour Party was increasingly dependent on support from Wales and Scotland to counter the effect of the strong Conservative vote in England. Now, however, even the loyalty of the Celtic fringe seemed threatened by the growth of rampant nationalism. In the same year that the SNP won its famous victory at Hamilton, Plaid Cymru also achieved successes in a by-election and in local contests against Labour. As the veteran nationalist, Oliver Brown, wryly observed, 'a shiver ran along the Labour backbenches looking for a spine to run up'.[2]

The Conservatives, already anxious about their declining popularity in Scotland, were the first to respond positively to the perceived nationalist menace. Richard Crossman noted in his diaries the comment of the Tory leader, Ted Heath, that nationalism was the 'biggest single factor in our politics today'.[3] As the party in opposition, the Conservatives may have exploited the constitutional issue to put further pressure on the Labour government because this was the background to Heath's remarkable Declaration of Perth in 1968 when, to the horror of many in the audience at the Scottish party conference, he committed the Conservatives to a devolved Scottish Assembly, thus reversing at a stroke an entire century of consistent Tory opposition to home rule.

After 1967 and 1968 Scottish politics would never be the same again. However, at first the SNP achievements did seem a mere flash in the pan. In the general election of 1970, while the nationalists doubled their vote, they lost Hamilton and gained only one seat, the Western Isles. The gains at local authority elections were quickly reversed as it soon became clear that many of the new SNP councillors were both inexperienced and ineffective. A vote for the SNP came to be regarded as an act of protest, a manifestation of Scottish discontent about government policy rather than any serious commitment to Scottish independence. All the opinion polls confirmed that only a small minority of those who actually supported the party in elections wished to see Scotland separated from the United Kingdom. Harold Wilson's policy of prevarication towards nationalism seemed to be amply justified by the course of events. He had appointed Lord Crowther to head a Royal Commission on the Constitution in 1969, but was in little doubt that this body would take a lot of time before producing a report and recommendations. The Prime Minister had once famously declared that Royal Commissions spent years taking minutes. The SNP performance in the 1970 general election, though its best to date, gaining 11 per cent of the vote but only one seat, confirmed the Labour government's view that delaying tactics on the Scottish constitutional issue were by far the most effective approach to this new and irritating problem.

However, the nationalist challenge had not quite run out of steam. Early indications that the SNP were once again on the move came in March 1973, when it polled 30 per cent of the vote in Dundee East, and again in November of that year, when the charismatic 'blonde bombshell and darling of the media', Margo MacDonald, won the rock-solid Labour seat of Glasgow Govan. In the first general election of 1974, the SNP broke through as a real parliamentary force in Scotland, gaining seven seats and 22 per cent of the vote. Within a week, the incoming Labour government embraced devolution as a real commitment despite having fought the election on a platform opposed to it. Even die-hard opponents of home rule like the formidable Secretary of State for Scotland, Willie Ross, the 'Hammer of the Nats', were forced to eat their words. In the second election of 1974 in October the SNP did even better by pushing the Tories into third place in Scotland and achieving 30 per cent of the vote. The party still had only eleven seats, but more alarming from Labour's point of view was the fact that the SNP had come second in no fewer than forty-two constituencies. As Michael Foot confided to Winnie Ewing: 'It is not the eleven of you that terrify me so much, Winnie, it is the 42 seconds'.[4] Within three months Labour published a White Paper, *Devolution in the UK – Some Alternatives for Discussion*, which set out five options for change. Even though many in the Labour Party in Scotland were opposed to this appeasement of the hated nationalists, the Cabinet was determined to press for some form of change, not in order to improve the UK constitution but to end the threat of separatism. Roy Jenkins, then Home Secretary, admitted:

> The fundamental trouble was that the Labour Party leadership, I think this was true of Wilson, I think it was true of Callaghan, I think it was to some substantial extent true of Willie Ross, saw the need for some declaration to avoid losing by-elections to the Nationalists, and not to produce a good constitutional settlement for Scotland and the UK. Any question of separation would be very damaging for the Labour Party because, while it might give Labour a very powerful position in Scotland, if you do not have Scottish members of parliament playing their full part in Westminster then the Labour Party could pretty much say goodbye to any hope of a majority ever in the UK.[5]

The Labour leadership was, therefore, enraged when in June 1974 the Scottish executive rejected all five options in the White Paper by a narrow margin at a meeting that was poorly attended, reputedly because it was held at the same time as a World Cup football match in which Scotland was playing! A special conference of the party was then ordered to be held two months later in the Co-operative Halls in Glasgow to reverse the decision. The debate was bitter and bad-tempered, with many arguing that nationalism was in direct conflict with socialism and that devolution would dilute the benefits of central planning which had brought so many economic benefits to Scotland since the end of the Second World War. In the end, the Union block vote was used to push through a motion in favour of devolution, the Scottish Trades Union Congress having for some time been an enthusiastic convert to home rule. Constitutional change for Scotland was firmly back on the political agenda within seven years of the SNP's historic victory at Hamilton and was due in large part to the two great surges of support for the party in 1967–8 and again in 1973–4.

Hamilton stands out as a landmark in the rise of the SNP but it did not come out of the blue. There were already clear signs of a revival in the party's fortunes earlier in the 1960s. Under the dynamic leadership of Arthur Donaldson as chairman, the number of branches rose from twenty in 1960 to 470 in 1969 and the party claimed an increase in membership from 1,000 to 125,000 over the same period. Organisation improved under the former farmer, Ian MacDonald, and was shown to good effect in by-elections at Glasgow Bridgeton in 1961 and West Lothian in 1962. One reason for Winnie Ewing's victory in 1967 was the ability of the SNP to flood the Hamilton constituency with an army of eager young canvassers and volunteers who proved more than a match for the semi-moribund local Labour Party organisation. The SNP in these years also entered into discussion with the Liberals with a view to possible cooperation against the two big parties.

The Liberals had already achieved early success, having been brought back from virtual oblivion by their solitary MP and leader, Jo Grimond, and they wrested three northern seats from the Conservatives in 1964, followed by the victory of the twenty-six-year-old David Steel in the Roxburgh, Selkirk and Peebles by-election a year later. In 1964 and 1967 both parties met to discuss an electoral pact. Though the talks foundered, they tellingly illustrated SNP ambitions and the growing force of third-party politics in Scotland. Labour and the Conservatives might stand for socialism and capitalism, but the very classlessness of the SNP gave it a distinctive appeal, especially for new voters and for those with no previous party affiliations.

A series of studies have shown that the SNP had a special attraction in this period for non-manual workers who had been upwardly mobile from the working classes, those who 'were renouncing the class of their homes, while not yet entering the middle class' and first-time voters.[6] The very vagueness of SNP policy on a number of issues (apart from the core factor of the constitution) also made the party an appealing vehicle for those who wanted a focus for a range of political discontents.

In the final analysis, however, the rise of the SNP and the new centrality of the Scottish question in national politics by the early 1970s was based not so much on the party's intrinsic attractions as on the broader historical context of the times. Few Scots, even at the height of the party's electoral popularity in 1974, wished to break the Union; the aim was rather to improve it to Scottish advantage. Opinion polls revealed that, while a third of Scots had voted for the SNP in that year, only 12 per cent supported independence. The SNP's success alarmed governments and was seen as an effective way of drawing attention to Scotland's problems. At the same time, however, deeper changes were under way which were to the party's advantage. 'Britishness' may have had less appeal than before. One perceived linchpin of the Union, the British Empire, was disintegrating at remarkable speed. India had gained independence in 1947 and a decade later even the African possessions, starting with Ghana, were winning freedom from British rule. Other former colonies followed in quick succession. Britain was seen to be a nation of declining influence on the world stage. Having won the war, the country seemed to be losing the peace. Successive governments had great power pretensions but that façade could not disguise the real erosion of Britain's standing. The Suez crisis in 1956 conclusively demonstrated the international dominance of the United States, with Britain tagging along merely as a junior partner in the 'special relationship'. In 1963 the British government of Harold Macmillan was humiliated when its application for membership of the Common Market was summarily rejected at the insistence of the French President, Charles de Gaulle, who dismissed the idea by claiming that the United Kingdom was unfit for full membership. Not until 1973 did the UK finally join. A year later, John Mackintosh argued in the *New Statesman* that whatever the other political parties offered to stem the SNP advance it would not be enough 'so long as there is no proper pride in being British'.[7] Ironically, it was the attempt to maintain Britain's status as a world military power that helped to alienate some in the new generation of Scots. In November 1960 Prime Minister Macmillan announced that the country's main nuclear deterrent, the Polaris submarine, would be based in the Holy Loch in Scotland, a decision confirmed in 1964 by the Labour government of Harold Wilson. These decisions boosted the membership of the Campaign for Nuclear Disarmament (CND) in Scotland, while opposition north of the Border had a particular force because of the realisation that the Scots would be in the front line in the event of nuclear war. This galvanised hostility across the political spectrum. Despite this, the SNP was the only party to voice outright opposition to nuclear weapons in the 1960s, especially after Hugh Gaitskell succeeded in reversing the policy of unilateralism espoused by Labour in 1960. Some leading figures in the SNP of future years, such as William Wolfe, Isobel Lindsay and Margo MacDonald had been members of CND. It was partly because of the success of the familiar CND symbol of the time that the SNP adopted its own equally recognisable image, the thistle-loop.

More fundamental – at least in the short term – than the issue of Britishness was the impact of economic change on the fortunes of the SNP. Harold Wilson's government had taken office in 1964 with the promise of bringing the 'white heat of the technological revolution' to bear on Britain's endemic problems. Planning was to be the panacea for both economic decline and regional disadvantage. Willie Ross, the Secretary of State, was the man responsible for ensuring that Scotland obtained at least its fair share of the resources to be dispensed through this strategy. Ross was in office from 1964 to 1970 and again from 1974 to 1976. He was the dominant Scottish politician of the day, an elder of the Kirk, and a former army major and schoolmaster who was a formidable champion of Scotland's cause in Cabinet. A ferocious opponent of the SNP, who was fond of referring to it as the Scottish Narks Party, he was yet utterly determined to fight Scotland's corner against all comers.

Under Ross, Labour in Scotland did deliver at first. Public expenditure rose spectacularly by 900 per cent to £192.3 million between 1964 and 1973 as the Secretary of State successfully extracted as large a share as possible from the public purse for Scotland. Identifiable public spending per head north of the Border moved to one-fifth above the British average. The whole of Scotland except Edinburgh was designated as one large development area within which over £600 million of aid was dispensed through a new Scottish Office Department. No part of the country was left untouched. The Highlands and Islands Development Board was set up in 1965 with executive authority over transport, industry and tourism. The north also gained when the Dounreay fast-breeder reactor started in 1966, followed by the Invergordon smelter in 1968. A huge new pit at Longannet was opened, bringing with it the promise of 10,000 new jobs. The Forth Road Bridge was completed in 1964 and the Tay Road Bridge in 1966. Achievements were by no means confined to infrastructure and industry. Following the publication of the Robbins Report in 1963, the number of universities doubled to eight with the foundation of Strathclyde (1964), Heriot-Watt (1966), Dundee (1967) and the only entirely new institution, Stirling (1968). There was a huge growth in the teaching profession of over 20 per cent between 1963 and 1973, which led to the opening of three teacher education colleges at Ayr, Hamilton and Falkirk in 1964–5. Technical colleges also boomed at the same time. In the 1960s, comprehensive schooling was introduced into Scotland, more successfully than in England. By 1974, under half the children south of the Border were in comprehensives, compared with 98 per cent in Scotland. The fact that so many of the larger education authorities were controlled by Labour helped facilitate the process. Local government itself was not immune from the wind of change. A Royal Commission was appointed under Lord Wheatley to recommend reforms in a system which had hardly altered since the 1920s.

The social and economic impact of all this activity can hardly be doubted. Scotland was gaining from the Union as public revenues were channelled north in the form of massive regional assistance and other benefits. Ross had demonstrated that, like Tom Johnston before him, the Union relationship could be maximised to Scottish advantage. Labour was rewarded with a general election victory for Wilson's government in 1966 in which the Conservatives lost three of their twenty-four seats in Scotland. This, however, was the lull before the storm. Planning and lavish state expenditure had created expectations which could not always be fulfilled. The vast Labour spending on the National Plan made it difficult to balance the budget. This in turn led to wage restrictions and increases in duties on foreign imports. A dockers' strike in 1966 compounded the problems and pushed sterling down further. The government was soon forced to devalue, but Harold Wilson's boast that 'the pound in your pocket' was still secure did not convince a sceptical electorate. This was the political background to the SNP's advances at the by-election in Pollok and the victory at Hamilton in 1967. Planning had now degenerated into crisis management and the state could no longer guarantee the employment levels and the material standards to which the Scots had become accustomed since the 1950s. This triggered support for the SNP in the short term, though much of it soon melted away. Articulate opponents, such as the eloquent and energetic Jim Sillars, then a prominent unionist member of the Labour Party, were able to launch a devastating attack on the SNP's Achilles heel, namely the absence of any coherent ideological position on social and economic issues. At the same time, the inept performance of many SNP councillors, some of whom resigned soon after their election, conveyed to the public the image of a party which had come much too far too fast. In the 1970 South Ayrshire by-election, Labour, with Sillars as its candidate, overwhelmed the SNP and effectively derailed their bandwagon. At the general election later that same year, the Tories triumphed under Ted Heath. It was unlikely, however, that the constitutional relationship between Scotland and the rest of the UK would disappear as an issue. Heath's new Secretary of State, Gordon Campbell, was the first since 1945 to belong to a government that did not possess a majority of votes or seats in Scotland. Before long, this and other factors were to cause trouble for the new incumbents.

A basic cause of the growing prominence of the SNP in Scottish politics in the 1960s and 1970s was the decline in the Tory Party as the most effective challenge to the hegemony of Labour in Scotland. The Conservatives stood above all for unionism. Indeed, it was only in 1964 that the Scottish party dropped the 'Unionist' label in favour of the more anglicised 'Conservative' one. For decades it had been a powerful vehicle north of the Border for the expression of British patriotism. Now the decay of the party gave nationalism its chance. The vote against Labour, which earlier might have gone overwhelmingly to the Unionists, now sometimes went to the SNP. The Liberals, despite their successes in rural Scotland, proved to be less significant than in England where in the two 1974 elections, when the SNP was at its peak, they took over 20 per cent of the vote compared with around 8 per cent north of the Border. The decline in Unionist popularity was as swift as it was sudden. As recently as 1955, the Unionists had attracted just over 50 per cent of all Scottish votes, the only party ever to have managed that electoral achievement. In 1959 the number of Unionist MPs fell from thirty-six to thirty-one, then to twenty-four in 1964, and dropped again to twenty in the 1966 general election. It was still not a disaster on the scale of the elections of 1987 and the 1990s, but it was nevertheless still an enormous humiliation for a party that had been the most successful in Scottish politics since the end of Liberal hegemony after 1918.

Increasingly the Unionists presented a remote elite and an anglicised image that seemed out of touch with current Scottish problems. In part, this was due to the combination of the difficulties of the older industries and the inexorable decline of indigenous control of manufacturing and enterprise with nationalisation, numerous mergers and the penetration of American capital. The great Scottish captains of industry and leaders of the Clydeside dynasties who had formerly ruled the party were fast disappearing and their place was once again being taken by lairds and aristocrats who had received an entirely anglicised education. The huge changes in urban housing after the Second World War also affected the party's fortunes. The massive working-class peripheral housing estates around Glasgow and Edinburgh established new Labour fiefdoms in former rural areas, while the flight of the middle classes to the suburbs eroded the Conservative vote in the heart of the cities. It may seem remarkable from the perspective of 2007, but as late as 1951 the Conservatives held as many as seven seats in Glasgow, only one less than Labour. By 1964, however, they were left with two, one of which was already very vulnerable.

The secret of Conservative success for much of the twentieth century had been the ability to reach out well beyond the middle classes to the respectable, skilled and semi-skilled working classes in Scotland. To them the party represented protestantism, unionism and imperial identity. Even in 1986, 45 per cent of the members of the Church of Scotland claimed to vote Tory. In Dundee in 1968, nearly 40 per cent of Protestant manual workers voted Conservative, compared with 6 per cent of Roman Catholics of the same class. These figures come from the period when the pattern of voting along religious lines – at least for Protestants – was already in decline. It is very likely that in the 1950s and early 1960s political and religious cleavages in Scotland were even deeper. Nevertheless, the bedrock Protestant working-class support for conservatism was crumbling in the 1960s and 1970s. The influence of the Kirk was ebbing. Church membership reached a peak in the mid-1950s and then went into serious decline. In 1956, 46 per cent of Scots had a formal Church connection. By 1994, this proportion had fallen to 27 per cent. The rate of decline for the Church of Scotland was even greater because, until recent years, the overall haemorrhage from the Catholic Church was much less. A 'membership catastrophe' occurred during the 'Swinging Sixties',[8] and many people lost contact with religion altogether. The numbers attending Sunday School plummeted and the proportion of marriages being religiously solemnised fell, especially from 1964/5. That Scotland was becoming a more secular society was also illustrated by the decline of sectarian employment practices, encouraged by the impact of new foreign-owned industry, the nationalisation and/or decay of the older staple manufactures, where discrimination against Catholics in skilled occupations had flourished, and the effect of full employment in the 1950s and early 1960s on the labour market. As a result, the Protestant monopoly of many skilled jobs was broken. Mixed marriages and the growing integration of the Catholic community into Scottish society as a result of better educational opportunities in colleges and universities after 1945 also diluted, although they did not yet end, the bitterness of historic religious divisions. It was a sign of the times when (the then) Archbishop Winning in 1975 became the first Catholic priest to address the General Assembly of the Church of Scotland, a body which just before the Second World War had campaigned vigorously against Irish Catholic immigration. Seven years later, Pope John Paul II met the Moderator under the statue of the great reformer, John Knox, during his historic visit to Scotland. There were occasional 'No Popery' demonstrations during the visit, but it was significant that most people regarded them as unrepresentative of Scottish public opinion as a whole. The Conservatives suffered most as a result of this growing tolerance and the associated secularisation of Scottish politics. As early as 1964, when they endured the shattering loss of the Pollok constituency in Glasgow, party managers first became aware that they were losing the old working-class religious vote. On the other hand, the Catholic Labour vote remained solid for another generation, while in the 1970s support for the SNP was overwhelmingly Protestant. The Tories were, therefore, squeezed by two forces: the desertion of many of their working-class supporters to new allegiances; and the still unquestioning loyalty to Labour of the Catholic population in numerous west of Scotland constituencies.

Nevertheless, in 1970 Scotland found itself once again under Conservative rule, although the party itself was now in a minority north of the Border. The new Prime Minister, Ted Heath, had been one of the first modern British politicians to acknowledge the importance of devolution for Scotland in his Declaration of Perth. However, the SNP performed poorly in the general election of 1970, winning only the Western Isles. Some thought it a spent force. Heath then took the opportunity to shelve the plans for a Scottish Assembly formulated by Lord Home's constitutional committee which he had appointed. From that point on, devolution had little appeal for the Tories. However, two factors during the period of Conservative administration rejuvenated the SNP and led to a spectacular performance in the two elections of 1974 which placed constitutional change once again at the centre of political debate for the rest of the decade. First, the Heath government tried to mount a radical assault on the interventionist economic policies that had sustained both Labour and Tories alike since 1945. There was to be more competition, industrial 'lame ducks' should not be propped up with taxpayers' money, overwhelming trades union power had to be crushed and a more discriminating approach undertaken to state welfare provision. The attempt to reform housing finance in Scotland under the Housing Financial Provisions (Scotland) Act 1972 provoked furious resistance from local authorities under Labour control, since low rents had been one of the key foundations of the vast post-war housing programmes around the Scottish cities. The Tories now proposed not only to raise them but also to end subsidised rents by demanding that local authorities balance the books on their housing accounts. This was political anathema. No fewer than twenty-five authorities refused to cooperate and came into line only when they were taken to court and fined for their truculence.

More serious was the plight of Upper Clyde Shipbuilders (UCS), one of two large combines established on the Clyde in 1967–8 to increase the competitive potential of a flagging industry. In 1971, UCS announced it was going into receivership with the potential loss of 8,500 jobs. Dole queues were already lengthening in Scotland during the first year of the Heath government, and the collapse of UCS was seen as a potentially mortal blow to the tottering edifice of the old industrial structure. Clydeside shipbuilding was seen as a Scottish icon, a great symbol of the country's glorious industrial past which could not be allowed to disappear and was now threatened with bankruptcy only because of the uncaring actions of a government for which the Scots had not voted. Under the charismatic and skilful leadership of two young Communist shop stewards, Jimmy Reid and Jimmy Airlie, a campaign of resistance to closure began which attracted widespread national support. In June 1972 an estimated 80,000 people marched to a rally in Glasgow in support of the workers' right to work. Nothing like it had been seen in this century, not even during the heyday of Red Clydeside. Reid himself later argued that the fight was initially to save the yards but it was eventually transformed into a wider struggle to protect the Scottish economy and the rights of the Scottish people to have some control over their destiny. UCS was reprieved and the government gave in. Protest was seen to work.

Secondly, the credibility of the government was undermined by economic crisis and industrial action. Heath's Industrial Relations Act 1971, far from curbing trades union power, swiftly unleashed an unprecedented wave of unrest in the workplace which culminated in the mighty National Union of Mineworkers' refusal to accept the government's pay policy. This led to an overtime ban, a state of emergency and finally to power cuts and a three-day week in the depths of the winter of 1973. Inflation stood at 18 per cent in November of that year and the balance of payments slipped into huge deficit as limits on oil production imposed by the Arab producers after the Yom Kippur War with the Israelis led to a quadrupling of prices. In early 1974, Heath was forced to go to the country on the issue of 'Who

Governs Britain?'. The nation was in acute crisis and there seemed little hope of recovery from the British disease of unemployment, balance-of-payments problems and poor labour relations.

However, the SNP argued that there was a way out of the spiral of decline if an independent Scotland took control of the enormous oil resources now becoming available in the North Sea. In October 1970, BP struck oil 110 miles off Aberdeen in what was to become the giant Forties field. The inflation in world oil prices after the Arab–Israeli War meant that even marginal fields could have huge potential value. Recovery of the 'black gold' and expansion in the area of exploration proceeded apace. The SNP oil campaign began in 1971 and brilliantly exploited the contrast between, on the one hand, the fabulous wealth found off Scotland's coasts and, on the other, the fact that by then the Scots had the worst unemployment rate in western Europe and were yoked to a British state that stumbled from crisis to crisis. Oil also gave the nationalist argument a new credibility by demonstrating that an independent Scotland could indeed survive from its own resources. In November 1973 Margo MacDonald's victory at Govan for the SNP, one of the safest of Labour seats, was the prelude to sweeping gains in the two general elections in 1974, including the scalp of the Tory Scottish Secretary, Gordon Campbell. Indeed, the nationalists did especially well in former Conservative seats. Nine of the eleven seats they won were from the Tories. The SNP was once again regarded as an effective instrument for exerting pressure on the London government to respond to Scottish grievances. However, its problem was that only a small minority of supporters agreed with the long-term strategy of full independence, while its voting strength was notoriously soft and volatile and liable to dissipate when grievances became less pressing. Nevertheless, the electoral success of the SNP in 1974 meant that home rule remained at the top of the UK political agenda for the next several years. Labour had gone to the country in October 1974 as a strong supporter of devolution, and its first attempt at honouring the election pledges came in 1975 when *Our Changing Democracy* was published, proposing a Scottish Assembly of 142 members, funded by a block grant and with control over most Scottish Office functions but with no revenue-raising powers.

Difficulties soon emerged when the Scotland and Wales Bill was finally presented in the House of Commons. To avoid intensifying damaging splits on the issue of devolution, the government was forced to concede a referendum. Michael Foot, who was responsible for taking the Bill through Parliament, admitted that this was forced on the Cabinet by threatened backbench disaffection. At least 140 MPs signed a motion urging a referendum and stating they would not vote for the Bill unless it was granted. A government with a tiny majority had no choice but to concede. The referendum was at best a delaying tactic and at worst a wrecking device; cheered by this victory, the anti-devoluntionists pressed on to other triumphs. The attempt to impose a guillotine on further parliamentary discussion of the Bill after its second and third readings failed, leaving opponents of the legislation with the opportunity to table amendments which could water down the original proposals even further. The most crucial of these was the motion proposed by the Labour MP for London Islington, the Scot George Cunningham, that if less than 40 per cent of those voting in the referendum voted 'yes' then an order should be laid before Parliament for the repeal of the Scotland Act. This amendment was passed on Burns Night, 25 January 1978. For those bent on destroying devolution it proved a potent weapon. Cunningham's coup has been described by some political scientists as the most significant backbench intervention in any Parliament since 1945. The Scotland Act was finally agreed by the Commons in February 1978. Now the verdict of the Scottish people was awaited.

When they gave their answer on 1 March 1979 it was inconclusive, ambivalent and confusing. The majority of those who voted did vote 'yes', 51.6 per cent or 1.23 million Scots, as against 48.4 on the 'no' side. On such a major constitutional issue, however, the margin of victory was very slim indeed and, since the 'yes' vote represented less than a third of the whole electorate, it was well below the 40 per cent required by the Cunningham amendment. This was hardly a ringing endorsement for home rule. Moreover, just 63.8 per cent of those entitled to vote did so, which does not suggest that the Scotland Act had engendered mass popular enthusiasm. More seriously, much of the rural north and south of Scotland voted against devolution. The Borders, Dumfries and Galloway, Tayside, Grampian and the Orkney and Shetland Islands all recorded 'no' majorities, suggesting they were more in fear of domination from the Labour-controlled cities of the Lowlands than of rule from London. The SNP launched a 'Scotland Said Yes' campaign to urge the government to press on with devolution, but the cause was lost. The truth was that less than a third of the electorate had actually voted for the most important constitutional change in Scotland's history since the Union of 1707 and the detailed results of the referendum demonstrated conclusively that the Scottish people were hopelessly divided on the issue.

Since the Callaghan government failed to deliver devolution and had proved incapable of controlling its backbenchers during the passage of the Bill through Parliament, the SNP thought it had no option but to table a motion of no confidence in an increasingly discredited administration. This succeeded by one vote and, in the general election that followed, the Conservatives under Margaret Thatcher swept to power with a radical agenda for curing Britain's ills in which constitutional change had no part. For the SNP, the election was a disaster. It lost nine of its eleven seats, thus confirming James Callaghan's famous gibe that the censure of the nationalist MPs on his government was the first recorded instance in history of turkeys voting for an early Christmas. The campaign for home rule which had dominated much of Scottish politics in the 1970s collapsed in acrimony, bitterness and disillusion. James Turnbull's cartoon in the *Glasgow Herald*, depicting the Scottish lion admitting, 'I'm feart', captured the mood of despondency in the pro-devolution camp.

Notes

1   This is a condensed and revised version of ch. 24 of my book, *The Scottish Nation, 1700–2000* (Harmondsworth: Allen Lane, 1999).
2   Quoted in Alan Clements, Kenny Farquharson and Kirsty Wark, *Restless Nation* (Edinburgh: Mainstream, 1996), p. 50.
3   Quoted in James Mitchell, *Conservatives and the Union* (Edinburgh: Edinburgh University Press, 1990), p. 55.
4   Quoted in Clements et al., *Restless Nation*, p. 66.
5   Clements et al., *Restless Nation*, pp. 63–4.
6   F. Bealey and J. Sewel, *The Politics of Independence: A Study of a Scottish Town* (Aberdeen: Aberdeen University Press, 1981), p. 160.
7   Quoted in James Mitchell, 'Scotland in the Union, 1945–95', in T. M. Devine and R. J. Finlay (eds), *Scotland in the Twentieth Century* (Edinburgh: Edinburgh University Press, 1996), p. 97.
8   Callum G. Brown, 'Religion and secularisation', in A. Dickson and J. H. Treble (eds), *People and Society in Scotland, Vol. III, 1914–1990* (Edinburgh: John Donald, 1992), p. 53.

10

THATCHERISM AND THE UNION

Richard J. Finlay

Modern folklore would have us believe that rather than a statue to Donald Dewar as the 'father of the nation' and the man responsible for the creation of the Scottish Parliament, that honour should instead go to Margaret Thatcher – no doubt made of iron. After all, Thatcher brought to an end the post-war consensus in which the state took responsibility for tackling the deep-rooted socio-economic problems that Scotland had inherited from before the Second World War. Ultimately this led to a growing political divergence between Scotland and England that helped to reduce the Scottish Conservative Party to the status of a fringe political movement and, most importantly, made most Scots question their faith in the efficacy of the existing constitutional relationship with the rest of the United Kingdom.[1] The 1980s witnessed the wholesale destruction of traditional Scottish heavy industry, higher rates of unemployment than the rest of the United Kingdom and the profound effect of social dislocation that followed in the wake of poor economic performance and profound economic restructuring. The prospect of an unchallengeable Conservative electoral hegemony in Britain after the party won its third general election in a row, especially when the Tories performed badly in Scotland, gave rise to what was known as the 'democratic deficit'.[2] After widespread tactical voting in 1987 which resulted in the Conservative Party winning only a handful of seats north of the Border, it seemed to many that the Scottish nation was doomed to perpetual Tory policies in spite of the fact that the Scottish electorate had rejected these policies at the ballot box. For the other unionist parties, home rule emerged as the best solution to the danger of a polarisation between unionism as represented by the Conservative Party and Scottish independence as represented by the SNP. This fear was given an added sense of urgency with the SNP's Govan by-election victory in 1988. After this time, the constitutional question would dominate Scottish politics and, as they say, the rest is history.

It is the purpose of this chapter, however, to test some of the common assumptions that underline the recent Scottish home rule narrative. First, there is the issue of chronology and the tendency to conflate cause and effect. This has particular resonance in dating the decline of the fortunes of the Conservative Party in Scotland and the issue of when the political momentum for home rule began to have effect. Too often, the Conservatives are portrayed as doomed to inevitable failure in Scotland with the advent of Thatcherism, which represented a decisive break with the Scottish political consensus.[3] Secondly, as with most recent history, the influence of the memoirs and statements of the main participants tends to weigh to heavily in the account and the impact of more diverse and impersonal socio-economic forces tends to get short shrift. This is especially the case in the construction of the idea of 'civic nationalism' or 'civil society' as a key factor in explaining both the rejection of Thatcherite policies and the growth of support for devolution.[4] As a theory, it has wide-spread support but little evidential underpinning. Also, the relation-ship between anti-Thatcherism and home rule is readily assumed to be symbiotic, but again there is only limited evidence for this. Thirdly, the role of Conservative Unionist ideology receives little attention.[5] It is commonly assumed that Thatcher had little understanding of Scotland and that the Conservatives did not really care what hap-pened in the northern kingdom. Home rule was given a boost by crass unthinking and insensitive Conservative politicians determined to impose their political will on the recalcitrant Scots.[6] As we shall see, however, there was a remarkable degree of ideological consistency in Conservative unionist policy that was neither as crass nor as insensi-tive as is often thought. Finally, the chapter will pull the various strands together to present a version of events that places socio-economic change at the heart of political change in Scotland during the 1980s and 1990s and reasserts the fundamental role of political ideology both in causing and engaging with that change.

As was pointed out by the sociologist, David McCrone, the socio-economic experience of Scotland and England began to converge in the late 1980s at precisely the time when home rule momentum was beginning to take off.[7] On a wide range of socio-economic indicators, the Scottish middle class was growing, standards of living were improving and the nation, once the worst of the depression of the early 1980s passed, was clearly becoming more prosperous.[8] Theoretically, this should have shored up Conservative support north of the Border as the bedrock of its socio-economic constituency increased in size. After all it worked in England and, if we regard socio-economic factors as the principal determinants of electoral behaviour, it should have worked in Scotland. Indeed, support for right-wing free market parties was increasing throughout the modern world at this time, and why it should not happen in Scotland presents the historian of comparative politics with a bit of a conundrum. Also, it is worth pointing out that Thatcherism was not quite such a disjuncture with the Conservative past as was previously thought and it actually represented the rank and file aspirations of Tories in the post-war era.[9] As Hutchison, the foremost political historian of modern Scotland, has noted the post-war Scottish Conservative Party was even more traditional in its outlook than its southern counterpart, and as such, might be expected to have responded even more warmly to the Thatcherite strictures against the 'Nanny State'.[10] Furthermore, as the number of home owners, self-employed and skilled workers increased, so too should have Conservative support. At the end of the day, there were more winners than losers in Scottish society as a result of the Thatcherite revolution.

Part of the explanation lies in the electoral first-past-the-post system which exaggerated the degree of Conservative decline. While it is possible to construct a case that the party was in decline in Scotland from the mid-1960s, the raw electoral data presents a more complex picture. In 1979, the Conservative Party did reasonably well in Scotland by increasing its share of the vote from 24.7 per cent to 30 per cent and its number of MPs from sixteen to twenty-two. This performance was well down on the overall United Kingdom Conservative performance of 43.9 per cent of the vote, but it is worth noting that initially Thatcherism did increase Scottish Conservative support. Labour won twice as many MPs with 42 per cent of the vote, a reflection of their historically higher vote efficiency in Scotland that had seen a consistently higher return of MPs per votes cast than their Conservative opponents. In 1983, the Conservative held up well, dropping only 1.6 per cent of the popular vote and losing one MP. Although their share of the vote was down about 10 per cent from the period 1959–74, the number of MPs was remarkably consistent (22.5 is the average from 1959 to 1974) and in 1983 the party won more Scottish seats than in 1966, October 1974 and gained the same number as February 1974. In the same election, Labour lost three MPs and saw a decline in its share of the vote from 42 per cent to 35.1 per cent. Although the 'Falklands Factor' undoubtedly played a major part in the election, the fact remains that at the height

of the depression, the voting differential between Labour and the
Conservatives in Scotland was not significantly different from its
post-war norm (6.5 per cent compared with 7.9 per cent for the
period 1955–79).[11] All this would seem to give lie to the claim that
Scottish Conservatism was doomed from the outset of the Thatcher
government. It also raises interesting issues regarding the political
impact of Thatcherite socio-economic policies. For example, 1983
witnessed the rise in unemployment to the historically significant
300,000 mark with a third of male and half of female under-25s
without work, all of which had little discernible effect on Tory performance in Scotland.[12]

Politically, it was the general election of 1987 that would bring the
constitutional issue into sharper relief. An examination of the main
party literature of the time shows that these issues were not at the top
of the agenda for the three main British parties in Scotland during the
election. The electoral system, however, translated a decline of 4.4 per
cent of the total vote into a loss of eleven Conservative seats, more
than half, and reduced the party of government to a humiliating ten
Scottish MPs. Secondly, while historically the Conservative Party was
used to not doing well in Scotland, the results of the 1987 election
could not be ignored and increasingly the wider United Kingdom
Conservative Party turned its attention north. It was after this date
that the widespread notion of the subsidy junkie was given currency
after a speech by the Chancellor of the Exchequer, Nigel Lawson, in
Glasgow, which drew attention to the higher rate of public expenditure in Scotland.[13] For many on the left, the results of the election
were a vindication of tactical voting in which the electorate punished
the Conservative Party for the way it had treated Scotland. According
to *Radical Scotland*, which had urged tactical voting, the election
demonstrated that there was a 'national' dimension at work in which
'there seems to be a simple egalitarianism emerging, wherein people
won't just vote Tory because they themselves would be better off'.[14]
This was used to explain why the Tories lost in Scottish seats with a
socio-economic profile that would have been fertile Conservative territory in the south. Undoubtedly anti-Conservative sentiment was an
important factor in explaining the elections results of 1987 – and
those who had proposed the policy of tactical voting certainly made
great play of it.[15]

Yet, it is important to emphasise that the Tory share of the vote was
perilously close to the threshold where seats would tumble even
without tactical voting due to the vagaries of the first-past-the-post

system. It is worth pointing out that the SNP with 18 per cent of the vote (7 per cent less that the Conservatives) could only notch up three seats. In a paradoxical way, vote efficiency worked to Labour's advantage in Scotland in the same way that it worked to the Conservatives' advantage in England, and vice versa. Also, it is worth emphasising that, at the time, many pointed out the 'inevitability' of Labour decline in England, as others were subsequently to claim happened to the Scottish Tories.[16] Although the Conservatives were bruised by the 1987 general election, they did not believe that as a party they were doomed to decline.[17] Indeed, they argued that the results of economic transformation, which were slower in coming to Scotland, were just taking longer to translate into political support. Furthermore, the rank and file was convinced that its community charge would be a vote winner and far from Scotland being used as a guinea pig, it was Scottish Tories in search of a popular policy to boost support who insisted that it be tried first in Scotland.[18] Finally, in examining the political landscape in 1987, it was far from clear that the Conservative Party would fail to recover. As party propagandists never tired of reminding the nation, the economy was growing faster, incomes were rising and Scotland showed no evidence of being adverse to popular capitalism on the ground.[19] Although not as many as in England, some 74,000 Scots bought their council home between 1980 and 1985, and even more would do so after 1987 at the height of Conservative unpopularity. By 1988, the figure had risen to 113,000. In 1988, the Conservatives claimed that twice as many Scots owned shares compared with 1979.[20] According to Thatcher 'Judged by cold statistics, Scots enjoy greater prosperity than anywhere in the United Kingdom outside the crowded, high-priced South East'.[21] The general election of 1987 was interpreted by Conservative Central Office as a temporary set-back and it saw no reason to change political direction.

The extent to which there was a genuine 'national' dimension to the results of the general election in 1987 tends to be assumed rather than proved. Statistically, the impact of the Scottish broadsheets and *Radical Scotland*'s readership to influence the outcome of the election was improbable given that the numbers were too few and most likely anti-Conservative in any case.[22] The effect of the result was to stimulate debate about the 'national' dimension in Scottish politics, but that is not the same as a 'national' dimension conditioning the outcome of the results.[23] The results of the election were enough to give the issue a political momentum. The fact that the economy had picked up and the socio-economic profile of Scotland started to converge with that of England – coupled with the fact that adverse economic conditions did not have too much impact on the 1983 election result – has in retrospect tended to confirm the idea that political culture or a notion of civic society was driving the anti-Conservative vote in Scotland (see below). Yet, the enormity of social dislocation of the 1980s had still not ended and more mundane socio-economic factors tend to get short shrift as an explanation for Conservative decline in Scotland. Although the depression was bad in 1983, it had still to run its full course. Unemployment, for example, was to peak in 1985 and a BBC opinion poll before the 1988 Govan by-election demonstrated that unemployment was the most important factor in determining how people intended to vote.[24] Furthermore, the election was fought under the shadow of the impending closure of Ravenscraig and the government's refusal to guarantee its survival beyond 1988.[25] While socio-economic convergence with England can be dated to 1987, it was by no means apparent to the electorate that the worst of the economic dislocation had passed.

Indeed, there is a case to be made that puts socio-economic factors at the heart of the explanation of Conservative unpopularity in Scotland in the late 1980s. Although the service sector was growing, the reformulation of census categories masks the fact that many of the new jobs that were created were low skilled and low paid. For example, more than half of all new jobs created in Scotland between 1985 and 1989 were taken by women, the vast majority of which were part-time and low paid.[26] This trend would continue into the 1990s with part-time women workers concealing the fact that, in terms of total employment, the number of Scottish men at work was in decline.[27] In short, Scottish families adapted to industrial decline by working longer hours. Also, the figures relating to unemployment were also recalculated with disability and Youth Opportunity schemes masking the true extent of those without work. In the much vaunted 'Silicon Glen' for example, most jobs were low-grade assembly work.[28] Not even the Scottish middle class remained unscathed. A survey of Scottish graduates revealed that 30 per cent of them had to leave Scotland to find work and the figure was even higher for those in the scientific and technical field. Indeed, the Scottish share of the graduate market declined from 9.4 per cent to 7 per cent at a time when the market was increasing.[29] Corporate takeovers, downsizing and relocation further dented Scottish middle-class security. Comparative figures demonstrate the extent to which the Scots were failing to benefit from the Thatcher revolution. Total employment in Scotland remained more or less static between 1983 and 1987 at 64 per cent, whereas the United Kingdom figure increased from 68 per cent to 70 per cent.[30] Furthermore, a significant gulf emerged between Scottish and British average earnings. Finally, the Tory flagship policy of 'right to buy' became more popular only when the economy began to settle after 1988, which perhaps indicates not so much a hostility to the policy *per se*, but more of wider pessimism of individual economic prospects.

Even when official figures showed that the economy was back on track and that the worse of the economic dislocation was over, things were not as rosy as the government liked to claim. In 1989, the Scottish low pay unit published figures that showed that half the labour force was earning less than £144 per week and as such were officially 'low paid'.[31] Even official figures highlighted the extent of poverty in Scottish society with some one and a half million Scots earning about the same as the minimum level of income support.[32] A central plank of government economic policy was to attract inward investment, but often high profile success stories could equally be marred by high profile withdrawals.[33] Whatever the success of government policy in restructuring the Scottish economy, and no matter how successful it was in the long term, the fact remains that it was not done without pain. As mentioned above, fear of unemployment rather than unemployment itself did more than anything to alienate the electorate. Also, the regional and local dimension of the Scottish economy has to be taken into consideration when considering the political impact of Thatcherite policy, especially in regard to the impact of closure in traditional industry. The numbers of workers involved in the Scottish steel industry at Ravenscraig and Gartcosh, for example, were fairly small in terms of total local employment, but the knock-on effect would impact on potential Tory recruits such as the self-employed and local small businesses. Indeed, it became standard practice in opposing industrial closure to emphasise its wider impact on the community and by 1987, there was an impressive roll-call of *communities* rather than *companies* that had suffered closure. In December 1987, the Proclaimers summed it up in their song *Letter From America* in which contemporary Scotland was experiencing an industrial clearance of the same historical magnitude as the Highland clearances: 'Bathgate no more, Linwood no more, Methil no more, Irvine no more, Lochaber no more.'

In charting the growth of the home rule movement in the late 1980s and early 1990s, civic nationalism or notions of civic society tend to be cited as the key factor in its establishment. Perhaps the most dramatic illustration of the phenomenon was the 'sermon on the Mound' speech by Margaret Thatcher to the Church of Scotland General Assembly in 1988. The hope that Presbyterian Scotland and the land of Adam Smith would approve her call for more robust individualism, greater independence from the state and more support for individual enterprise was, to say the least, misguided.[34] The audience listened in stony silence and at the end, the Moderator presented the Prime Minister with a series of reports from the Church which highlighted the divisive nature of her policies. While Mrs Thatcher may have chosen to emphasise wealth creation, the Church chose to emphasise widespread poverty. In many ways, the event came to symbolise all that was wrong with Thatcherism in Scotland. For many, the incident was a telling metaphor on how the Prime Minister misread not only her audience, but the nation as a whole.[35] The fact that the Kirk, that most traditional bastion of Scottish society, had cold shouldered the Iron Lady was taken as proof that her policies were alien even to traditional Scottish society. Yet, this ignores the fact that since the 1960s the Kirk had increasingly been moving to the liberal left in an endeavour to shore up its credibility in the face of declining membership.[36] The sermon was taken as further evidence that Thatcher had no interest in society and that the speech was simply an endorsement of greed. The Scottish press and media led the chorus of condemnation. Shortly afterwards, in July 1988, the Scottish Constitutional Convention published its *Claim of Right*.

An important component in putting the case that civic society was a key aspect in the demand for Scottish home rule was the fact that the Convention was cross-party and included representatives from the Scottish Churches, trades unions and other civic organisations and forums. Crudely put, it is argued that the Scots rejected Thatcherism on account of this strong civic identity (which was strong enough to band together in this way) and as such, this civic identity needed a parliament to best represent the wishes of the Scottish people. Yet, an important aspect of the Convention which tends to be forgotten, is that it was fundamentally designed to preserve the Union and that while anti-Thatcherite in its rhetoric, it was equally anti-Scottish nationalist in its political objectives. In the section on the quality of life that the parliament could offer the people, it stated that 'No modern economy can be viewed in isolation from the others in which it is entwined by ties of trade and owner-ship – one reason why Scotland has to remain within the United Kingdom, which is by far its biggest marketplace'.[37] For the non-nationalist opposition parties, there was a danger that the political debate in Scotland would polarise between nationalism and union-ism. The nationalist victory at the Govan by-election in 1988 added weight to fears that Conservative intransigence, coupled with oppos-ition impotence, would turn the electors towards the SNP. Indeed, the Conservative Party goaded the opposition on the issue that reform of the constitution of the United Kingdom could only come through the democratically-elected British government and if they wanted a Scottish parliament then they should stand on a separatist ticket.[38] In fact, the Conservative Party was quite happy to exploit the Labour Party's discomfiture, particularly as the party had won fifty seats in the 1987 general election in Scotland and had a hardcore of anti-poll tax activists within its ranks.[39] In a world of diminishing political opportunities and widespread popular discontent at the political impotence of the majority of Scottish MPs, the Convention, whatever the deeply held conviction of its members, was as much a vehicle for political survival for the non-Conservative Unionists parties in a world that might become polarised between take-it-or-leave-it union-ism as espoused by the Tories and independence-or-nothing national-ism as espoused by the SNP.

Indeed, evidence of the failure of conventional party politics can be seen from the growth of extra parliamentary pressure groups. It was the inability of the Unionist opposition parties to stop the imposition of Trident and the poll tax that led to the emergence of groups deter-mined to pursue a more direct form of opposition that often involved non-legal means. Similar populist opposition manifested itself in the referendum on the proposed privatisation of water, which was organ-ised by Strathclyde Regional Council, to demonstrate popular hostil-ity to the Thatcherite policy of privatisation of public utilities.[40] The emergence of popular activism against Thatcherite policy and its imposition on a reluctant Scottish people can be cited to demonstrate the fact that there was growing engagement with politics, and hence the existence of a strong sense of civil society. But an equally plausi-ble explanation is that it was precisely the impotence of conventional party politics which turned many to activism. What the advocates of home rule were able to do was take the mounting evidence of dis-content with government policies and publicly mould it into an image of national discontent. A crucial propaganda push to the home rule cause was to use the message of the nation united in opposition to government policies. However, the extent to which the various disparate groups had anything else in common tends to be assumed rather than proved. Furthermore, the fact that there was opposition to the government need not necessarily translate itself into support for home rule. Home rule was a common denominator in a society that was becoming increasingly politically divided. Crudely put, in the 1987 general election the Tories won just under 750,000 votes, Labour about 1,250,000, the Alliance just over 500,000 and the SNP just under 500,000. It is worth pointing out that both in terms of MPs and share of the vote the Conservative Party was still Scotland's second largest party. To coalesce the opposition around the issue of home rule, which almost included the SNP by default, was the major achievement of the Convention.

The main criticism of the Thatcher government was that its policies damaged the fabric of civil society and that a key reason why the Scots rejected the Tories was their desire to protect their civic society. Yet, how strong was civic society at the grass roots? There is no doubt that it existed in the minds of its proponents, but how far it stretched into the masses is another question. As we have seen, the Scots were not averse to taking advantage of Tory policies such as the right to buy and share ownership, and as was reported regularly at Conservative Party conferences in the late 1980s, opinion polls showed that the vast majority of young people now aspired to private ownership of their home. Like other parts of the modern developed world, Scottish society experienced what might be called the atomisation of society with individualism and consumerism just as widespread as elsewhere. Furthermore, the gulf between 'haves' and 'have-nots' was growing as large 'sink estates' began to emerge. Traditional family and communal ties often began to disintegrate with the development on new private housing estates and the growth in divorce and the rise of single-parent families.[41] What the proponents of civil society as a bastion of anti-Thatcherism nicely fudge is the extent to which it was a cause, rather than a consequence. On the basis of empirical evidence, civil society was an aspiration rather than a reality.

Home rule climbed up the political agenda as much on account of its expedient value, as a cohesive glue for the anti-Thatcher forces in Scottish society which formed disparate groups into a coalition, as on its own merits. The idea of civic society or a distinctive Scottish political identity that opposed Thatcherism that was founded on the altruistic notions of community and public service rather than individualism and greed was a convenient way of masking that fact that numerous elements within Scottish society were in decline and losing their social and political relevance. It is probably stretching things too far, but the cynic might point out that self-interest and survival was as much a motivation for the coalition that formed the Convention. The opposition parties of the Labour and the Alliance/Liberal Democrats were impotent in a constitutional arrangement in which they thought they would always be out-voted by the superior numbers of English elected MPs. The Scottish Trades Union Congress had seen its membership and its influence shrink under the onslaught of free market policies which worked against the bastions of traditional heavy industry.[42] The Churches had likewise witnessed a diminution in membership and influence as society became more secular.[43] Local government saw its authority and finance decline under an onslaught of legislation.[44] Large sectors of state employment were vulnerable to the threat of privatisation. In short, the post-war structures of the corporate state were under threat in Scotland and their ability to coalesce into a united front in the absence of a British political solution in the shape of a defeat of the Conservative Party at the polls, is a remarkable testament to how well entrenched they were in Scottish society. As the cynic might observe, the notion that Scotland was immune to the selfish impetus of the Thatcher onslaught that was so successful in the south effectively masked the self-interests of the home rule coalition. In a world of growing uncertainties, the prospect of a self-governing parliament within the United Kingdom was probably a safer bet than unbridled Thatcherism. Furthermore, an often forgotten aspect associated with the rise of the home rule movement is the growth of globalism, in which the state (whatever its political complexion) was becoming less and less important.

A key problem facing the Convention (given its Unionist basis) was the extent to which it would feed nationalist aspirations. Again civic nationalism was a useful ploy in that it could couch its pronouncements within a nationalist language, but claim that this was not based on ethnicity or exclusion of the English. The Convention had to tread a careful line by using the language of Scottish distinctiveness, but at the same time not providing succour to the nationalists. Certainly, the winner of the Govan by-election, Jim Sillars, believed that the Convention would fail and the home rule momentum when it was thwarted would divert into nationalism.[45] In many ways the reason why the Conservative Party became a political pariah in Scotland was its inability to deal with the 'national' dimension in Scotland, or rather its response to it, coupled with the negative impact of restructuring the economy, which was not going to win thanks in any case. It proved a devastating cocktail. The Conservatives were blamed for administering the medicine that, in retrospect, all agreed was necessary, but, at the same time, they allowed their political opponents to portray them as anti-Scottish. At the end of the day, it is difficult to avoid the conclusion that the Scottish Conservatives and their leader were largely the authors of their own misfortunes in Scotland.

In explaining the unpopularity of the Conservative Party in Scotland, the role of Thatcherite political ideology needs to be emphasised, in particular the enthusiasm with which it was pushed and the political dividends it was expected to deliver. In spite of the impact of industrial closure, 'the Lady' was definitely 'not for turning'. In her speeches in Scotland before the 1983 election there was no doubt in her mind about the efficacy of her policies. Indeed, she was quite unapologetic in promoting the idea that the international free market would rectify the problems of the Scottish economy, rather than government intervention:

> For Scotland's pioneering achievements in the first industrial revolution left the Scots economy dangerously dependent on industries like coal which faced natural exhaustion, and shipbuilding which faced cyclical decline . . . And while successive post-war governments – and particularly Tory governments, be it noted – have devoted large resources to diversify employment this side of the border, much of it has inevitably come from branch factories which have proved dangerously vulnerable to the cold winds of worldwide recession.[46]

At the party conference before the general election of 1983, Thatcher told delegates that the collapse of the old industries was to be regretted, but it was a necessary step before a new economy could flourish. Indeed, there was little acknowledgement that the Scottish economy was in bad shape:

> Scotland has battled through recession with determination and enterprise. In the 1930s it was the new generation of consumer goods industries – the motor car and washing machine – which led to recovery from the slump, and too much of it was located in the South of England, passing Scotland by. This time, by contrast, it is precisely the products of the next generation – transistors and computers, the micro chip and the

semiconductor – which have chosen Scotland as their preferred base for the European market. 'Silicon Glen' has earned a second meaning – more appropriate indeed than the first. And so Scotland now greets the recovery of world markets with a new industrial base – the broadest you have known since you pioneered the first industrial revolution.[47]

At the party conference of 1985, Thatcher was even more blunt and in a not too subtle way told her audience that there were too many ships in the world, and that 'Scotland no longer depends on the heavy industries of the past, but on the enterprise culture of tomorrow'.[48] Even following the general election of 1987, there was still a refusal to accept that government economic policy had an adverse effect on the outcome:

> Government promised to insulate Scotland from the reality of industrial change . . . But they couldn't and they didn't. Shipyards closed. Factories closed. Men lost their jobs. Whole areas turned to wasteland. And the money that might have been invested in new industries, new opportunities, went instead in trying to keep yesterday's jobs alive.[49]

In short, the problem in Scotland lay with the post-war corporate policies and the official Conservative line was that the real success stories were not being promoted enough. Devolution, it was claimed, was not an urgent matter.[50] This hardline attitude on the economy was an important factor in the portrayal of the Conservatives as uncaring and insensitive to the needs of the Scottish nation. The problem for the Conservative Party was its refusal to accept that its policies were taking a toll in Scotland. This dogmatic approach to economic issues was arguably a critical factor in hardening attitudes. The refusal to temper the harsh realities of market forces coupled with a near contempt for the system of economic management that had served Scottish society, if not the economy, well in the post-war era made the Tories vulnerable to opposition claims that they were anti-Scottish.[51] Indeed, efforts to ally economic liberal policies with Scottish identity sounded patronising at best and Victorian at worst. The frequent incantation of Adam Smith, an appeal to traditional Scottish values such as hard work and thrift and harking back to the era of Scottish economic and technical progress in the nineteenth century failed to strike a chord with the Scottish electorate.[52] In reality, it probably made things worse as that very world of heavy industry was suffering most from economic restructuring. Furthermore, the record on new jobs and new technology was never anything more than a list of inward investment. While the opposition after 1987 made great play of the negative consequences of Thatcherite economic policy in a Scottish context, the Tories were never able to construct a positive Scottish counter-argument. Mostly policy was presented as a wider aspect of British and government development, devoid of any significant Scottish dimension. There was even an element of cockiness following the 1987 defeat: 'I am sometimes told the Scots don't like Thatcherism. Well, I find that hard to believe – because the Scots invented Thatcherism, long before I was thought of'.[53] This was political condescension at its worst.

The ideological fervour with which economic policy was applied was equally apparent in Thatcherite attitudes to the Union. In the Scottish context, it is often forgotten that Thatcher was a dyed in the wool Unionist, as her handling of the situation in Northern Ireland in the early 1980s illustrates.[54] Indeed, it is possible to argue that Thatcher's Unionist strictures were even more severe in Scotland than in Northern Ireland where there was at least some form of negotiation and compromise.[55] In Scotland, the Union was sacrosanct and not up for discussion. With as much dogmatic certainty, Thatcher refused to concede that there was a 'national' dimension to Scottish politics and believed that the issue was simply between unionism and nationalism. She accused devolutionists of seeking 'separation by degrees' and accused them of wanting to 'tear the kingdom apart'. For her, there was no half-way house: 'As long as I am leader of the party, we shall defend the Union and reject legislative devolution unequivocally'.[56] At party conferences and speeches to the Scottish media, Thatcher had little to say on the issue of devolution, other than to associate it with increased bureaucracy and higher taxes. Indeed, it is quite remarkable the degree to which the Conservative Party refused to engage with the issue. It occupied little more that a few summary statements in party literature and defence of the Union and more often than not rested on historical foundations, with the Scottish role in Empire and economic development singled out for praise.[57] Arguably making matters worse was the tendency of Thatcher to equate Tory policy with providing the Scots with 'real independence' by reducing the role of the state, while at the same time her Scottish ministers were forever reminding the Scots that they could not survive on their own as they depended on a subsidy from the United Kingdom.[58] At the end of the day, the party of the Union could come up with no better defence than it was 'necessary' to ensure English subsidies. Furthermore, it is clear from reading party conference speeches that the key element in Thatcherite policy in Scotland was to focus on economic success in finance, electronics and tourism as if this would somehow overshadow all other political considerations.[59] But, as Mrs Thatcher constantly reminded everybody, governments did not create jobs. Although the Scottish economy could report many 'positive' stories, it is hard to avoid the conclusion that memories of the harsh restructuring were still raw and the Tories were not forgiven. This lack of imagination contrasted unfavourably with their devolutionist and nationalist opponents. Indeed, at the end of the day, it is difficult to avoid the conclusion that a major problem with the Conservative Party in Scotland was its failure to engage imaginatively with the Scottish dimension. The unapologetic attitude towards economic restructuring and the uncompromising position on the existing constitutional arrangement effectively painted the Tories into a corner. Labour and the Alliance/ Liberal Democrats were both more adaptable. They were able to embrace the 'social market' once Thatcher had taken the opprobrium for its consequences and by using constitutional change they were able to mask their political impotence.[60] The nationalists simply waited for their opportunity. By the time of John Major's premiership the damage had been done. The decision to host the European Union summit in Edinburgh and return the Stone of Destiny were largely empty symbolic gestures. In many ways it was an almost belated recognition that Scotland was different.[61] However, the Tories had no answer to the question of how to accommodate that difference. 'Scottishness' was hijacked by the opposition.

Notes

1 Standard accounts include T. M. Devine, *The Scottish Nation, 1700–2000*, 2nd edn (London: Allen Lane, Penguin Press, 2006); D. McCrone, *Understanding Scotland: The Sociology of a Nation*, 2nd edn (London: Routledge, 1991); L. Paterson, *The Autonomy of Modern Scotland* (Edinburgh: Edinburgh University Press, 1997); Alice Brown, David McCrone and Lindsay Paterson, *Politics and Society in Scotland*, 2nd edn (Basingstoke: Macmillan, 1998) and David Denver, James Mitchell, Charles Pattie and Hugh Boche, *Scotland Decides: The Devolution Issue and the Scottish Referendum* (London: Frank Cass, 2000).

2 On the economy see G. C. Peden, 'The managed economy: Scotland 1919–2000', in T. M. Devine, George C. Peden and Clive Lee (eds), *The Transformation of Scotland: The Economy Since 1700* (Edinburgh: Edinburgh University Press, 2005) and C. Lee, *Scotland and the Union: the Economy and the Union in the Twentieth Century* (Manchester: Manchester University Press, 1995). The issue of the 'democratic deficit'

is discussed in Owen Dudley Edwards et al., *Claim of Right for Scotland* (Edinburgh: Polygon, 1989). For a contemporary account of the 'democratic deficit', although the term is not used, see 'Can Labour grasp the thistle?', *Radical Scotland*, 29, October/November 1987, pp. 6–9.

3 For example, see Paterson, *Autonomy of Modern Scotland*, pp. 168–70. and Brown et al., *Politics and Society*, pp. 21–2.

4 Paterson, *Autonomy of Modern Scotland*, p. 12; Brown et al., *Politics and Society*, p. 122 and Lindsay Paterson and Richard Wyn Jones, 'Does civil society drive constitutional change?', in Bridget Taylor and Katrina Thomson (eds), *Scotland and Wales: Nations Born Again?* (Cardiff: University of Wales Press, 1999), pp. 169–99.

5 The notable exception is James Mitchell, *Conservatives and the Union* (Edinburgh: Edinburgh University Press, 1990).

6 This is a common theme in many contemporary accounts of modern Scottish political history; for example, see Arnold Kemp, *The Hollow Drum* (Edinburgh: Mainstream, 1993), p. 189 in which Thatcher described Scotland as 'nothing but problems'.

7 McCrone, *Understanding Scotland* deals extensively with this theme.

8 For an in-depth analysis of the extent of social change see Lindsay Paterson, Frank Bechhofer and David McCrone, *Living in Scotland: Social and Economic Change Since 1980* (Edinburgh: Edinburgh University Press, 2004).

9 E. E. H. Green, *Ideologies of Conservatism* (Oxford: Oxford University Press, 2002), pp. 214–40.

10 I. G. C. Hutchison, *Scottish Politics in the Twentieth Century* (Basingstoke: Palgrave, 2001), pp. 104–17.

11 These figures are based on the average differential in the share of the total proportion of the vote won by both the Conservative Party and the Labour Party in Scotland.

12 Central Statistics Office, *Regional Trends*, 29, 1994, p. 81.

13 *Glasgow Herald*, 24 November 1987.

14 *Radical Scotland*, 29 October/November, 1987, p. 6.

15 *Radical Scotland*, 29, October/November, 1987.

16 For a discussion of vote efficiency see R. Johnston et al., 'Labour electoral landslides and the changing efficiency of voting distributions', *Transactions of the Institute of British Geographers*, (2002), 27(3), pp. 336–61.

17 Margaret Thatcher in an interview with the *Aberdeen Press and Journal*, 3 September 1987. Likewise at the Scottish Conservative Party Conference in 1988, the election results were described as a temporary setback: *The Scotsman*, 14 May 1988.

18 This was especially the case at the 1987 Scottish Conservative Party conference when it was described as a long overdue reform: *The Scotsman*, 12 May 1987.

19 This way the key theme that emerged during Scottish Party conferences throughout the period.

20 *The Scotsman*, 14 May 1988.

21 *Scotland on Sunday*, 15 May 1988.

22 In spite of inflated claims, the probable combined readership of the broadsheets was probably only 300,000 and heavily biased towards the cities.

23 The most extensive debate on this issue was carried out by *Radical Scotland* which argued that a national dimension was at work.

24 Quoted in Alice Brown, 'Introduction', *The Scottish Government Yearbook 1989* (Edinburgh: Edinburgh University Press, 1989), p. 8.

25 Margaret Thatcher in interview with STV, 3 June 1987.

26 Scottish Executive, *Scottish Economic Statistics*, 'Economic activity by gender, Scotland, 1985–2000' (Edinburgh: HMSO), p. 102.

27 Scottish Executive, *Scottish Economic Statistics*.

28 Peter Payne, 'The economy', in T. M. Devine and R. J. Finlay (eds), *Scotland in the Twentieth Century* (Edinburgh: Edinburgh University Press, 1996), pp. 24–9.

29 Isobel Lindsay, 'Migration and motivation: A twentieth-century perspective', in T. M. Devine (ed.), *Scottish Emigration and Scottish Society* (Edinburgh: John Donald, 1992), pp. 166–8.

30 *Scottish Economic Statistics*, 'Employment rates, Scotland and the United Kingdom, 1960–2000', p. 97; 'Average earnings of employees: Scotland and Great Britain', p. 99.

31 Robin Smail, *STUC Review*, 42, 1989.

32 Cited in *Radical Scotland*, 39, June/July 1989, p. 16.

33 For example, the decision by Ford not to invest in Dundee in March 1988 not only illustrated the precarious nature of foreign investment but both Labour and the Tories blamed one another for the debacle.

34 *The Scotsman*, 23 May 1988. See also her memoirs, *The Downing Street Years*, for her perplexed response to Scottish attitudes to her economic policies.

35 Report from *The Scotsman*, 23 May 1988.

36 A good example is William Storrar, *Scottish Identity: A Christian Vision* (Edinburgh: Handsel Press, 1990).

37 Scottish Constitutional Convention, *Scotland's Parliament: Scotland's Right* (Edinburgh: 1995).

38 Margaret Thatcher, speech to Scottish Conservative Party Conference, 12 May 1989.

39 *Scotland on Sunday*, 6 November 1988.

40 In March 1994, 97 per cent voted against water privatisation.

41 R. Finlay, *Modern Scotland* (1994), pp. 386–9.

42 John W. Leopold, 'Trade unions in Scotland: forward to the nineties', in Brown (ed.), *Scottish Government Yearbook 1989*, pp. 71–4.

43 Callum Brown, 'Religion and secularisation', in A. Dickson and J. H. Treble (eds), *People and Society in Scotland: Vol. 3, 1914–1990* (Edinburgh: John Donald, 1992), pp. 48–80.

44 Arthur Midwinter, *Local Government in Scotland: Reform or Decline?* (Basingstoke: Palgrave, 1995).

45 *The Scotsman*, 1 July 1989.

46 Speech to Scottish Conservative Party in Edinburgh, 26 November 1982.

47 *The Scotsman*, 14 May 1983.

48 *Glasgow Herald*, 17 May 1985.

49 *The Scotsman*, 14 May 1988.

50 *Aberdeen Press and Journal*, 3 September 1987.

51 This was not helped by the Party Conference speech of 10 October 1986 in which Mrs Thatcher wore the 'Red Rose of England'.

52 See David McCrone, 'Scottish opinion polls 1988', in Brown (ed.), *Scottish Government Yearbook 1989*, pp. 344–61.

53 Speech to Scottish Conservative Party Conference, 13 May 1988.

54 See Alvin Jackson, *Ireland, 1798–1998* (Oxford: Oxford University Press, 1999), p. 413.

55 See Alvin Jackson, *Home Rule: An Irish History, 1800–2000* (London: Weidenfeld and Nicolson, 2003), pp. 293–4.

56 Speech to Scottish Conservative Conference, 13 May 1988.

57 See, for example, the 1994 publication, *Scotland and the Union: A Partnership for Good*.

58 Finlay, *Modern Scotland*, p. 372.

59 For example, every speech by Thatcher at the Scottish Conservative Party conference has a large litany of investment and business growth, coupled with a denunciation of Labour economic policy. At the 1988 Scottish Party Conference, for example, the economy started the speech and, together with agriculture, accounted for about half the total.

60 See, for example, Gordon Brown's *Where There is Greed* (1989) in which he acknowledges the need for public and private intervention and that the market ought not to be suppressed.

61 This theme is explored in greater depth in R. J. Finlay, 'Thatcherism, civil society and Scottish home rule', in A. Murdoch (ed.), *Politics and Identity: Essays in Honour of William Ferguson* (Edinburgh: Birlinn, 2008).

11

THE DEATH OF UNIONISM?

W. L. Miller

After a Scottish Parliament election that, for the first time put the Scottish National Party (SNP) into office, if not into power (the party holds only forty-seven of the 129 seats), it is tempting to link the supposed 'death of unionism' with the supposed 'rise of nationalism'. That would make an attractively simple story: 'Unionism killed by the rise of nationalism'. Unfortunately, the evidence does not support that simple story.

Much of the evidence suggests that Scots have, indeed, become somewhat more nationalist and less unionist since the 1960s – but more so in terms of voting than in anything else. It has got easier to vote nationalist and more difficult to vote unionist – in part because the meanings of both nationalism and unionism, as defined by the parties, have changed. So even if there had been no change at all in public opinion, there would probably have been a significant change in public behaviour.

The option of a nationalist vote has become more available as the SNP contested more seats, more credible in the context of a Scottish Parliament and a proportional election system, and less frightening as the SNP has adopted a much more moderate and inclusive definition of nationalism. In policy and rhetoric, nationalists have become very much less nationalist.

On the other side, unionism has been redefined in a way that makes it much less attractive to the Scottish voter. Until the 1960s, unionism still represented a tradition that combined respect for Scottish heritage and commitment to the Scottish national interest with pragmatic support for the Union – sometimes described as 'Unionist Nationalism', defined as using the Union for Scottish advantage. Under Thatcher's leadership of the Conservative Party however, unionism was redefined as British nationalism in opposition to Scottish nationalism – instead of being an historic form of Scottish nationalism.

The evidence suggests, therefore, that the apparent 'death of unionism' owes more to Thatcher's redefinition of unionism than to the changing attitudes of the Scottish public. Also the 'rise of nationalism' in elections owes more to institutional changes and the SNP's moderate, internationalist and inclusive redefinition of nationalism than to rising nationalist sentiment among the public.

MORE NATIONALIST SCOTS?

What is the evidence that Scots have become more nationalist since the 1960s? We can look at trends in voting, trends in constitutional preferences, trends in political culture and values and trends in national identities.

Trends in voting

A chart of party shares of the vote at UK general elections in Scotland shows a steady decline in unionist voting since its peak in 1955, a decline that was interrupted only by a brief and very partial recovery in 1979 and 1983. Incidentally, what later became the Conservative Party in Scotland called itself the Unionist Party from 1912 to 1965. (Where it can cause no confusion and yet serve to clarify my argument, I will use the term 'Unionist Party', irrespective of the date.) It was that explicitly 'unionist' vote that exceeded 50 per cent in 1955 – an achievement that has never been matched by any other party since the introduction of universal suffrage in 1918. Until the 1960s this unionist vote in Scotland closely matched the Conservative percentage vote in England, but thereafter the two diverged. So there was something peculiarly Scottish that eroded its support.

Within Scotland, the rise in nationalist votes seems to mirror the decline in unionist votes. There was a spectacular surge to a peak of over 30 per cent in 1974, followed by a rapid decline until 1983, and a modest recovery thereafter – so that nationalist votes eventually stabilised at around 20 per cent in UK general elections. Clearly there was a long-term trend towards nationalist voting in Scotland, albeit a somewhat erratic trend rather than a steady advance.

However, was there really such a trend in Scots' willingness to vote nationalist? Do the simple trends in votes mislead? That rising trend in nationalist voting looks a lot less impressive if we take account of the growing number of SNP candidates up to 1974. If we chart the SNP vote in places where they fielded a candidate, the trend since 1945 is still visible, but quite shallow. Moreover, if we extend the

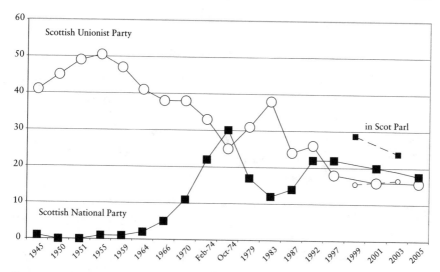

Sources: Colin Rallings and Michael Thrasher, *British Electoral Facts 1832–1999* (Aldershot: Ashgate, 2000); David Butler and Dennis Kavanagh, *The British General Election of 2001* (London: Palgrave Macmillan, 2002); David Butler and Dennis Kavanagh, *The British General Election of 2005* (London: Palgrave Macmillan, 2005).

Figure 11.1   Unionist and nationalist votes, 1945–2005

chart back to the inter-war years 1929–35 the trend is very shallow indeed. Nationalist candidates could expect 10–15 per cent of the votes whenever they stood. Viewed in the longer term from 1929 to 2005, 1974 looks like an aberration, not the culmination of a steadily rising trend. February 1974 was a crisis election with the miners' strike and a government-imposed 'three-day week'. There was a huge 'neither of the above' vote which went to the Liberals in England (who got 24 per cent in seats they contested) and to the SNP in Scotland (who got only 22 per cent in the seats they contested). Polls also showed that just a couple of weeks before election day, SNP support was running at only 15 per cent – its historic baseline level since the inter-war years.[1]

Thus, the SNP vote of 22 per cent in February 1974, rising to 30 per cent in October 1974, reflected a short-term crisis in British politics, not a steady rise in nationalist voting preferences. A decade later, there was another 'neither of the above' reaction against both Labour and the Conservatives who were both seen as drifting to (opposite) extremes. However, in 1983 that 'neither of the above' vote went to the LibDems in Scotland as well as in England. Within Scotland, the

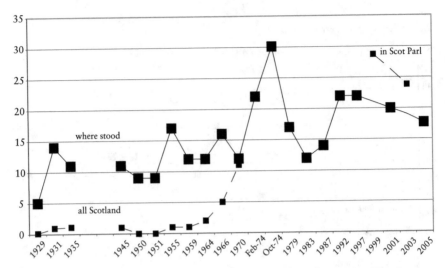

Sources: Frederick W. S. Craig, *Minor Parties at British Parliamentary Elections 1885–1974* (London: Macmillan, 1975); Colin Rallings and Michael Thrasher, *British Electoral Facts 1832–1999* (Aldershot: Ashgate, 2000); David Butler and Dennis Kavanagh, *The British General Election of 2001* (London: Palgrave Macmillan, 2002); David Butler and Dennis Kavanagh, *The British General Election of 2005* (London: Palgrave Macmillan, 2005).

Figure 11.2   Nationalist votes, 1929–2005

LibDem vote in 1983 (24.5 per cent) was over twice as high as the SNP vote (11.8 per cent).

Under the new institutional – and also new electoral – arrangements for the Scottish Parliament, the SNP vote has been consistently higher than in UK elections. The SNP is clearly a more credible contender within a Scottish context, and under a proportional representation (PR) electoral system. In 2007 it took top place in the Scottish Parliament elections and formed a minority government.

None the less, when comparing like with like, the SNP vote in the 2005 UK election was only 18 per cent – just 3 per cent higher than their vote in 1955 in the places where they had candidates. Indeed, taking the comparison back to the inter-war years, the nationalist vote in 2005 had risen by no more than 7 per cent over a period of seven decades. There has been a real trend towards higher levels of nationalist voting, but it has been a very modest, shallow and erratic trend: averaging 1 per cent per decade. By contrast, the decline in unionist voting has been much more consistent and dramatic than the rise in nationalist voting.

Increases in nationalist votes reflect institutional factors more than rising public enthusiasm. These increases have been driven by increasing numbers of candidates, by the new setting of a Scottish Parliament elected under a PR system, and in 1974 by a crisis election that prompted a 'neither of the above' vote in Scotland as it also did in England.

Trends in constitutional preferences

Public support for independence ran at 21 per cent in 1974 when the first data were collected, dropped after the unsuccessful 1979 referendum, peaked at 37 per cent after the very different 1997 referendum, and thereafter dropped back to stabilise at around 27 per cent. Over three decades, therefore, public support for independence increased by less than 6 per cent, while support for devolution increased by 11 per cent, and opposition to a Scottish Parliament declined by 21 per cent. Echoing the voting trends, the decline in opposition to a Scottish Parliament has been much more dramatic than the increase in support for independence.

Trends in culture and values

The myth of a peculiarly Scottish political culture is just that: a myth. In 1991 a team at Glasgow University undertook a comprehensive survey of Scottish and English attitudes towards a very wide range of issues to do with the principles and practice of liberty and equality.[2] It found that age, education and religiosity had a huge impact on attitudes towards liberty, and that both class and gender had a huge impact on attitudes towards equality. However, living in Scotland or England had no significant impact on public attitudes to issues of either liberty or equality, especially once account was taken of social background. In short, there was no significant difference between the culture and values of those who lived in Scotland and England.

Since that survey, recurrent studies have reached broadly the same conclusion.[3] Scots voted for left-wing parties more than the English, but they did not have particularly left-wing values. Since devolution, Scots keep telling interviewers that they want more powers for the Scottish Parliament. Yet in the 1997 referendum, they showed some lack of enthusiasm for the powers on offer: 74 per cent voted for a Scottish Parliament, but only 64 per cent voted for it to have even

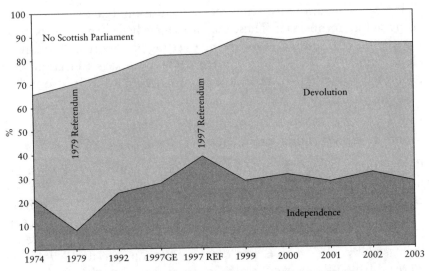

Sources: Paula Surridge, Alice Brown, David McCrone and Lindsay Paterson, 'Scotland: constitutional preferences and voting behaviour', in Geoffrey Evans and Pippa Norris (eds), *Critical Elections: British Parties and Voters in Long-term Perspective* (London: Sage, 1999), p. 229; Alison Park and David McCrone, 'The devolution conumdrum?', in Catherine Bromley, John Curtice, David McCrone and Alison Park (eds), *Has Devolution Delivered?* (Edinburgh: Edinburgh University Press, 2006), p. 16.

Figure 11.3   Constitutional preferences, 1974–2003

marginal powers of taxation – and no Scottish Parliament has so far dared to use even these marginal tax-raising powers.

Most recently, the British Social Attitudes Survey (BSAS) has been asking whether the public in England and Scotland support 'increased taxes – to spend on health, education and welfare'. That is only a single question but, none the less, it is a key indicator of left-wing tendencies. In a five-year study, the BSAS found that Scots were more left-wing than the English in three of the five years, but more right-wing than the English in the other two years.[4] On average, across the five years, Scots were just 2 per cent more left-wing than the English.

In short, there is no significant difference, and no evidence of a trend towards any significant difference, between the broad political values of the Scots and the English. In particular, Scots are not, in fact, significantly more egalitarian (though they may think they are), nor significantly more willing to pay taxes than the English.

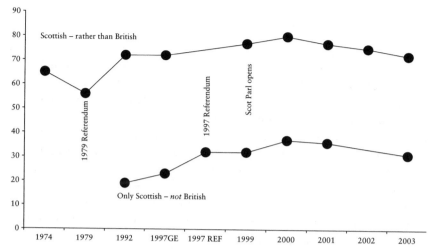

Sources: John Curtice, 'Brought together or driven apart?', in William L. Miller (ed.), *Anglo-Scottish Relations from 1900 to Devolution and Beyond* (Oxford: Oxford University Press for the British Academy, 2005), pp. 167–8; Paula Surridge, 'A Better Union?', in Catherine Bromley, John Curtice, David McCrone and Alison Park (eds), *Has Devolution Delivered?* (Edinburgh: Edinburgh University Press, 2006), p. 38.

Figure 11.4   National identities, 1974–2003

Trends in Scottish identities

What does distinguish the Scots from the English is identities, not values.[5] So if it is not value differences that explain the decline in unionist or Conservative voting in Scotland, could it be a rising sense of Scottish identity? Since the question was first asked in 1974, a majority of Scots have described themselves as 'Scottish rather than British'. The numbers fell from two-thirds in 1974 to just over half immediately after the unsuccessful 1979 referendum. They peaked at 80 per cent just after the successful 1997 referendum, before falling back thereafter. The much smaller number who regarded themselves as exclusively Scottish and not at all British followed similar trends, and also peaked just after the successful 1997 referendum.

Clearly, the consistently high level of Scottish identification is far more striking than the relatively minor and undulating trends. Scots' identities were only a little more nationalist in 2003 than in 1974. So these trends in nationalist identities could not possibly explain the dramatic fall in unionist voting over those years.

Summary

Have the people changed? Have they become more nationalist? Their broad political culture and values remain almost indistinguishable from those in England. Their support for a Scottish Parliament – always strong – was more for devolution than independence, it increased only modestly and it is now past its peak. Their identification with Scotland – always strong – also increased only modestly and it is also past its peak. The greatest change has been in voting, rather than constitutional preferences, broad political values, or national identities; and the decline of the unionist vote has been more striking than the rise in nationalist voting. So none of these potential causes of voting change has changed as dramatically as voting itself: behaviour has changed more than opinion.

Redefining unionism and nationalism

Redefining unionism and nationalism suggests a very different explanation: perhaps the parties have changed more than the people? Perhaps the decline in the unionist or Conservative vote reflects the increasing identification of the Conservative Party with England, rather than the increasing identification of the Scottish public with Scotland?

The changing nature of unionism

Paradoxically, unionism was always nationalist – so much so that some use the term 'unionist nationalism', by which they mean 'unionist Scottish nationalism', defined as using the Union for Scottish advantage.[6]

In the 1920s and 1930s, De Valera was accused of wanting 'a Catholic state for a Catholic people', while Lord Craigavon, his counterpart in Northern Ireland, was accused of wanting 'a Protestant state for a Protestant people'. Let me set aside the issue of whether either or both were misrepresented. The relevant point here is not whether they were 'guilty as charged', but rather the 'nature of the charge'. It was that those who wanted 'a Catholic state for a Catholic people' or 'a Protestant state for a Protestant people' were nationalists, and the worst kind of nationalists: 'ethnic nationalists', who defined the nation exclusively in terms of a common heritage, a common ancestry and a common religion. Such 'ethnic nationalists' would be inherently conservative, and would oppose cultural change and development as much as they opposed cultural diversity.

So how should we describe those who supported a Union that guaranteed 'for all time coming', not only a Protestant state, but a Presbyterian state for a Presbyterian people – as unionists, as nationalists, or as 'unionist nationalists'? That Union was explicitly designed to protect Scotland not only from the scourge of Continental catholicism, but also from the scourge of Anglican episcopalianism. As Linda Colley argues, we decide who we are, by who and what we are not.[7] And the Union defined Scots as neither Catholic nor Episcopalian.

That Union was a marriage of convenience not a marriage of affection. Tom Devine (see Chapter 7) links the Union to the opportunities it provided 'for presbyterianism and plunder'. Through the Union, he argues, Scots were able not only to preserve and indeed export their presbyterianism, but also to import 'an indecent share of the spoils of Empire'. That unionist tradition was inherently Scottish nationalist in a way that the Labour tradition, built on class and the socialist claim that 'the workers have no country', could never be. Though they lost the Protestant working-class vote over the following two decades, as late as the 1970s the unionist vote in Scotland was defined far more by religious traditions than by class.[8]

Until the 1960s, unionism also retained at least the rhetoric of Scottish nationalism in a way that Labour was reluctant to emulate. Addressing a rally in the Usher Hall, Edinburgh just a week before the 1950 election, Winston Churchill declared that he 'would never adopt the view that Scotland should be forced into the serfdom of socialism as the result of a vote in the House of Commons'. And this celebrated parliamentarian continued: 'the socialist menace has advanced so far as to entitle Scotland to further guarantees of national security and internal independence'.[9] In his attack on the supremacy of Parliament, this unionist leader was happy to apply the terms 'national' and 'independence' to Scotland. Later on unionist leaders Edward Heath and Alec Douglas-Home drafted proposals for devolution and at the election of October 1974 the unionists (as well as Labour) advocated a parliament for Scotland.

The turning point in public perceptions of the Scottish unionists came after Mrs Thatcher took over as leader. Addressing a rally in Glasgow in February 1975, on her first major public appearance since being confirmed leader, she formally confirmed her party's support for devolution but then focused on 'the unity of the UK', warned about

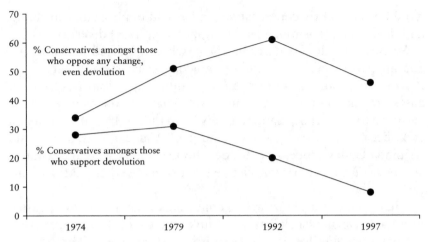

Sources: Paula Surridge, Alice Brown, David McCrone and Lindsay Paterson, 'Scotland: Constitutional Preferences and Voting Behaviour', in Geoffrey Evans and Pippa Norris (eds), *Critical Elections: British Parties and Voters in Long-term Perspective* (London: Sage, 1999), p. 231.

Figure 11.5   Losing the devolutionists

the dangers of 'fragmenting Britain', advised her audience 'not to look smaller but to enlarge our vision of the world' and concluded by asserting – inaccurately but significantly – that 'Conservatives are and always have been, British Nationalists'.[10] As late as the 1979 referendum she was still formally in favour of devolution, but never in favour of any specific proposal for it. The tactic was unconvincing. When she imposed a three-line whip in 1976 against the government's proposals for devolution only six of the sixteen Scottish Conservative MPs obeyed – and two of those six retired before the next election.[11]

Thereafter the Conservative Party did better and better among the declining numbers of Scots who opposed devolution, but they lost their previously strong support among the increasing numbers of Scots who supported devolution.[12]

Thatcher had no real sympathy with that Scottish 'internal independence' and Scottish 'national security' that had come so readily to the lips of Churchill. Her victory in 1979 was followed by eighteen years of ideological and insensitive government (including the imposition of the hated poll tax in Scotland before it was imposed on England) by a party that had been decisively beaten in Scotland. Her redefinition of unionist nationalism in opposition to Scottish nationalism – instead of being an historic form of Scottish nationalism – allowed the SNP to depict unionist nationalism as not merely 'British nationalist' but as essentially 'English nationalist'. At least in party terms, that was the 'death of unionism' in its historic form; and the assassin was Thatcher, not the Scottish public.

To a lesser extent, however, those eighteen years of Thatcherism helped to redefine Labour in the unlikely role of a Scottish nationalist party instead of a centralising socialist party. They gave Labour a partisan incentive to accept the convenience, if not the ideological desirability, of a more Scottish nationalist stance. Devolution was no longer seen a device to protect Labour from the SNP (as it had been in 1974), but instead it became a device to protect Labour in Scotland from Conservative governments at Westminster.

The changing nature of nationalism

It is not just unionism that has been redefined since the 1960s, however. Nationalism has also been redefined – and redefined in two ways. First, the concept of independence has been redefined and secondly, and equally important, the concept of the nation has been redefined.

Redefining independence

The SNP has always been troubled by the concept of independence. That is its core policy. But what does independence mean? For the first few decades of its existence, the party, and the wider national movement, was divided between those who sought full independence and those who sought something more like devolution. By the 1960s and 1970s the party had come to favour complete independence, and it was antagonistic towards membership of the emerging European Union. Nationalists were quite properly described as 'separatists', who wanted independence outside both the UK and the EU.

For several years after the failure of the 1979 referendum, and a dismal SNP performance in the 1979 and 1983 elections (it was reduced to a poor fourth place with under 12 per cent of the vote in 1983) there was a fierce battle between rival factions within the party – which briefly included the expulsion of Alex Salmond. However, by 1988 the party had adopted Jim Sillars' policy of 'independence within Europe' by a majority of eight to one. Donald Dewar responded by describing Labour plans for devolution – in almost Churchillian terms – as 'independence within the UK'. Andrew Marr commented that 'independence no longer meant quite what it used to mean' and described the new policy as 'that mysterious mixture, an Internationalist Nationalism' – as complex, as apparently self-contradictory, and yet as coherent as traditional 'Unionist (Scottish) Nationalism'.[13]

By 1997 less than a quarter of SNP voters were separatists, in favour of complete independence outside both the EU and the UK.[14] Even for SNP voters, independence was no longer a matter of black and white, but a matter of shades of grey – ranging from independence outside the EU (23 per cent), through independence within the EU but outside the UK (37 per cent), to independence within the UK (34 per cent) in the Churchillian or Dewar sense. So, just as the 'death of traditional unionism' might be attributed to Thatcher rather than the voters, the 'death of traditional nationalism' should be attributed to the new SNP leadership rather than the voters.

Redefining the nation

Less obviously, the SNP in recent years has sought to redefine the nation and national identity. The party has travelled all the way from a nationalism that stressed history, people and heritage, to a new nationalism that now stresses:

- the future rather than the past;
- the land rather than the people; and
- multiculturalism rather than heritage.

It is a long way to travel. In the 1950s, nationalists blew up red post-boxes that bore the symbol 'E II R', because the new Queen Elizabeth was not the second of that name, neither for Scotland nor for the UK. Nationalists also removed the 'Stone of Destiny' (reputedly the Scottish coronation stone) from Westminster Abbey, prompting the Archbishop of Canterbury to state: 'there can be no simpler, more elemental illustration of the spiritual causes of the world's evil than the stealing from Westminster Abbey of the Coronation Stone'.[15] Arguably that was an over-reaction, but such nationalist actions did reveal a romantic, backward-looking, heritage-based and fundamentally 'ethnic' vision of the nation. By contrast, today's nationalist leaders explicitly describe themselves as 'civic nationalists' rather than 'ethnic nationalists'. Some observers, including myself, would go further and describe them as 'multicultural nationalists':

- who not merely welcome new recruits to the nation as 'civic nationalists' might do, but go beyond that to welcome the diversity and cultural change that new recruits to the nation might bring with them; and
- who look to a developing and changing national culture rather than attempting to conserve a culture based on a single heritage.

There is some hard evidence to support this argument that nationalism has become less nationalist, and that it has moved on from an ethnic to a civic, or even to a multicultural vision of the nation.

SNP manifestos

Murray Leith has recently completed a comprehensive study of the changing content of SNP manifestos over the last thirty-five years. Using statistical content analysis he reached the conclusion that recent SNP manifestos are only 'half as nationalist' as they were three decades ago.[16]

A less statistical and more qualitative approach revealed a progressive change from an 'ethnic' vision of the nation in the 1970s to a more 'civic' vision later on. Also, from 1992 onwards, SNP manifestos put forward an explicitly 'multicultural' vision of the nation. The anti-English tone of earlier manifestos was eventually replaced by a less ethnic and more political attack on the Conservative Party for being anti-Scottish. The English themselves were no longer attacked as they had been in the 1970s (for taking student places at Scottish universities, for example) and negative statements about England or anglicisation 'almost disappeared'. Coded phrases like 'new Scots', 'new Scotland', even the more explicit 'multicultural society' crept in.[17] Furthermore, words were followed by deeds: the first Asian to sit in the Scottish Parliament was elected from the SNP list in 2007.

Street-level nationalism

'Internationalist nationalism' or 'multicultural nationalism' may be magnificent, but are they still nationalist? Leith goes on to speculate that SNP attempts to 'stretch the boundaries' of the nation have gone so far that they may 'alienate the Party's core support'. So does the 'multicultural nationalism' of the party elite reach down to the grass roots of the party and indeed further, to SNP voters? Research with Asifa Hussain shows that SNP voters are more Anglophobic than

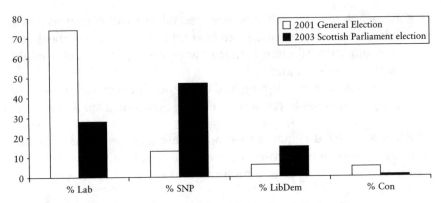

Source: Asifa Hussain and William Miller, *Multicultural Nationalism: Islamaphobia, Anglophobia and Devolution* (Oxford: Oxford University Press, 2006), p. 165.

Figure 11.6   Scottish Muslims switch to SNP

those of any other party. At street level there remains a correlation – fairly modest but indisputably detectable – between Anglophobia and SNP voting.

We also looked, however, at a range of other street-level phobias: about Europe; asylum-seekers; Catholics; and Muslims. On every one of these it was Scottish Conservative voters, not SNP voters, who displayed the highest levels of fear and prejudice. So with the single, though important, exception of attitudes towards the English, SNP voters seem more multicultural than Scottish Conservatives – or, in other words, nationalist voters are more inclusive and multicultural than Unionist Party voters.[18]

Corroboration

We also found corroborating evidence from the minorities themselves. For decades most ethnic minorities throughout Britain have tended to vote Labour, but after the invasion of Iraq Muslims switched away from Labour. That is not in the least surprising. What is remarkable, however, is not their departure point but their destination. At the 2003 Scottish Parliament election, Muslims switched overwhelmingly to the SNP. That a visible and cultural minority should switch their votes to the local nationalist party is a remarkable endorsement of the SNP's claim to have embraced a multicultural vision of the nation. That switch is far more significant for what it tells us about the nature of contemporary Scottish nationalism than for what it tells us about the voting preferences of Muslim voters.

The voting evidence is reinforced by evidence of national identity. English immigrants find it exceedingly difficult to identify with Scotland and typically identify with 'Britain' rather than Scotland even if they wish to downplay their English identity. But other minorities do not. In particular, Muslim Pakistanis identify strongly with Scotland rather than Britain – and do so irrespective of whether they were born in Scotland or not.[19]

CONCLUSIONS: NATIONALISM RAMPANT; UNIONISM DEAD?

All the evidence suggests that the decline in Scottish unionism and the rise in Scottish nationalism have not been driven by changing public sentiment so much as by changing party strategies. That is not to say that public sentiment is unimportant. Quite the reverse. Public sentiment has been powerful but relatively stable. The parties that aligned themselves more with that relatively stable public sentiment reaped a reward, while those that ignored, irritated or insulted that relatively stable public sentiment have been punished.

The Nationalist Party recovered popular support after its disastrously low point in 1979–83 by redefining nationalism to make it less separatist, less backward-looking, less extreme, less narrow, more inclusive, altogether less frightening, remarkably multicultural, and, in the eyes of seasoned observers like Andrew Marr, much less nationalist. However, inclusive 'multicultural nationalism' is an unlikely combination. The redefinition of nationalism that occurred in the early 1980s could be reversed. Nationalism could once again become more nationalist, narrow, separatist and exclusive. The liberal, genuinely multicultural, leadership could lose its influence over streetlevel nationalists, especially if the SNP victors in the 2007 Scottish Parliament election are at any stage removed from office by a coalition of their opponents. Students of nationalism tend to be sceptical and critical. Gellner, for example, sees 'nationalist sentiment' as at root 'a feeling of anger'; Breuilly argues that it is 'not often sweetly reasonable'; Vincent that it 'easily collapses into shallow expressions of blood, soil and xenophobia'; Pulzer that it 'is often inspired by the urge to emancipate . . . but degenerates . . . into its logical conclusion, a paroxysm of destructiveness'.[20] Brian Porter's study of nineteenth-century Polish nationalism is particularly chilling because it traces in great detail the development of a nationalism from an earlier inclusive and 'multicultural' phase to a later exclusive and 'ethnic' phase.[21] For the moment, however, and perhaps against the odds, Scotland has succeeded in becoming somewhat more nationalist and more inclusively multiculturalist at the same time, although only because nationalists have redefined nationalism.

Conversely, the Unionist Party lost public support in the 1970s when Thatcher redefined unionism in opposition to Scottish nationalism rather than recognising that unionism was an historic form of Scottish nationalism. That allowed its opponents to depict the party as foreign to Scotland and what was worse, unsympathetic to Scots and Scotland. Classic unionism, which combined a perhaps overly romantic respect for Scottish heritage with hard-headed commitment to Scottish national interests and pragmatic support for the Union was killed off by Thatcher. It might be possible to gradually erode contemporary perceptions of the Conservatives as an English party but that is far short of re-establishing its image as a party of the Scottish interest.

Now that Labour has abandoned centralist socialism it is at least as able as even the post-Thatcher Conservatives to combine commitment to the contemporary Scottish interest with pragmatic support for the Union. Labour has little respect for a specifically Scottish national heritage, but after its long experience of Thatcherism it is more committed than before to a specifically Scottish interest. So it now comes close to inheriting the role of classic unionism, disregarding Scottish tradition but none the less combining commitment to the strictly contemporary Scottish interest with pragmatic support for the Union. So, somewhat transformed, much (though not all) of the unionist spirit has survived the decline of the Unionist Party by migrating to the Labour Party.

The new unionism defined by Thatcher, and firmly based on British nationalism rather than Scottish nationalism might be fostered by the post-9/11 climate of a war on terror. Somewhat transformed, that too might migrate to the Labour Party, as the party holding power in government. The new Labour Prime Minister, Gordon Brown, is keen to push the idea of Britishness, not like Thatcher in contrast to Scottishness, but in contrast to the rest of the world. That could emphasise Britishness without irritating Scots as much as Thatcher, but possibly with increasingly exclusive overtones, or with an emphasis on assimilation into a British culture rather than integration into a developing multicultural society. It could, therefore, be much closer to the narrow heritage-based (albeit now a more clearly British heritage rather than a merely English heritage) nationalism so criticised by students of nationalism than to the new, open, inclusive and multicultural nationalism of the SNP. It is worth recalling that it was not SNP voters who were the most phobic towards Europe, asylum-seekers, Catholics and Muslims. Scottish nationalism has been redefined over the last few decades to become less nationalist. There is now a possibility that under the pressures of the war on terror, British unionism will be redefined to become more nationalist.

Notes

1 William L. Miller, *The End of British Politics? Scots and English Political Behaviour in the Seventies* (Oxford: Oxford University Press, 1981), pp. 65–6.
2 William L. Miller, Annis May Timpson and Michael Lessnoff, *Political Culture in Contemporary Britain: People and Politicians, Principles and Practice* (Oxford: Oxford University Press, 1996), *passim*, but especially pp. 364–73 and pp. 436–48.
3 Alice Brown, David McCrone and Lindsay Paterson, *Politics and Society in Scotland* (London: Macmillan, 1998), p. 165; Alice Brown, David McCrone, Lindsay Paterson and Paula Surridge, *The Scottish Electorate: The 1997 General Election and Beyond* (London: Macmillan, 1999), p. 112; Paula Surridge, Alice Brown, David McCrone and Lindsay Paterson, 'Scotland: constitutional preferences and voting behaviour', in Geoffrey Evans and Pippa Norris (eds), *Critical Elections: British Parties and Voters in Long-term Perspective* (London: Sage, 1999), p. 235; John Curtice, 'Brought together or driven apart?', in William L. Miller (ed.), *Anglo-Scottish Relations from 1900 to Devolution and Beyond* (Oxford: Oxford University Press for the British Academy, 2005), p. 162.
4 John Curtice, *Anglo-Scottish Relations from 1900 to Devolution and Beyond*, pp. 153–70.
5 Miller et al., *Political Culture in Contemporary Britain*, p. 370.
6 Brown et al., *Politics and Society in Scotland*, p. 11.
7 Linda Colley, *Britons: Forging the Nation, 1707–1837* (New Haven: Yale University Press, 1992).
8 Brown et al., *Politics and Society in Scotland*, p. 156.
9 Miller, *The End of British Politics?*, pp. 21–2.
10 *The Times*, 22 February 1975 accessed on www.margaretthatcher.org.
11 Miller, *The End of British Politics?*, p. 242.
12 Surridge et al., *Critical Elections*, p. 231.
13 Andrew Marr, *The Battle for Scotland* (London: Penguin, 1992), p. 192.
14 Brown et al., *Politics and Society in Scotland*, p. 162.

15 Richard J. Finlay, 'Scotland and the monarchy in the twentieth century', in William L. Miller (ed.), *Anglo-Scottish Relations from 1990 to Devolution and Beyond* (Oxford: Oxford University Press for the British Academy, 2005), p. 30.

16 Murray Leith, *Nationalism and National Identity in Scottish Politics* (Glasgow: Doctoral thesis in Glasgow University Library, 2006), ch. 3, s. 7.

17 Leith, Doctoral thesis, ch. 6.

18 Asifa Hussain and William Miller, *Multicultural Nationalism: Islamaphobia, Anglophobia and Devolution* (Oxford: Oxford University Press, 2006), p. 82.

19 Hussian and Miller, *Multicultural Nationalism*, p. 156.

20 Ernest Gellner, *Nations and Nationalism* (Oxford: Blackwell, 1994), pp. 1–2; John Brueilly, *Nationalism and the State* (Manchester: Manchester University Press, 1993), pp. 5–7; A. Vincent, 'Liberal nationalism: an irresponsible compound?', *Political Studies*, (1997), 45(2), p. 294; Peter Pulzer, *The Rise of Political Anti-Semitism in Germany and Austria* (Cambridge, MA: Harvard University Press, 1988), p. 287.

21 Brian A. Porter, *When Nationalism Began to Hate* (New York: Oxford University Press, 2000).

PART FOUR

DEVOLUTION AND THE FUTURE

12

WHERE STANDS THE UNION NOW? SCOTTISH–ENGLISH RELATIONS AFTER DEVOLUTION

Charlie Jeffery

INTRODUCTION

Devolution is both a response to problems of managing the Union of the four nations of the UK, and a challenge about the future character of that Union. It responded to perceived problems in Scotland, Wales and Northern Ireland surrounding the legitimacy of a political system concentrated on UK political institutions in Westminster and Whitehall and dominated by its largest component, England. The challenge it has unleashed was exemplified in the processes of government formation following the devolved elections of spring 2007: Scotland now has a government in Scotland run by a party, the Scottish National Party, which is committed to independence from the UK; the Northern Irish government is co-led by a party, Sinn Fein, committed to the unification of the island of Ireland; and Wales is now governed by a coalition of Labour with the nationalist Plaid Cymru which is committed to a referendum on further-reaching devolution for Wales.

These election outcomes suggest that the territorial configuration of political community in the UK remains contested. They also give the lie to claims made by some of the architects of Scottish devolution that the reforms reflected a 'settled will' (John Smith and Donald Dewar), or would 'kill nationalism stone dead' (George Robertson). More accurate was the telling phrase by the former Secretary of State for Wales, Ron Davies, that devolution was a 'process, not an event', not a one-off enactment of constitutional change, but rather a dynamic whose trajectory was open and whose endpoint was unclear. This chapter takes the Davies' view further, arguing that the way devolution was implemented has opened up, rather than 'settled' the scope for debate about political community in the UK, leaving the different purposes and the inter-relationships of structures of government representing different scales of political community at the devolved and UK levels in disequilibrium.

That open-endedness is especially clear in the relationship of the Scottish to a UK level of government which has interconnected UK-wide and England-specific roles. This chapter explores the institutional forms which connect Scottish and UK/English government, arguing that a piecemeal and loosely coordinated approach to enacting devolution has produced a post-devolution political system which lacks equilibrium and is vulnerable to territorial mobilisation on either side of the Anglo-Scottish border.

DEVOLUTION AS PIECEMEAL PROCESS

Devolution was very easy to introduce. It built on a long-standing tradition of differentiated territorial administration in the UK. Though the 'sovereign' Westminster Parliament has unusually far-reaching power, that power was not used (in contrast, say, to French unitarism) to create a territorially uniform state. Adapting the terminology of the 'union state',[1] Mitchell has dubbed the UK a 'state of unions' in which different terms of membership of the UK state were struck (re-struck in the case of Ireland/Northern Ireland) between a dominant England and the other nations at different times and in different political contexts.[2] The territorial arrangements for the administration of UK policy outside England reflected and embedded those different terms of membership. By 1997, those arrangements were carried out mainly through UK central government departments for Scotland, Wales and Northern Ireland, that is, the Scotland, Wales and Northern Ireland Offices. These were cabinet-level departments with a remit of policy implementation in their respective nations. There was no equivalent territorial department for England.

The devolution reforms built on the residual territorial non-uniformity of the 'state of unions'. What devolution has done is to transfer the different sets of territorial competences formerly exercised from within central government by the territorial departments to separate devolved governments established by new electoral processes. It has transformed a system of territorial *administration* indirectly accountable through UK elections, into one of territorial *politics* in which new Scottish, Welsh and Northern Irish democratic processes co-exist alongside that at UK level. These changes leave the UK central government responsible for a residual mix of UK-wide and England-specific functions, though the territorial departments live on in central government in modified and truncated guise as conduits for intergovernmental relations between UK and devolved political arenas.

Two significant consequences arise from projecting this tradition of differentiated territorial administration forward into the structure of devolution. The first is that devolution has been a piecemeal project. Different UK government departments introduced institutional reforms defined by the historical scope and purposes of territorial administration in each of the non-English nations. This means the reforms are asymmetrical. It also means, rather more importantly, that devolution has been a project of the parts, not the whole. There was limited coordination of reforms across government departments, next to no consideration of how reform in one part of the UK might have implications in any other part of the UK and negligible thought about the systemic properties of a post-devolution state, that is, the relationships between UK and devolved tiers of government, including mechanisms for resolving conflict or for agreeing and implementing common objectives.

The second consequence concerns the rump territory not affected by devolution reforms, that is, England. Unlike the devolved territories, England had no territory-specific institutional arrangements before devolution. England was, and remains, administered directly by functional departments of UK central government (health, education, transport, etc.) which mix (in largely unplanned and often unacknowledged ways) UK-wide and England-specific functions. No coordinated territorial system for governing England has emerged. The failure, beyond the Greater London Assembly (which has only modest responsibilities in policy coordination across the London city-region), to regionalise the government of England means that a centralised England will remain the preponderant part of a lopsided UK for the foreseeable future. The devolved nations together account for just 15 per cent the UK's population and gross domestic product and England the rest. Few other states have the same pattern – or, perhaps better, imbalance – in which the preponderant part is governed centrally while the peripheral parts have significant devolved powers.[3] That lopsidedness creates both challenges of coordination across jurisdictions and raises new questions about 'the English' and the representation of their interests in the post-devolution state.

PROBLEMS OF PIECEMEAL DEVOLUTION

No other such significant territorial constitutional reforms have been conceived and implemented in such a piecemeal way and with such little consideration of their state-wide implications as has devolution in the UK. There are five ways in which piecemeal devolution appears problematic:

1. Unmanaged divergence

First, it has a logic of unmanaged divergence, or what Greer has called a 'machinery' for territorial policy divergence.[4] The structure of devolution is unusually permissive of policy-making autonomy in each of the component parts of the UK. In Scotland (and Northern Ireland, with Wales headed in the same direction) devolution is based on the separation of devolved legislative powers from those of the UK Parliament. Within the framework of devolved powers there is in principle unlimited discretion, with no provision for the UK Parliament to require minimum standards or set framework conditions to achieve UK-wide objectives. That high degree of policy-making autonomy is underlined by a system of territorial finance which awards an unconditional block grant to the devolved administrations, again lacking any mechanisms for pursuing UK-wide objectives, and a system of intergovernmental relations which lacks structure and sanction (see further under point 4, below).

That permissiveness is amplified by the different dynamics of government formation produced by the distinctive party and electoral systems in operation outside England. In Scotland the classic left–right axis of party competition is supplemented by an additional axis of nationalism versus unionism. The presence of nationalist parties exerts a pull on the UK-wide parties (Labour, Conservative and Liberal Democrat), giving, say, Labour in the Scottish Parliament a different strategic landscape to negotiate than Labour in Westminster.[5] The broadly proportional electoral system in Scotland underlines the strategic pull away from UK-level party considerations by requiring greater degrees of cross-party cooperation in the coalition and minority government situations that Scotland has seen since 1999.

The outcome of this permissive institutional and political context is a growing degree of territorial policy variation. This is, of course, to an extent what devolution was for, to open up the prospect of distinctive policies better reflecting devolved preferences. Somewhere, however, there is a tipping point where the scope for autonomy begins to rub up against the content of common citizenship which membership of a union implies. There are, for example, periodic concerns in England about the different regimes for National Health Service prescription licensing and charging on either side of the Scottish and English border (with Scottish policy more generous), and the arrangements for charging tuition fees at universities in which Scottish residents studying at Scottish universities pay less than English residents who choose to study in Scotland (while, in order to comply with rules on *international* mobility across the EU, students from other EU member states share Scottish privileges denied to the English).

Two issues emerge from this, and both are examined further below: public opinion across the UK does not appear to endorse this institutional logic of policy divergence; and the piecemeal approach taken to devolution means there is no institutional structure capable of recognising and regulating the tension between the expression of distinctive devolved preferences and the realisation of common citizenship rights irrespective of location.

2. Displacing legitimacy problems

A second feature of piecemeal devolution is that of displacement of legitimacy problems. Because the devolution reforms were each introduced in a self-contained way to address a problem in one part of the UK, they were blind to the possibility that there might be spillover effects on other parts of the UK.[6] In Scotland devolution was introduced to restore for Scots the legitimacy of UK government – and it has done so. Devolution is consistently the leading constitutional preference of the Scots at 50 per cent-plus, the Scottish Parliament is much more trusted to act in Scottish interests than the Westminster Parliament, and Scots would rather see Westminster's influence in Scotland fall, and the Scottish Parliament's grow further.[7]

However, especially in the last year or so, there has emerged a growing sense in some parts of political, media and public opinion in England that Scottish devolution is unfair to the English, both in terms of the distribution of public spending and of political representation. Piecemeal devolution may in other words solve one problem, but end up creating another. For historical reasons not driven by measures of objective spending needs, there is significantly more public spending per head in Scotland than in England, although Scotland now comes in at fourth place (out of twelve) in the UK's regional economic league tables, behind only the booming regions of southeast England. For that reason there is now a groundswell of support across political parties and in public opinion for revisiting the terms of financing devolved spending.[8] The perception of unfairness in representation concerns the so-called West Lothian Question, that is, the capacity of Scottish Westminster MPs to vote on, say, health policy for England, while English MP's cannot on health policy in Scotland, because health policy there is a devolved responsibility beyond Westminster's remit. One proposed remedy – which is the policy of the Conservative Party – is to exclude Scottish MPs from voting on England-only business at Westminster. Whether this would be a workable solution is unclear; and in any case it might end up creating further grievances by establishing Scots as 'second class' members of the UK Parliament.[9] Adding piecemeal reform on to piecemeal reform is unlikely to be a recipe for equilibrium.

3. The English problem

The third and perhaps biggest problem of piecemeal devolution is the 85 per cent rump of England. England is governed by central institutions in Westminster and Whitehall which combine and at times confuse England-only and UK-wide roles. Within the framework of a UK single economic market, a single welfare state and a single security area it is inevitable that decisions taken for the preponderant part of those single areas will have impacts outside of England. A striking example emerged during the 2005 UK election campaign, when healthcare performance indicators designed for England shaped the election debate in Scotland and Wales, even though they are issues of devolved competence and beyond the remit of UK-level politics. Another concerns policies on immigration in Scotland. The Scottish government is committed to an immigration policy to counter population decline, but is dependent on a UK government reluctant to allow territorial flexibility to a UK immigration policy increasingly understood in policy debates in England as a matter of internal security not population replacement.

Many of these English spillovers are inadvertent, reflecting the preoccupations of UK government departments with England as 'core business' and an inadequate mainstreaming of devolution sensitivity in civil service training programmes. Some also reflect the UK-wide agenda-setting capacity of a highly centralised media industry whose main focus is on Westminster politics (which explains how English healthcare indicators went out-of-area to Scotland and Wales in

2005). At times, though, 'Anglo-UK' has more wilfully acted against devolved interests, normally when early sight of a policy initiative of the UK Labour government which had implications for Scotland fell into an area for which the Liberal Democrats provided the responsible minister in the 1999–2007 Labour–Liberal coalitions in Scotland.[10] In the latter circumstances the instincts of adversarial politics at Westminster (not sharing information with a Westminster opposition party) collided with the need for coordination across levels of government (which may require cross-party coordination). Needless to say this was not a promising foundation for cooperation between the UK Labour government and the SNP minority government elected in Scotland in May 2007 and a number of disputes have resulted.

4. The UK's borderless public opinion

The fourth problem of piecemeal devolution is that it superimposes political borders on what, in large part, is a borderless public opinion across the UK. With few exceptions there are at best marginal differences in the values that the Scots and the English (or, for that matter the Welsh and Northern Irish) hold on the role of the state or the balance of market and state, or on preferences on some of the headline issues which have seen territorial policy variation since devolution like free personal care for the elderly or tuition fees (Table 12.1). Also, confirming anecdotal concern about 'post-code lotteries' in the provision of public services, most people across the UK appear to dislike the idea that policy standards might diverge from place to place as a result of devolution.[11] To put this another way: devolution in Scotland (or Wales or Northern Ireland) did not reflect public demand for a different policy agenda than that favoured by the English; it was much more a demand for proximity and ownership of decision making, a sense that Westminster was too remote and unresponsive.

There might appear to be a contradiction here between a preference for uniform policy standards and a demand for 'proximate' devolved government which, logically, is likely to produce diversity of policy standards. That contradiction is not unusual. It plays out in other states which have tiers of regional government and is often described as balancing uniformity and diversity. The difference is that those other places have well-established techniques of intergovernmental coordination which maintain that balance.

Table 12.1 Policy attitudes in Scotland and England

	1999 (%)	2000 (%)	2001 (%)	2002 (%)	2003 (%)
(1) *Benefits for the unemployed are too low and cause hardship*					
Scotland	36	43	41	41	45
England	32	40	34	28	36
(2) *Increase taxes and spend more on health, education and social benefits*					
Scotland	55	54	63	60	58
England	58	51	60	61	51
(3) *Ordinary working people do not get their fair share of the nation's wealth*					
Scotland	58	71	61	64	54
England	60	61	58	61	60
(4) *No students or their families should pay towards the cost of their tuition fees while studying*					
Scotland	–	38	31	–	29
England	–	30	33	–	28
(5) *Government should be mainly responsible for paying for the care needs of elderly people living in residential and nursing homes*					
Scotland	86	–	88	–	88
England	80	–	86	–	84
(6) *All children should go to the same kind of secondary school, no matter how well or badly they do at primary school*					
Scotland	63	–	63	–	65
England	49	–	51	–	48

Source: Charlie Jeffery, 'Devolution and social citizenship. Which society, whose society?', in Scott Greer (ed.), *Territory, Democracy and Justice* (London: Palgrave Macmillan, 2006), pp. 67–91.

5. Weak intergovernmental co-ordination

The UK has, at best, an underdeveloped approach to intergovernmental coordination. Though special mechanisms were set up to coordinate the work of UK and devolved governments – 'concordats' setting out everyday rules of the game for coordination, and a Joint Ministerial Committee (JMC) for developing coordinated policy initiatives and resolving disagreements – they have been barely used. There is little strategic policy discussion at senior official or ministerial levels in which the balance of UK-wide and devolved objectives in, say, health policy or transport, is problematised. Asymmetrical devolution also encourages bilateral rather than multilateral (that is, UK-wide) discussion of policy ideas and objectives. Intergovernmental relations have so far worked mainly through informal linkages among officials with related functions in devolved and UK administrations. However, these discussions are not transparent, their subject matter and impact unclear, and their content unaccountable to either UK-level or devolved democratic processes. They depend on personal working relationships, which need to be re-invented as officials move on.

In large part this understated and fragile practice of intergovernmental relations reflects the pre-history of devolution and, like the wider pattern of piecemeal devolution, the decision to project forward pre-devolution practices into the post-devolution era. Before 1999 Scottish concerns were coordinated with English/UK-level concerns in largely informal processes of discussion between departments of central government. That *intra*governmental practice of informal territorial accommodation has been projected forward into an *inter*governmental practice for the post-devolution era with minimal adaptation, and within a framework of collegiality provided by a common home (that is, British, covering England, Scotland and Wales) civil service. That tradition of 'home' collegiality, while appropriate for the pre-devolution era of territorial *administration*, appears problematic in the new context of territorial *politics*. Already in 2003 one of the most insightful observers of the civil service, Richard Parry, identified signs that once elections produced different government formations in different places, traditional commitments to collegiality and informality would be insufficient to contain intergovernmental dispute between, say, the Scottish and UK governments.[11] Others – including the only official inquiry into devolution so far by the House of Lords Constitution Committee[12] – have come to similar conclusions arguing that a more fully institutionalised approach to intergovernmental coordination would be necessary to contain future conflicts.[13] Strikingly, one of the first demands of the new nationalist government elected in Scotland in May 2007 was to convene the JMC as a regular forum for intergovernmental exchange. Devolution commentators pursued the same line, trundling out their favoured institutional mechanisms for coordinating UK and devolved interests.[14]

THE UK AS (PART-)DEVOLVED STATE: WHAT'S IT ALL FOR?

It is not clear, though, that simple institutional tinkering will address the problems that the UK's haphazard and incomplete approach to the territorial dimension of constitutional change has opened up. What the devolution reforms have lacked is a conscious attempt to rethink the relationships between political community at the scale of the UK state and political community in Scotland, or Wales, or Northern Ireland. It is clear enough why varying degrees of autonomy have been devolved to Scotland, Wales and Northern Ireland – to re-legitimise the UK system of government, to give better voice to peripheral identities, to provide an institutional framework for the peace process in Northern Ireland, and so on. There has, however, been no systematic articulation of what the UK as a whole in its post-devolution format is for, what the role of the centre should be, how it now relates to the devolved territories, how the parts now add up to make a whole.

Hazell and O'Leary set out a clear prescription on the launch of devolution in 1999:

> The trick will be to identify and understand what items need to be held in common throughout the kingdom as constants of UK citizenship; and what items can be allowed to vary . . .
>
> This . . . is a matter on which the Government needs to give a lead, in its actions and in its words, to bind the Union together in order to counterbalance the centrifugal political forces of devolution. The Government needs to understand and allow political space to those forces, and the regional and national loyalties that underpin them; but it also needs to understand and articulate clearly a sense of the wider loyalties which bind us together at the level of the nation state.[15]

Attempts to meet these challenges, to offer new visions of what the Union is for, what the division of labour of the post-devolution UK institutions and those of the devolved nations should be, have been at best thin and half-hearted. Tony Blair rarely spoke about devolution after its introduction in 1999, and never in any depth. Only Gordon Brown, Blair's Chancellor and then successor as Prime Minister has shown a sustained interest in devolution in a series of speeches on 'Britishness'. In part these have been interpreted as an opportunistic attempt to reaffirm his credentials as a Scot to be UK Prime Minister in the post-devolution state. In part they have grappled with the issue Brown himself set out, in his 1981 doctoral thesis, of how to reconcile statewide and devolved interests after devolution:

> No theorist attempted in sufficient depth to reconcile the conflicting aspirations for home rule and a British socialist advance. In particular no one was able to show how capturing power in Britain – and legislating for minimum levels of welfare, for example, could be combined with a policy of devolution for Scotland.[16]

By 1999 Brown claimed to have the answer by emphasising how core components of the post-war welfare state in health, education and labour market policy remained 'British', or as Hazell and O'Leary put it, 'items held in common' despite devolution:

> Today when people talk about the National Health Service whether in Scotland, Wales or England people think of the British National Health Service . . . And its most powerful driving idea is that every citizen of Britain has an equal right to treatment regardless of wealth, position or race and, indeed, can secure treatment in any part of Britain . . . When we pool and share our resources and when the stronger help the weak it makes us all stronger . . . I believe that the common bonds and mutual interests linking our destinies together is as real for other public services: the ideal that every child in Britain should have an equal opportunity in education. And the equally strong belief, widely felt throughout the country, that everyone in Britain who can work has the right and responsibility to do so. When Scots, English or Welsh talk of the right to work, they do not normally distinguish between the rights of the Scottish, Welsh or English miner, computer technician, nurse or teacher.[17]

Brown's claims about the strength of common, Britain-wide beliefs are, as was noted above in the discussion of the UK's borderless public opinion, in large part well-founded. The problem is that the realities of educational opportunity, labour markets and health care provision increasingly do not match the Britain-wide reach of those beliefs, but, as a marker of the unmanaged divergence of post-devolution policy-making, instead vary significantly by national territory. In Scotland, for example, there is less selection in secondary education than in

England, teachers are paid more and health care is delivered differently. Though some of these differences pre-date devolution, they have grown significantly since. As Greer concludes from his study of divergence in health policy across the four nations, devolution has 'already had an impact on the meaning and rights associated with citizenship in the UK'.[18]

The failure of Brown to acknowledge the contradiction between his arguments about the benefits of sharing welfare risk on a UK-wide scale and the erosion in practice of UK-wide commonalities is striking. It is indicative of a mindset in UK central government which remains curiously unchanged since and by devolution. That mindset sees devolution as a minor tweak to the UK constitution. It has been facilitated by the institutional continuities of the devolution reforms, the piecemeal approach to those reforms which have fragmented any sense of a 'bigger picture' of reform across the UK and the preponderance of England, where, in fact, nothing much has changed, in the business of Westminster and Whitehall. Put simply the institutions of the UK centre have not (yet had to) adapt much of what they do because of a devolution process confined to the UK periphery. The institutional expression of political community at a UK scale remains largely uncoupled from the institutional expressions of political community at the devolved scale. UK and devolved politics talk past one another.

The contrast with other regional and federal states is instructive. Over the last thirty years there have been extensive reforms to regional institutional structures in Belgium, Spain and Italy. There have also been protracted debates (though limited actual reforms) on the institutional configuration of federalism in Canada, Germany, Austria and Switzerland. These debates on the formal institutional structures of the state have generally had a wider social resonance. They have been conducted more or less transparently in formal institutions and/or set-piece negotiations involving central state and regional actors, and accompanied by wide debate in national and regional media. They have articulated tensions between competing judgements about what is right and just in the balance of meeting state-wide objectives and territorial claims to distinctiveness and autonomy, in the balance of state-wide and regional political community. In Germany strong decentralist pressures from the wealthy south have challenged, though not (yet) transformed the legacy of post-war commitments to state-wide 'uniformity of living conditions'. In Canada and Belgium centrifugal pressures based in distinctive identity (Quebec, Flanders) and declining inter-regional solidarity (Alberta, Flanders) have opened up scope for the pursuit of narrow territorial objectives, but are still bound by enduring state-wide commitments to Canadian 'social union' and a Belgium-wide understanding of social security. In Italy, Austria and Switzerland themes of autonomy, identity and desolidarisation have also played into debates on rebalancing the central state and the component units.

The UK has had no general forum for the discussion of constitutional reform (although Scotland had a territory-specific forum in the Scottish Constitutional Convention). There has been no sustained discussion of the structures and implications of devolution in UK-wide media (although plenty of such discussion in the Scotland-specific media outlets). There has been no general articulation of the balance of state-wide (and within that English) political community and the political communities that exist within the UK outside of England. As a result devolution lacks generally understood, generally accepted rules of the game which might mark out the limits of policy divergence, offer a general rather than piecemeal framework for addressing the legitimacy problems claimed by different territorial communities in the UK, conceptualise the government of England and connect it to government outside of England, manage the contradictory impulses of public opinion and inform a framework of intergovernmental relations capable of identifying state-wide objectives and balancing them against devolved autonomy.

The absence of a general debate on the rules of the game needed to make sense of and underpin the institutional reforms passed so quickly in 1997–9 marks out the devolution process as incomplete and unstable. The post-devolution constitution remains hobbled by the path dependencies of pre-devolution administrative arrangements and, in all likelihood, ill-equipped to express and contain the new dynamics of territorial politics that devolution has begun to set in motion. That those dynamics have been contained so far is a result of a transitional party political congruence: the fact that Labour led the governments in Westminster and in Edinburgh (and Cardiff) from the launch of devolution in 1999 through to 2007. Where there were overt differences of interest and priority between UK and Scottish governments – arising from the impact of cross-party cooperation and/or the competitive pull of nationalism, or unintended or deliberate spillovers from Anglo-UK – they could be finessed within the Labour Party family. The election of a nationalist government in

Scotland in 2007 takes the territorial dynamics out of 'family' politics and brings a mutually reinforcing partisan and territorial cleavage into UK–Scottish relations. At the same time a new focus in Conservative opinion on articulating English dissatisfactions with Scotland's place in the post-devolution state may deepen that territorial cleavage. The prospect of a Conservative UK government ranged alongside a nationalist Scottish government after the next UK election in 2010/11 is not improbable. As we move away from pan-British Labour hegemony the robustness of a post-devolution constitution in which institutional reform has not been accompanied by a more general rethinking of the purposes and balances of a Union that brings together different scales of political community will be sorely tested.

Notes

1 Stein Rokkan and Derek Urwin, *The Politics of Territorial Identity* (London: Sage, 1982).

2 James Mitchell, 'Evolution and devolution. Citizenship, institutions and public policy', *Publius. The Journal of Federalism*, (2006), 36:1, pp. 153–68.

3 Ronald L. Watts, 'The United Kingdom as a federalised or regionalised union', in Alan Trench (ed.), *Devolution and Power* (Manchester: Manchester University Press, 2007.

4 Scott Greer, 'The fragile divergence machine: citizenship, policy divergence and devolution', in Alan Trench (ed.), *Devolution and Power* (Manchester: Manchester University Press, 2007.

5 See, for example, Jonathan Hopkin and Jonathan Bradbury, 'British statewide parties and multi-level politics', *Publius. The Journal of Federalism*, (2006), 36:1, pp. 135–52.

6 James Mitchell, 'Devolution's unfinished business', *Political Quarterly*, (2006), 77:4, pp. 465–74.

7 Alison Park and David McCrone, 'The devolution conundrum', in C. Bromley et al. (eds), *Has Devolution Delivered?* (Edinburgh: Edinburgh University Press, 2006), pp. 15–28.

8 Charlie Jeffery and Drew Scott, *Scotland's Economy: The Fiscal Debate* (Edinburgh: Scottish Council for Development and Industry, 2007).

9 Robert Hazell, 'The English question', *Publius. The Journal of Federalism*, (2006), 36:1, pp. 37–56.

10 See, for example, Michael Aron, *EU Business: Reviews of Engagement with Europe and of EU Office*, internal memorandum of the Scottish Executive, 2007.

11 Richard Parry, 'The Home Service after Devolution', *The Devolution Policy Papers*, No. 6. http://www.devolution.ac.uk/Policy_Papers.htm.

12 House of Lords Select Committee on the Constitution Session 2002–03, 2nd Report, *Devolution: Inter-Institutional Relations in the United Kingdom*, HL Paper 28 (London: The Stationery Office, 2002).

13 Alan Trench, 'Intergovernmental relations a year On', in Robert Hazell (ed.), *The State of the Nations 2001. The Second Year of Devolution in the United Kingdom* (Thorverton: Imprint Academic, 2001), pp. 153–74: Robert Hazell, 'Conclusion. The devolution scorecard as the devolved assemblies head for the polls', in Robert Hazell (ed.), *The State of the Nations 2003. The Third Year of Devolution in the United Kingdom* (Thorverton: Imprint Academic, 2003), pp. 285–302: Charlie Jeffery, 'Devolution and social citizenship. Which society, whose citizenship?', in Scott Greer (ed.), *Territory, Democracy and Justice* (London: Palgrave Macmillan, 2006), pp. 67–91.

14 Alan Trench, 'We need joined-up "Intergovernment"', *The Scotsman*, 22 June 2007: Katie Schmuecher, 'How will we cope with the battle of Britain to come?', *The Herald*, 8 May 2007.

15 Robert Hazell and Brendon O'Leary, 'A rolling programme of devolution: slippery slope of safeguard of the Union', in Robert Hazell (ed.), *Constitutional Futures. A History of the Next Ten Years* (Oxford: Oxford University Press, 1999), pp. 21–46.

16 Gordon Brown, *The Labour Party and Political Change in Scotland 1918–1929: The Politics of Five Elections*, PhD dissertation, University of Edinburgh, 1981, p. 527, cited in James Mitchell, 'Evolution and devolution. Citizenship, institutions and public policy', *Publius. The Journal of Federalism*, (2006), 36.1, p. 163.

17 Gordon Brown, speech at the Smith Institute, 15 April 1999.

18 Scott Greer, 'The fragile divergence machine: citizenship, policy divergence and devolution', in Alan Trench (ed.), *Devolution and Power* (Manchester: Manchester University Press, 2007.

13

HOW FIRM ARE THE FOUNDATIONS? PUBLIC ATTITUDES TO THE UNION IN 2007

John Curtice

INTRODUCTION

For many of its advocates devolution was supposed to strengthen the Union.[1] By showing that the United Kingdom could accommodate the distinctive needs and wishes of Scotland, it was hoped that Scots would be persuaded that they could pursue their aspirations and secure political recognition of their distinctive national identity within the framework of the Union. Yet on 3 May 2007, just eight years after the creation of the devolved Scottish Parliament, the Scottish National Party (SNP), the principal advocates of Scottish independence, topped the poll and its leader, Alex Salmond, was elected the country's First Minister. It would seem that the most crucial foundation of the Union of all – public support – is now close to collapse.

This chapter considers whether the SNP's 'victory' in May 2007 does, indeed, indicate that the introduction of devolution has served to undermine public support for the Union in Scotland. We begin by looking at trends in national identity. Ultimately, for many nationalists the key reason why Scotland should be independent is that it is a distinct nation whose people have a distinct sense of identity, and this should be recognised in the form of independent statehood.[2] At the same time, however, the United Kingdom is a multinational state that has developed a state-wide identity, Britishness, a sentiment that might be expected to underpin a wish to maintain the British state, and thus the Union. However, given that the devolved institutions themselves give expression to Scotland's distinctive national identity, perhaps their creation has served to reinforce that distinctive identity at the expense of any sentiment of Britishness.[3] Which of these perspectives is correct is the first question that we address.

Still, it is perfectly possible for someone to feel Scottish without wanting this identity to be expressed by independent political institutions.[4] Moreover, the debate about independence is not simply about how Scotland's sense of nationhood should be recognised. It is also about whether membership of the Union or going it alone would best serve Scotland's economic, strategic and cultural interests.[5] So even if the pattern of national identity has changed little since devolution, perhaps the balance of opinion on the practical consequences has changed, thereby resulting in increasing support for independence. Perhaps, for example, devolution is thought not to have delivered what it was hoped it would achieve, with the result that more people have come to doubt the wisdom of remaining in the Union. So our second task is to look at trends in constitutional preferences in recent years, and how these might have been affected by perceptions of the effectiveness of devolution.

It would of course, be simplistic to presume that public opinion about the Union can simply be divided into support for or opposition to the Union. After all, the many years of debate about devolution prior to its introduction in 1999 were about the form that Scotland's membership of the Union should take. Perhaps that debate has not ended. After all, a commission chaired by the first Presiding Officer of the Scottish Parliament, Sir David Steel, put forward proposals for amending the devolution settlement, principally by strengthening the powers of the devolved institutions.[6] Indeed, in initiating a 'national conversation' about the country's constitutional future the newly installed SNP administration in Edinburgh recognised that Scots might prefer to do down the path of increased powers for a devolved parliament rather than embark on the journey towards independence.[7] So, even if we were to conclude that people in Scotland still want to remain part of the Union, this does not mean that there are not pressures for constitutional change, pressures that certainly might help to put the Union under strain. Thus, the third and final question that we consider is how far there are such pressures.

Our evidence comes primarily from the Scottish Social Attitudes (SSA) survey. Inaugurated in 1999 as the devolved institutions came into being, the survey aims to provide high quality data on public attitudes north of the Border with a view both to informing the development of public policy and the academic study of public opinion.[8] Conducted annually among a representative sample of around 1,500 adults aged eighteen plus, it has closely charted how public attitudes towards devolution and the country's constitutional status have developed over the first eight years of devolution. Moreover, at the time of writing we have access to initial provisional data from the 2007 survey, which was conducted in the weeks after the May 2007 election.[9] The SSA series, therefore, provides us with a unique body of evidence with which to examine whether public support for the Union has been eroded since the advent of devolution.[10]

NATIONAL IDENTITY

So, to which identity do most people in Scotland adhere? Table 13.1 shows one answer. It shows the proportions who, when forced to choose just one national identity out of an array of possible identities including Scottish, British, English and European, pick either Scottish or British, the only two options chosen by more than a handful of respondents. Moreover, because this question was asked on surveys as long ago as 1974, when the SNP first came to political prominence, we can compare recent trends in national identity with those over a much longer time period.

Clearly, of the two identities, feeling Scottish has long been the more popular throughout the last thirty years. Moreover, there is no evidence of a consistent trend in one direction or the other since the advent of devolution. In the 1997 survey, conducted in the period between the general election held in May 1997 and the devolution referendum the following September, 72 per cent said that they were Scottish, while 20 per cent said they regarded themselves primarily as British. The figures for the most recent survey, 2007, conducted in the weeks after the Scottish election, are almost identical at 71 per cent and 20 per cent, respectively. While in the intervening period the proportion saying they are Scottish has often been somewhat higher, and the proportion claiming to be British correspondingly lower, there has not been a consistent secular trend.

On the other hand, it does appear as though Scots' commitment to a British identity was seriously eroded during the years of Conservative government at Westminster from 1979 onwards. On no occasion from 1992 onwards has the proportion claiming to be British approached anything close to the 30–40 per cent range observed in both 1974 and 1979. So while devolution itself may not, so far at least, have eroded the sense of British identity north of the border, the debate about devolution in the 1980s and 1990s was accompanied by a marked change in Scots' sense of national identity. As a result by the time that the devolved institutions were in place the sense of identity that might have been thought to

Table 13.1 Trends in forced choice national identity

	1974 (%)	1979 (%)	1992 (%)	1997 (%)	1999 (%)	2000 (%)	2001 (%)	2002 (%)	2003 (%)	2004 (%)	2005 (%)	2006 (%)	2007 (%)
Scottish	65	56	72	72	77	80	77	75	72	75	79	78	71
British	31	38	25	20	17	13	16	18	20	19	14	14	20

Source: Scottish Election Studies 1974–97; Scottish Social Attitudes Survey, 1999–2007. Data for 2007 are provisional.

have provided a source of affective attachment to the Union already appeared rather weak. Perhaps in this respect at least the foundations of public support for the Union have long been beyond repair.

However, this analysis makes one important but key assumption: that people in Scotland can only feel either Scottish or British. Yet perhaps these are not regarded as 'exclusive' identities? Maybe people feel both? As an identity that is supposed to embody Scottishness as well as being English, Welsh, or someone from Ulster, perhaps being British is simply regarded as an extension, albeit perhaps a subsidiary one, of feeling Scottish. In any event, one line of questioning that allows for this possibility is the so called Moreno question.[11] Rather than forcing people to chose one identity, survey respondents are invited to chose one of five options, as detailed in Table 13.2, that between them enable people to say either that they are exclusively Scottish or British or, alternatively, some mixture of the two.

As the table reveals, many a Scot feels both Scottish and British. In 1992, around three-quarters (76 per cent) said that they were some mixture of Scottish and British. In the most recent survey, again around three-quarters (73 per cent) did so. True, in every year (apart from 2007 as it happens) more than half of this group said that feeling Scottish meant more to them to feeling British, thereby confirming the impression that British national identity is often subsidiary to people's sense of Scottishness. Equally, however, only a minority of around a third of Scots feel Scottish to the exclusion of some sense of being British. Moreover, there certainly is not any evidence that that minority has been growing since the advent of devolution.

So if, indeed, public support for the Union rests on the pedestal of adherence to a British national identity, the foundations of that support certainly do not appear strong. A majority of Scots may feel some sense of British identity, but for most it plays second fiddle to their sense of Scottish identity. Moreover, while the introduction of devolution has evidently not instigated any decline in British national identity, that identity is clearly weaker now in Scotland than when the constitutional debate first acquired prominence in the 1970s.

But how far does support for the Union depend on someone's sense of national identity? In part it clearly does. Among those who when, forced to choose, said in 2006 that they were British just 10 per

Table 13.2 Trends in Moreno national identity

	1992 (%)	1997 (%)	1999 (%)	2000 (%)	2001 (%)	2003 (%)	2005 (%)	2006 (%)	2007 (%)
Scottish not British	19	23	32	37	36	31	32	33	26
More Scottish than British	40	38	35	31	30	34	32	32	30
Equally Scottish and British	33	27	22	21	24	22	22	21	28
More British than Scottish	3	4	3	3	3	4	4	4	5
British not Scottish	3	4	4	4	3	4	5	5	6

Source: Scottish Election Studies, 1992, 1997; Scottish Social Attitudes Survey, 1999–2007. Data for 2007 are provisional.

cent indicated that they supported some form of independence for Scotland. In contrast as many as 35 per cent of those who said they were Scottish gave that response. Nevertheless, this, of course, means that even among those who say they are Scottish a clear majority would prefer to stay in the Union. Indeed, even if we confine our attention to those who say they are Scottish and not British, a little under half (45 per cent) indicate support for independence. So perhaps the weakness of British national identity north of the Border need not be a fatal blow to public support for the Union. We evidently need to look directly at Scots' constitutional preferences and how they might have been affected by devolution.

CONSTITUTIONAL PREFERENCES

Table 13.3 shows how over the last decade people in Scotland have responded when asked to choose between one of five options for their country's constitutional future. The first two of these options are independence outside the European Union and inside it; those giving one of these two answers have been combined into a single row in the table. The second pair of responses comprises support for having an elected Scottish Parliament within the UK, either with or without taxation powers. The final option is remaining within the UK without any kind of elected parliament for Scotland.

As measured by this line of questioning independence always has been, and still remains, a minority passion. Over the last ten years typically only around three in ten Scots have said that they would prefer Scotland to be independent. The most popular option has consistently been some form of devolution within the framework of the United Kingdom. Moreover, there is not any sign of a trend over time, gradual or otherwise, towards greater support for independence. While there was some indication in 2005 that this might be happening, with support reaching 35 per cent, the independence tide has subsequently ebbed again. Indeed, despite the SNP's success in the 2007 election, the initial survey reading for that year suggests that support for independence is now actually lower than it has been at any time in the last decade.

That last result might seem too paradoxical to be credible. Indeed, it certainly has to be borne in mind that the answers obtained by surveys of people's views about independence depend heavily on how the question is phrased. In particular, more Scots will say they are in favour of independence if simply asked to say whether they support

Table 13.3 Trends in constitutional preferences, 1997–2007

	May 1997 (%)	Sept 1997 (%)	1999 (%)	2000 (%)	2001 (%)	2002 (%)	2003 (%)	2004 (%)	2005 (%)	2006 (%)	2007 (%)
Scotland should –											
Be independent, separate from UK and EU or separate from UK but be part of EU	28	37	28	30	27	30	26	32	35	30	23
Remain part of UK with its own elected Parliament which has some taxation powers	44	32	50	47	54	44	48	40	38	47	55
Remain part of the UK with its own elected Parliament which has no taxation powers	10	9	8	8	6	8	7	5	6	7	8
Remain part of the UK without an elected Parliament	18	17	10	12	9	12	13	17	14	9	10

The two independence options, one where Scotland remains within the European Union (EU), and one that it does not, were offered to respondents separately. The first row of the table shows the combined total choosing either option.
Source: Scottish Election Study 1997; Scottish Referendum Study 1997; Scottish Social Attitudes Survey, 1999–2007. Data for 2007 are provisional.

Table 13.4 Whose economy benefits most from the Union, 2000–7?

	2000	2001	2003	2005	2007
England	43	38	30	36	26
Equal	36	39	40	34	39
Scotland	16	18	24	21	27

Source: Scottish Social Attitudes, 2000–7. Data for 2007 are provisional.

or oppose independence rather than if they are asked to choose between a variety of options, and especially so if those options lay any stress on the fact that independence means Scotland being 'separate' from the rest of the UK.[12] However, while this pattern suggests a need for caution in claiming that any particular proportion of people in Scotland back independence, it also suggests that the meaning of the term is not necessarily as clear in the public mind as advocates (or indeed opponents) of independence are inclined to assume. In any event, one of the striking features of the opinion polls that were taken during the 2007 election campaign is that, irrespective of the phrasing of the question they asked, in every case support for independence fell.[13] So the decline in support for independence between 2006 and 2007 recorded in Table 13.2 is, in fact, consistent with many another survey findings.

Why might support for independence have not increased and perhaps if anything fallen back most recently? Table 13.4 provides us with one possibly important clue. Just a year after the creation of the Scottish Parliament, over twice as many people felt that England's economy benefited the more 'from having Scotland in the UK' as believed that Scotland did. Now, in the most recent survey, the proportion that feels that Scotland benefits the more is much the same as the proportion that feels that England does. This change seems to suggest that the arguments sometimes used by SNP politicians and others that Scotland loses out economically from the Union and would be better off as an independent country have become less convincing in the eyes of the public in recent years.

Indeed, this conclusion is bolstered by the answers to a question on whether people in Scotland feel they do or do not get a fair share of government spending across the UK (see Table 13.5). Although identifiable public spending per head has long been higher in Scotland than in England, the creation of the Scottish Parliament has resulted in much greater media discussion and commentary about whether

Table 13.5 Perceptions of fairness of government spending, 2000–7

	2000 (%)	2001 (%)	2003 (%)	2007 (%)
Compared with other parts of the UK, Scotland's share of government spending is –				
Much more than fair	2	2	3	3
Little more than fair	8	8	8	14
Pretty much fair	27	36	35	39
Little less than fair	35	32	35	25
Much less than fair	23	15	13	10

Source: Scottish Social Attitudes, 2000–7. Data for 2007 are provisional.

Table 13.6 Perceived impact of Scottish Parliament on Scotland's voice in the Union

	2000	2001	2002	2003	2004	2005	2006
Made voice stronger	52	52	39	49	35	41	43
No difference	40	40	52	41	55	50	49
Made voice weaker	6	6	7	7	7	6	6

Source: Scottish Social Attitudes, 1999–2006.

this discrepancy is fair. For some commentators at least it was one thing for Scotland to enjoy higher public spending when English MPs had some say in how that money was spent, but quite another for it to do so when English MPs no longer have any say in how Scotland's schools and hospitals are run. It seems as though this debate has had some impact on public opinion north of the Border. True, in the most recent survey only 17 per cent believe that Scotland gets more than its fair share of government spending, whereas twice as many (35 per cent) feel it gets less than its fair share. However, these figures compare with 10 per cent and 58 per cent in the early days of devolution in 2000. Again, it seems that Scots are less likely to feel that they are losing out from the Union.

Meanwhile, Table 13.6 suggests a further possible reason why support for independence has at most been steady since the creation of the Holyrood parliament. Around two in five people in Scotland are of the view that creating the Scottish Parliament has strengthened Scotland's voice in the UK. Little more than one in twenty reckon that it has weakened that voice. True, the proportion that feels that Scotland's voice has been made stronger has been smaller in recent years than it was in the immediate wake of the creation of the Parliament. But perhaps a judgement made after some years is of greater import than one made in the immediate wake of the excitement of the Parliament's early days. In any event, it appears that the advent of devolution has persistently been seen as a development that has strengthened Scotland's position within the Union, and thus may have helped to persuade some people of the merits of Scotland's continuing membership.

Indeed, devolution is more likely to be regarded as having had a favourable rather than an unfavourable impact on a number of measures.[14] Thus, in 2006 37 per cent said that having the Parliament gave ordinary people more say in how the country is governed, while only 5 per cent said less. Equally, 30 per cent reckoned that devolution had helped improve the standard of education in Scotland while only 6 per cent reckoned it had helped to make standards worse. Also, while just 22 per cent said that the creation of the devolved institutions had resulted in improvements in the health service, this was still higher than the 9 per cent who said that it had made them worse.

So despite the relatively weak and low levels of adherence to a British national identity, there still appears to a considerable level of commitment to staying within the Union. The perceived record of devolution's achievements certainly appears to have been good enough not to drive people to the conclusion that independence is necessarily the only solution to achieving the country's aspirations, while the experience of many years of economic growth (albeit growth not necessarily at the same pace as in some parts of England) may well have helped persuade Scots that they are no longer losing out economically from the Union after all. However, this still does not necessarily mean that there are not potential pressures on the current shape of the Union.

THE PRESSURE FOR CHANGE

Although in many respects Scots are inclined to regard the impact of devolution favourably (or at least are disinclined to do so unfavourably), this does not necessarily mean that devolution has lived up their expectations. While a majority may not want independence, a clear majority do feel that Holyrood, not Westminster,

Table 13.7 Who ought to have most influence over the way Scotland is run, 1999–2006?

	2000 (%)	2001 (%)	2003 (%)	2004 (%)	2005 (%)	2006 (%)
Scottish Parliament/ Scottish Executive	72	74	66	67	67	64
UK government	13	14	20	12	13	11
Local councils	10	8	9	17	15	19
European Union	1	1	1	1	1	1

From 2000 to 2003 answer codes referred to the Scottish Parliament, From 2004 onwards answers referred to the Scottish Executive.
Source: Scottish Social Attitudes, 2000–6.

should be the centre of power in Scotland, but they are far from convinced that this is what devolution has delivered.

Table 13.7 shows where Scots feel that power ought to lie in Scotland. In 2006 nearly two-thirds (64 per cent) said that the devolved institutions should have most influence over the way that Scotland is run, with only a little over one in ten (11 per cent) feeling that the UK government should. True, the former figure has declined somewhat since the early years of devolution, but this is not because there has been an increase in the proportion who would like power to reside at Westminster, but rather because of an increase in the popularity of local councils. Few want Westminster ruling the roost in Scotland.

Yet this is precisely what many people feel actually happens. As seen in Table 13.8, in 2006 nearly two in five (38 per cent) felt that the UK government actually has most influence over how Scotland is run. In contrast, just under a quarter (24 per cent) believe that the devolved institutions have most influence. True, this gap has narrowed considerably. The proportion believing the devolved institutions have most influence has nearly doubled since the first year of devolution, while the proportion that believe the UK government has most influence has nearly halved. Evidently the devolved institutions have slowly but consistently made a greater impression on the Scottish public. Nevertheless, for many people there is evidently still a large gap between what they think ought to the case and what they feel actually happens.

It should then, perhaps, come as little surprise that there appears to be persistent support for more powers for the Scottish Parliament. In all but one of the surveys represented in Table 13.9 around

Table 13.8 Who has most influence over the way Scotland is run,
1999–2006?

	2000 (%)	2001 (%)	2003 (%)	2004 (%)	2005 (%)	2006 (%)
Scottish Parliament/ Scottish Executive	13	15	17	19	23	24
UK government	66	66	64	48	47	38
Local councils	10	9	7	19	15	18
European Union	4	7	5	6	8	11

2000–3: 'Which of the following do you think *has* most influence over the way Scotland is run?' Answer codes refer to the Scottish Parliament.
2004: 'Which of the following do you think *has* most influence over the way Scotland is run?' In one half of the sample answer codes referred to the Scottish Parliament, in the other half to the Scottish Executive. No difference was found between the two sets of results.
2005–6: 'Which of the following do you think *has* most influence over the way Scotland is run?' Answer codes refer to the Scottish Executive.
Source: Scottish Social Attitudes, 2000–6.

Table 13.9 Trends in demand for more powers for Scottish Parliament

	1999 (%)	2000 (%)	2001 (%)	2003 (%)	2005 (%)	2007 (%)
The Scottish Parliament should be given more powers –						
Agree strongly	14	23	20	13	17	22
Agree	42	43	48	46	47	44
Neither agree nor disagree	20	15	14	18	17	16
Disagree	18	12	13	17	13	14
Disagree strongly	4	5	4	6	5	3

Source: Scottish Social Attitudes, 1999–2007. Data for 2007 are provisional.

two-thirds agreed with the proposition that 'the Scottish Parliament should be given more powers', while typically only around one in five have disagreed. Much the same results were obtained by other surveys that carried the same question in 2005 and 2006.[15]

So while a majority of Scots want to remain in the Union, they apparently still want greater autonomy within that Union than many of them feel they have been given so far by the current devolution settlement. Not surprisingly nearly everyone who would like Scotland to be independent (93 per cent of them in the 2007 survey) believes the parliament should have more power. More importantly, however, this is the view of a majority of those who say they are in favour of devolution. In the most recent survey no less than two-thirds (66 per cent) of those say they prefer Scotland to have a devolved parliament with taxation powers. Indeed, even half (51 per cent) of those who say they would like a devolved parliament without taxation powers are also of the same view.

As a result it appears that remaining within the Union but giving Holyrood greater powers is now the most popular constitutional option. As we have already seen, according to the 2007 survey 23 per cent support independence. If we then divide the remaining respondents according to their answers in response to the question on more powers we find that those who support more powers but wish to remain in the Union constitute 42 per cent of all Scots, while those who would like to remain in the Union but do not back more powers comprise just 30 per cent. On the basis of these figures it seems that a more powerful parliament within the framework of the Union would most likely emerge the winner in any future 'multi-option' referendum in which people in Scotland are invited to choose between independence, a more powerful version of devolution and the status quo.

Perhaps the feature of the current devolution settlement that has been the subject of most criticism is the way in which the devolved institutions are financed.[16] Apart from its right to vary the basic rate of income tax by up to three pence in the pound, and its ability to influence the level of council tax, the amount of money that the devolved institutions have to spend is determined by the UK government. Some critics argue that this arrangement does not give the Scottish government and Parliament sufficient incentive to pursue policies that would enhance the tax base or consider the fiscal consequences of the public spending decisions that they make. Others in contrast argue that the current arrangements constrain the devolved institutions too tightly and leave them subject to the whim of decisions made by UK government ministers who may not be in political sympathy with the administration in Edinburgh.

In any event, it seems that there is considerable public support for changing the way in which the devolved institutions are financed. As Table 13.10 shows, in recent years over half have consistently agreed with the proposition that 'now that Scotland has its own parliament, it should pay for its services out of taxes collected in Scotland'. Only around a quarter appear to be opposed. This is despite the fact that

Table 13.10 Trends in support for 'fiscal autonomy', 2001–7

	2001 (%)	2003 (%)	2007 (%)
Now that Scotland has its own parliament, it should pay for its services out of taxes collected in Scotland			
Strongly agree	7	5	7
Agree	45	46	50
Neither agree nor disagree	18	16	15
Disagree	25	25	21
Strongly disagree	3	4	3

Source: Scottish Social Attitudes 1999–2007. Data for 2007 are provisional.

government statistics suggest (albeit not uncontroversially) that current levels of public expenditure in Scotland outstrip current tax revenues.[17]

So while a clear majority of Scots may want to remain in the Union, and while there is some evidence that they may have become more persuaded of the economic and financial benefits of membership, this does not mean that there is not pressure for change. The Scottish Parliament is widely regarded as weaker than it should be, and as a result there is considerable public support for increasing the powers of the institution, including its financial powers. Evidently, a key challenge now facing the Union is whether it can accommodate this public mood.

CONCLUSION

We have presented a very different picture of public attitudes towards the Union in Scotland than the one we might have been expected to paint in the wake of the SNP's success in the May 2007 election. The SNP may be committed to making Scotland independent, but its election to office does not seem to have signified growing public discontent with the Union. If anything in some respects at least the Union now appears to be regarded in a somewhat more favourable light than it was eight years ago.

This finding is not, in fact, as paradoxical as it might seem. First, it should be remembered that while the SNP came first in the 2007 election, it still won less than a third of the vote. Its tally was just 32.9 per cent in the constituency contests and 31 per cent on the list vote.

The party was simply the largest minority in that election rather than anything approaching a majority. Secondly, while the SNP's share of the vote in the 2007 election might have been some nine to ten points above the tally the nationalists achieved in 2003, support for other parties that favoured independence, most notably the Greens and the far left, fell back substantially. Taken together the increase in support for parties favouring independence was a far more modest three points on both ballots.[18]

Indeed, while fewer people may have backed independence in 2007, those that did were far more likely to vote for the SNP than they were four years previously. In 2003 only just over half (51 per cent) of those who said they favoured independence voted for the SNP on the regional list vote. In 2007 no less than three-quarters (76 per cent) did so. This change more than compensated for the impact of the apparent decline in support for independence. At the same time, however, the SNP also won an important slice of additional votes among the much larger group of people who supported devolution. Nearly a quarter of those who favoured some form of devolution voted for the SNP, up by nine points on 2003.

Given the mood among many who support devolution, the ability of the SNP to secure the support of those who do not support independence should not surprise us. For many devolution was not providing as powerful a symbol of Scotland's distinctive national identity as they would like to see. And it appears to have been among this group that the SNP did relatively well; those in favour of devolution but also backing more powers were twice as likely to vote for the SNP (28 per cent did so on the list vote) as those not in favour of more powers (14 per cent).

The SNP has always outpointed other parties in Scotland when people are asked how closely the various parties look after the interests of people in Scotland. For example, in 2007, nearly a quarter (24 per cent) said that the SNP looked after those interests 'very closely', while well under one in ten said the same of any other party. It has thus, perhaps, always had the potential to appeal to those who, while still supportive of the Union, would like the apparent balance of power between Westminster and Holyrood reversed. Meanwhile, now that it has taken office the SNP minority government has proven willing to state its disagreements in public with policy stances being taken by the UK government, in stark contrast to the rather coy approach taken by the previous Labour–Liberal Democrat coalition. But if in so doing the SNP can persuade people in Scotland that the devolved institutions can be made more effective and that Scotland's voice in the Union is now being heard more loudly, perhaps they might be encouraged to believe that devolution within the Union can deliver – so long, perhaps, as the institutions are invested with a little more autonomy. By causing more friction within the Union the SNP could ironically help persuade the public that remaining within that Union continues to be worthwhile.

Notes

1 C. Bromley, J. Curtice, D. McCrone and A. Park, 'Introduction', in C. Bromley et al. (eds), *Has Devolution Delivered?* (Edinburgh: Edinburgh University Press, 2006).

2 E. Gellner, *Nations and Nationalism* (Oxford: Blackwell, 1983).

3 M. Billig, *Banal Nationalism* (London: Sage, 1995).

4 M. Rosie and R. Bond, 'Identity matters: the personal and political significance of feeling Scottish', in C. Bromley, J. Curtice, K. Hinds and A. Parks (eds), *Devolution – Scottish Answers to Scottish Questions* (Edinburgh: Edinburgh University Press, 2003).

5 J. Murkens with P. Jones and M. Keating, *Scottish Independence: A Practical Guide* (Edinburgh: Edinburgh University Press, 2003).

6 D. Steel (chairman), *The Steel Commission: Moving to Federalism – A New Settlement for Scotland* (Edinburgh: Scottish Liberal Democrats, 2006).

7 Scottish Government, *Choosing Scotland's Future: A National Conversation: Independence and Responsibility in the Modern World* (Edinburgh: Scottish Government, 2007).

8 C. Bromley et al. (eds), *Devolution – Scottish Answers to Scottish Questions*: C. Bromley et al. (eds), *Has Devolution Delivered?*

9 These data comprise the responses from the first 1,300 people interviewed by the survey. While there will be small differences between the results reported here and those reported from the final version of the data set, they are unlikely to be sufficiently large to overturn any of the conclusions reached here.

10 Some of the questions included in the SSA series were previously asked on Scottish Election Study surveys that comprise part of the British Election Study series. W. Miller, *The End of British Politics? Scots and English Political Behaviour in the Seventies* (Oxford, Clarendon Press, 1981); L. Bennie, J. Brand and J. Mitchell, *How Scotland Votes* (Manchester: Manchester University Press, 1997); A. Brown, D. McCrone, L. Paterson and P. Surridge, *The Scottish Electorate* (Basingstoke: Macmillan, 1999). This means that in some cases we can consider trends in opinion over a longer time period.

11 L. Moreno, 'Scotland and Catalonia: the path to home rule', in D. McCrone and A. Brown (eds), *The Scottish Government Year Book 1988* (Edinburgh: Unit for the Study of Government in Scotland, 1988).

12 J. Curtice, *So Where Stands the Union Now? The Lessons of the 2007 Scottish Parliament Election* (London: Institute for Public Policy Research, forthcoming). Available at: www.ippr.org/publicationsandreports.

13 J. Curtice, *So Where Stands the Union Now?* (forthcoming).

14 R. Ormiston and C. Sharp, *Scottish Social Attitudes Survey 2006: Core Module: Report 1: Attitudes towards Public Services in Scotland* and *Report 2: Perceptions of Government in Scotland* (Edinburgh: Scottish Government, 2007) Available at: www.scotland.gov.uk.

15 gfkNOP Social Research and J. Curtice, *Scotland – Poll Position: Public Attitudes towards Scottish Parliamentary and Local Government Elections* (London: Electoral Commission, 2006).

16 See, for example, P. Hallwood and R. MacDonald, *Fiscal Federalism* (Glasgow: Fraser of Allander Institute, 2004): M. Fitzpatrick et al., *Calling Scotland to Account?* (Edinburgh: Policy Institute, 2006).

17 Scottish Executive, *Government Expenditure and Revenue in Scotland 2004–5* (Edinburgh: Scottish Executive, 2006).

18 J. Curtice, *So Where Stands the Union Now?* (forthcoming).

14

FUTURE OF AN UNLOVED UNION

Neal Ascherson

Few people celebrated the tercentenary of the Anglo-Scottish Union in May 2007. They were too fascinated by what was happening to the Union, almost week by week, to light bonfires. Anyway, it would have been like lighting a bonfire on a melting ice-floe. An SNP minority government took over at Holyrood, ending nearly fifty years of Labour hegemony and releasing a torrent of initiatives which washed the opposition off their feet. In Wales, Plaid Cymru joined a coalition administration with Labour. In London, a Scot succeeded Tony Blair as prime minister – and started talking about constitutional reforms which would make possible a reinvented 'Britishness', a new patriotism constructed around loyalty to British institutions, and especially to what Gordon Brown calls 'British values'.

It was a strange moment to choose. The United Kingdom, as a multinational state, is beginning to show signs of disintegration. Even in England, opinion is growing rapidly impatient with the whole constitutional structure. Why is there no English parliament? Why do Scottish MPs vote on English matters? Why should Gordon Brown, a Scot from a Scottish constituency, be allowed to rule Britain as Prime Minister?

The London-based media make three assumptions. One is that English resentment against the Scots is increasing rapidly. A second is that a waning sense of British nationhood and British values must be restored. A third, involving the state we still call the United Kingdom, is a gathering expectation that the Scots will march out of it. All three propositions, as I see it, are misunderstandings – some of them wilful deceptions, others defects of political imagination.

The first topic is Scotophobia. For the last eighteen months, an intelligent Scot reading the London papers, or watching London-made political TV shows, could only conclude that sharp dislike of Scots and Scotland is spreading across south Britain on a scale without parallel since the eighteenth century. The ignorance and nastiness of some of this journalism has been startling. The *Daily*

Telegraph wrote of Scotland as 'trapped in the squalor of dependency' and asserted that 'until recently an English voter hearing Gordon Brown's Fifeshire accent would simply have said to himself "Labour"; now, he says "Scottish". The lopsided devolution settlement has created a sense that the Scots are having their cake and yet guzzling away at it'.

Since then, the papers have railed on. They accused a Scottish mafia of dominating Tony Blair's last Cabinet. They suggested that Scottish ministers, from the safety of northern constituencies, were driving through measures hateful to the English, such as tuition fees in higher education (Brown now proposes to cut them). They picture Scotland as pampered by unjustified English taxpayers' subsidies (an inaccurate summary of the admittedly ramshackle Barnett Formula) and yet nagging for more. On the *Daily Telegraph* website, hatred of the European Union is closely associated with resentment of Scotland. Ending the older Union is seen as the precondition for ending the newer one. 'Time to disband the 1707 Union, let the Scots join the Euro, kowtow to the French for extra subsidies &c and let England move on to its destiny . . .'. Some Tory MPs and their friends in the London commentariat even proclaim that parliamentary government will be raped and trampled now that an MP from a Scottish constituency is Prime Minister.

How real is all this fury, and does it reflect what English people think about Scotland and the Scots? I am certain that on the whole it does not. Southern views of the Scots over the last hundred years have been mildly derisive – 'chippy, lacking in humour, slow to unbend' – but on the whole affectionate. (Contrast English attitudes to Welshness which, for reasons I am not sure of, are often genuinely hostile.) The English have also shown noticeable tolerance, taking on board that some Scottish touchiness was justified. The days when an Englishman could comfortably refer to the Highlands as the most beautiful part of England are now unimaginable (though actually not that long ago). As for Scottish independence, polls as far back as the 1970s showed that most English people thought that it would be 'a pity, after all we've been through together, but if they want that, I suppose they have a right to it'. Unionist politicians must have found that absence of panic unnerving. They still do.

In other words, this present flare of Scotophobia began as little more than a media ramp, fuelled by and to some extent coordinated with the Conservative Party. Its motives are transparent. When the bombardment opened last summer, it was obviously targeted to damage and disable Gordon Brown, the Conservatives' future adversary, before he reached 10 Downing Street. It is fascinating that professed Unionists were ready, in order to knock out an adversary, to touch off this barrage against Scottishness in general and Brown's Scottishness in particular, against those damned Scots who are such fragments of grit in the otherwise creamy perfection of Britain's constitutional arrangements.

None the less, relentless repetition of these grievances does begin to wear a dent into public opinion. Iain MacWhirter, political commentator for *The Herald* papers in Glasgow, received a torrent of cross and sometimes abusive posts – over 1,300 of them – when he tried, late last year, to explain Scotland's political and financial realities on *The Guardian*'s (left–liberal) website. It was the usual stuff: Scots whining while they grab our money, abusing our parliamentary system and taking over England. As MacWhirter comments, 'the idea of a Scottish "Raj" running England is . . . so extraordinary that it's difficult to say anything coherent about it'. But the really interesting point about these emails, like those on the *Telegraph* site, was this: that all but a handful saw the solution to their complaints in ending the Union.

This isn't Scotophobia. It's Anglophilia. The ICM poll of November 2006 suggested that 59 per cent of English respondents would prefer Scotland to be independent, while 68 per cent of them wanted an English Parliament of their own. While the media and political campaign against the Scots has not apparently made the English more anti-Scottish in any general, xenophobic way, it has had the effect of boosting the slow resurgence of English national self-awareness which first became noticeable some ten or twelve years ago.

Was that effect intended by the new Tory leadership? It's hard to know. In the short term, there are Tory votes to be gained in the south by calling for a ban on Scottish MPs voting on English matters ('English votes for English laws'). In the longer term, the prize the Conservative Party could win by evicting the Scots from British politics altogether is so enormous – so overwhelming, in fact – that it makes most Tory MPs nervous.

Since the 2005 elections, Labour holds 286 of the 529 English seats at Westminster, a clear majority. However, these results from Westminster's 'first past the post' electoral system conceal the fact that the Conservatives actually won more English votes than Labour. The lesson is that any serious Tory revival could carry the party to an almost impregnable domination of English politics – as long as those Scottish MPs aren't there to spoil it.

Tempting in theory – but would anyone dare to pick up that prize? In 1997, John Major tried to make 'the defence of the Union' (no to devolution!) his main election plank. It fell hopelessly flat; nobody cared. Today, opinion polls show that the Union is unpopular both north and south of the Border. Yet I suspect that a question worded: 'Do you want the break-up of Britain?' would get a different response in England, at least in the next few years. For the moment, I cannot imagine any Westminster–British political leader bold enough to propose dissolving the 300-year-old Union Treaty. None the less, as I want to show later on, a truly ambitious, coldly clear-sighted leader – once in power – could now bring about a situation in which the Union would unravel and it could be made to seem to be all the fault of the Scots.

Scotophobia in England is largely a media invention and has not been very effective in its own terms. It has, however, accelerated a current of English national grievance, political and cultural, which was already flowing. And the object of this grievance is not so much Scotland as Britain itself.

In the film *Monty Python and the Holy Grail*, King Arthur rides up to a muddy peasant woman and announces: 'I am the King of the Britons'. She asks: 'King of the who? Who are the Britons?' The king answers rather uncertainly: 'We are *all* Britons!' Well, perhaps we are now all muddy peasant women, because – in spite of Gordon Brown's exhortations – the notion of Britain is plainly growing less convincing. The last British Social Attitudes survey showed how, in the ten years up to 2005, the English sense of British identity had declined by 8 per cent to less than half the sample, while primary identification as English had risen by 9 per cent. (The far steeper decline in Scots prioritising British identity – now down to 14 per cent – has been known and written about for many years now.)

It is now nearly ten years since 'Diana Week' in London revealed how English nationalism was returning. Central London was a sea of red-and-white English flags, with scarcely a Union Jack to be seen. St George's Cross has become the flag of the heart for millions of English families, a symbol of allegiance which has now spread far beyond the football stadiums. The big questions about the future of this particular nationalism – whether it will find serious and effective leadership in the English professional classes, and how far it will edge along the spectrum from sullen, xenophobic, 'ethnic' feelings towards more 'civic' programmes for reform and emancipation – are being avoided by the Brown government. No wonder! This new consciousness begins to challenge Britishness just when Gordon Brown sets out to deepen it. There is a growing conviction among the English that, although they form 90 per cent of the UK population, the British state structure condemns them to be its victims and losers.

There are parallels, of course. One was the Habsburg Empire in which the core imperial population group – the Germanic inhabitants of Austria – began to lose their identity in the age of rising nationalisms. Robert Musil put this well in his great novel about the last decades of Austria-Hungary, *A Man Without Qualities*: 'within the Empire, the Czechs knew they were Czech and the Hungarians knew they were Hungarians, but the Austrians were just . . . Habsburgers?' I thought of Musil when I read a passage from Sir Keith Ajegbo's recent 'Diversity and Citizenship' report. The investigator was talking to a small Year 3 girl in a London school, who was the only English child in her class. When all the others had talked about their origins, she said sadly: 'I come from nowhere!'

We must allow for differences, of course. The Germans were a minority in their state, the English are an overwhelming majority in theirs. And terminology comes into it. People in the Habsburg Empire, weird old patchwork as it was, knew the difference between a nation and a state. In recent history, the Irish, Scots and Welsh never had much difficulty distinguishing the two, but the English never grasped it and few do so even today. It is only in the last ten years or less that you come across Westminster politicians referring to the UK as a 'multinational state'.

The muddle over words is significant. Nor has it always been an exclusively English habit. In the eighteenth and early nineteenth centuries, many successful Scots were happy to describe themselves as 'English' to the outside world, and did not make much fuss when southerners referred to the whole island as 'England'. Sir John Seeley wrote his prophecy of global imperial destiny in 1883 under the title: 'The Expansion of England'. For generations, the fact of England's numerical predominance within 'Great Britain' was hidden behind the image of the island English as the heroic founding few, outnumbered by the millions inhabiting the British Empire.

It was only in the late twentieth century that civil servants and educators began to insist that English people should be polite enough to refer to themselves as 'British', in order not to offend Welsh and Scottish sensibilities. Patiently, they did so, only to find that the Scots and the Welsh still identified them as English and found all this 'Britishness' stuff rather evasive. Conceived as a well-meaning stroke of political correctness, it had the effect of concealing the truth that the English still used their wealth and numbers to call the shots in the UK. And almost inevitably, the English backlash slowly began. Who are all these eggheads and Eurocrats and Scottish carpetbaggers to tell us who we are and how we should think in our own country? Why should we, the majority, be the victims whose tax money is spent by people we didn't elect? Why can't we have a parliament too?

English self-assertion is the most intimate of all imaginable threats to the 'Ukanian' power structure. So the Britishness campaign (or campaigns, because there are several) sprang up in rebuttal. They propose that Britain is a nation, like Holland or Hungary, which possesses some essential cultural identity and 'typical values'. But I have to say that if you want to get to Britain, I wouldn't start from here. You will squelch into some really bad history. Seven years ago, the BBC History Department made an ass of itself by naming its Millennium TV series 'A Thousand Years of British History' (suggestions that a more accurate title would be 'A Thousand Years of English Expansion' were coldly received). Even now, it seems that not enough people have digested Professor Linda Colley's work: 'Britishness was superimposed over an array of internal differences in response to contact (and conflict) with the other', that is, with Catholic and then republican France. In other words, Britishness can exist when the nations of the UK face a common external threat or challenge: in war, in the armed forces, in the East India Company or the Indian Civil Service, in a British embassy abroad, and so on. But do these challenges have to be exclusively external? Could a moment of Britishness be sparked by something domestic – like an irresistible cry for social justice?

Many years ago, when Gordon Brown had only just joined Tony Blair's government, he tried to give some body to vapid New Labour slogans about unity. Brown began to analyse possible objects of patriotism, and he proposed that the National Health Service should be such an object. It was a common achievement, a great moral reform done in the name of fairness and justice, and all the inhabitants of the United Kingdom should be proud of it and ready to defend it. (I'm glad he didn't say 'die for it'.) This remains to me the most impressive thought Mr Brown has ever put forward, since he edited the *Red Paper on Scotland* back in 1975. It's impressive because what it implies is utterly subversive. Patriotism gathered round an institution of reform created in the name of the people is a *republican* concept, not an Ancient British one. And that leads to an even more shocking thought.

Does it follow that the only way to muster a united New Britain would be around a programme of interventionist state socialism?

Since then, however, Brown on Britishness has followed a more conventional pattern. In a *Daily Telegraph* interview in 2006 (in which he praised the patriotism of Mrs Thatcher and Winston Churchill, but of nobody in his own party), he defined British virtue thus: 'Most nations subscribe to universal values like freedom, but it is how these values come together – in Britain's case, in liberty married to social responsibility and to a belief in what Churchill called "fair play" – and then are mediated through our institutions and our history, that defines the character of the country'.

Attractive, but not really solid enough to form the pedestal for a new patriotism. Jack Straw, Foreign Secretary under Blair and now Brown's Minister of Justice, trying to identify 'British values' in what he called 'a nation of nations', listed the following: 'the core democratic values of freedom, fairness, tolerance and plurality that define what it means to be British'. But don't they also define what it means to be Norwegian? Alan Johnson, when he was Blair's Education Minister, also had a try: 'Free speech, tolerance, respect for the rule of law, which are not exclusively British [values] . . .'. Or Slovenian, or Irish, or Australian?

He was commenting on the Ajegbo report about 'Diversity and Citizenship'. That report suggested compulsory lessons for eleven to sixteen year olds on British values, emphasising respect for other cultures and tolerance of religious differences, and discussing freedom and justice. *The Times* snorted: 'This proposal is less Elizabeth I and Winston Churchill than Barney the Dinosaur meets the Commission for Racial Equality . . . whatever Britishness may be, it is surely not the "mush" that is now being proposed'. All that one can say is that the 'mush' spoken about Britishness matches the 'mush' thought about Britishness by the inhabitants of this archipelago.

In a chapter of the British Social Attitudes report I mentioned earlier, the research team found that their sample was baffled by an invitation to define British values. They had no idea what these might be. Pressed to rate institutions by their importance to British identity, most of them thought the monarchy and trial by jury were really important, but they didn't think that free speech mattered very much and were not impressed by the way government worked. Make of that what you will. Yet note, too, that nobody, and certainly not one of the politicians, counts 'equality' in their list of British values. 'Plurality' is on sale, and 'fair play', but not the equality which mattered so much to English radicals in the seventeenth century – and to the British Labour movement in the twentieth century.

So where do these so-called British values come from – whose are they really? An interesting question. I was reading an *Observer* review by Rafael Behr of Peter Mandler's *The English National Character*, and I came across this: 'The Victorians were a bit snooty about European nationalism (which reeked of peasants, pitchforks and revolutionaries in grubby breeches). They didn't want to be just a nation, so they promoted themselves to the status of "civilisation".' There's something in that. And Behr goes on: 'As a consequence of this canny national re-branding, many of the characteristics people think of as primordially "British" are actually Victorian: austere, eccentric, industrious, beloved of fair play, liking a good pageant, respectful of the monarch, obsessed with decency and propriety, redoubtable, stoical, in possession of a stiff upper lip.' A month later, Adam Nicolson wrote almost exactly the same in the *Daily Telegraph*: 'There is a propriety to British [*sic*] nationalism that betrays its Victorian origins: austerity, industriousness, respect, stoicism, fortitude, fairness, regularity, decency. . . there is nothing particularly British about them. They are the virtues of a Victorian middle class . . .'.

If these bourgeois values attach to a class and a period, did they also attach to other classes? We can be certain now that they were widely shared, at least as aspirations. But the banker in his comfortable family villa in Otley or Bridge of Weir would probably have denied that, regarding the lower orders as improvident, unreliable and inclined to expect something for nothing: that Other who is the mirror-opposite of one's own virtues. If these so-called British values are, then, no more than the values of one social class in one particular epoch, how can they be called 'national'? Or was that Victorian bourgeoisie a sort of nation in itself, a roughly uniform social group to be found distributed across a British territory whose other inhabitants were culturally diverse? And here we get to the next proposition. Is it possible that a beast called *Homo Britannicus* can exist, has existed and may survive in dense woodlands even today?

I believe that it did. Professor Chris Stringer, the famous palaeontologist, has just written a book with this title. He is not describing recent history, but the repeated failure of human groups to establish a permanent settlement in what was to become the British Isles until the end of the Younger Dryas glaciation, some 11,500 years ago. But he is, symbolically, showing that being British has been a discontinuous business, with no manifest destiny about it.

From a political point of view, to be recognised as Danish or Welsh or British requires evidence of some bond with a place identified as 'home'. From a cultural point of view, it requires the existence of a bundle of attributes which are perceived to be shared – in varying proportions – by members of this community. Some of these attributes may be external and material – tribal costume, hunting equipment – others will be to do with language, with dietary preferences and taboos, or with techniques of social interaction and courtship. Entry to such a group is proclaimed to depend mostly on birth and lineage, but in practice the group maintains its vigour by a continuous process of fosterage and the acculturation of outsiders.

I am talking, as some of you have guessed, about the 'British Gentleman'. In the course of the nineteenth century, and through the socially-transforming engines of the Victorian 'public schools', there was created a ruling elite with a common culture. This culture, originally modelled on the mores and kit of the English landowning aristocracy, came to be carried mainly by the children of the new industrial and financial middle class. That process is well understood now, but I think it is important to reflect how the cultural identity of this group transcended local particularity.

Until very recently, whether you rambled at Land's End or John O'Groats, you would probably have been halted by the most threatening tribal challenge in the English language: 'Can I help you?' This landowning figure might be called MacGregor, Griffiths, Penhaligon or Smith; but although his grandfather might well have spoken with a Gaelic, Yorkshire or Welsh accent, he would speak in precisely the same public-school tones whether he lived in Caithness or Cornwall. His clothes, his taste in food, the way he carried his gun and addressed his dogs, the coiffure of his wife, the newspaper he read were all non-local, part of the culture of a universal class in which Scottishness or Irishness, backgrounds in land or trade, were transcended in a higher Hegelian synthesis: the global empire of countless races and tongues and customs which he or his relations would serve as officers or governors. No wonder that the question which made a true 'Gent' despise the questioner was: 'Where are you from?' A universal 'Gent' did not 'come from' anywhere. He might have a town house and a country house, but he didn't *come* from London or the local market town. He just *was*. That was enough for him – although not enough for that little English girl who didn't want to come from nowhere.

What can we call this gentleman culture but 'British'? It's not the only example of such a culture. Most multinational empires evolve something comparable. In the mere seventy years of the Soviet Union's existence, *Homo Sovieticus* appeared and multiplied; men and women of European, Caucasian, Turkic or Mongolian appearance sat in the same offices from the Baltic to the Pacific, under portraits of the same autocrat, sipping standard glasses of tea, smoking the same cigarettes, lifting identical black telephones to say '*Nyet!*' in the same dead tone. They too had transcended ethnic and familial differences in the universality of a great empire. *Homo Sovieticus* was, however, generally despised as a moronic automaton, while *Homo Britannicus* is remembered for reasonably fair dealing and unpredictable moods of leniency.

Is he extinct? No, but – at a time when Eton boys have begun to speak with the regional accent of southeast England – he is endangered and has long ceased to be the power-bearing caste. And with the retreat of *Homo Britannicus*, there dissolves the last living proof that Britishness was for a time not just a citizenship but a tangible culture, tiny in numbers and yet absolutely distinct – almost a transnational nationality.

To resume, I have been describing a country – a multinational state – in which the richest and most powerful section of the population has grown discontented with its relationship to the other nations. Those other nations, meanwhile, press for more autonomy and a larger share of state wealth. But in spite of some startling opinion polls, it is still pretty unlikely that the component nations are yet ready to vote for the break-up of the state in a referendum.

And what country is that? Yes, it's Czechoslovakia in 1992. The third proposition I wanted to examine was that the Scots are preparing to march out of the Union. But the story of the 1992 'Velvet Divorce' between the Czechs and the Slovaks suggests that we may be looking at that possibility from quite the wrong angle. I recommend a masterly book on the subject by Abby Innes,[1] *Czechoslovakia: The Short Goodbye.*

When Londoners think about Scottish independence, they probably imagine half a million Bravehearts standing in Princes Street and roaring: 'Freedom!' That's improbable. Independence can happen by metropolitan push as well as nationalist pull. Much more likely, a series of disputes between Westminster and Holyrood about money and reserved powers will seize up the weak and ill-maintained machinery of devolution. Then the London negotiators may lose patience and tell the Scots that, if they still want more, they should go off and have their own state – by that stage, the simplest solution. That's a fatalistic scenario: institutional defects working out their own logic. But what about agency? What if some politician in England decided that he or she had an interest in making that machinery seize up?

The background to the Czechoslovak split was certainly both institutional and political. After the collapse of communism in 1989, Slovak nationalism had revived, but mainly as demands for greater autonomy rather than full independence. Meanwhile, the public in both nations felt sceptical about the existing federal government structures, redesigned in the 1968 constitution after the Warsaw Pact invasion. But the motive power for the split – the agency – was provided by the Czech politician Vaclav Klaus (today the President of the Czech Republic).

An ambitious and crafty neo-liberal, Klaus concluded that Slovak needs and demands would always obstruct his own plans in a federal Czechoslovakia. In an independent Czech state, on the other hand, he would be relatively unhindered. The difficulty was that neither the Czech nor the Slovak public wanted the federation to break up. Instead, although discontented with the present structure, they looked forward to a better one.

What Klaus achieved, in the years leading to the final breach in late 1992, was to provoke a series of unacceptable proposals from either side which would end in a separation apparently caused by Slovak nationalist intransigence. In this dance, his tango partner was the Slovak politician Vladimir Meciar, who did not originally want Slovakian independence but fell into almost all the traps dug for him by Vaclav Klaus. The journalist Theodore Draper wrote, 'It was as if Meciar pounded on Klaus's door without really wanting to knock it down; to Meciar's surprise, Klaus opened the door and Meciar fell in'. As Abby Innes comments, 'it was the Czech and not the Slovak will to separation that proved implacable'. Both sides declared that negotiations on a new federal or confederal relationship had failed, and that independence was the only conclusion. Both sides, quite scandalously, refused to hold referenda on Slovak independence or the dissolution of the federation because they knew they would lose them. Czechoslovakia ceased to exist on 1 January 1993.

This story puts conventional predictions about the Anglo-Scottish Union in a new light. The congruencies of that Czech–Slovak divorce with the topics I have been discussing are obvious, and the old Klaus/Meciar script can be re-run with a new cast in the British present. First, politicians and journalists with an agenda have tried to foment a general Scotophobia. Directly, they have failed, but they

have encouraged English ethnic awareness and drawn English attention to the defects of the Union as expressed in the devolution settlement. For the purposes of the phobia-mongers, that can count as
success. Secondly, there is now discontent with the 1997 devolution
settlement on both sides of the Border. The 1707 Union itself is no
longer perceived in England as an indispensable pillar of parliamentary democracy. Thirdly, the notion of 'Britain' is weakening as identity politics – already embedded in Scotland and Wales – take root in
England. 'Britishness', as the common culture of a group of human
beings exercising social and political leadership, has almost ceased to
be tangible. The gentlemen class has left the public stage, and the
repackaging of Victorian bourgeois ethics as 'British values' is too
vapid to be a substitute.

So far, the resemblances between us and 1990s Czechoslovakia are
striking, if never total. But now comes the most delicate question.
Does England have a Klaus? Could he already be leading a party? The
role of Klaus is implicitly offered to David Cameron, the new leader
of the Conservatives. So far, though, it does not look as if he has the
power hunger, or the political imagination, to accept it. But it must be
plain that almost all the preconditions for what Vaclav Klaus did, with
the stumbling assistance of Vladimir Meciar, are now being rolled out
in the United Kingdom. Already, since May 2007, different parties are
governing in London and Edinburgh. In a few years, the SNP administration led by Alex Salmond may be facing David Cameron as British
Prime Minister.

From now on, the real strain will begin to bear down on the devolution settlement after its first easy decade. The stage will be set. And
all it will then lack is a leading actor, an English or Scottish politician
ruthless enough to divide in order to rule.

This is an updated version of the Orwell Lecure given at Birkbeck
College, London in 2006 and subsequently published in part in the
London Review of Books (www.lrb.co.uk).

Note

1 Abby Innes, *Czechoslovakia: The Short Goodbye* (New Haven and
London: Yale University Press, 2001).

INDEX

Note: f stands for figure, t for table